a
sense
of
honor

remembrances of WWII veterans

expanded edition

Ronald G. Perrier

*Published by Archie Publications, P.O. Box 50154,
Minneapolis, Minnesota 55403.
Telephone (612) 333-7922.
Web address: www.archiepub.com*

Cover design by Lance Jeffrey Olson, Arclight Creative Group,
Los Angeles, California.

Printed by Sentinel Printing, Inc., St. Cloud, Minnesota.

First Printing: September 2005

ISBN 0-9704064-9-5

Dedication

I dedicate this book to the wonderful people whose stories appear here. They were willing to share with me the experiences which they had during that tumultuous time of the Second World War more than 60 years ago. Some of their memories were painful for them to talk about, but all of their memories are justifiably laced with feelings of considerable pride and accomplishment.

Along with the countless thousands of their World War II colleagues, these people do indeed possess an enviable sense of honor. I have profound respect for all of the heroes whose stories unfold in the following pages.

Ronald G. Perrier

Acknowledgments

I am grateful to Ms. Stacy Bray for her excellent transcription of the interviews from audio tape to written form. Her language skills, patience, and good humor were a great comfort to me.

I thank Ms. Karen L. Mrja for her thoughtful and intelligent work as my editorial assistant on the entire manuscript for this book.

I thank Lance Jeffrey Olson for creating the stunning cover design. Its clean and clear yet hauntingly abstract imagery suggests not one war but all wars, from antiquity to the present.

I also thank Brian Wise, Denise Rossman, and the friendly staff at Sentinel Printing for their fine assistance in the production of this book.

I extend special thanks to Debbie Brown, Jill Helmin, and the rest of the staff at Copy Central in St. Cloud for their superior service and support of this project.

Many people provided me with names of friends and relatives who were involved in World War II. I appreciate their helpful guidance in directing me to many interviewees.

Of course, I thank all the people who agreed to be interviewed for this book. They are some of the finest people I have ever met, and I appreciate how pleasant and patient each one of them was with me in our conversations. These people who lived through the World War II era are a rich national treasure, and their stories must be preserved for future generations to savor.

Methodology

As one would do in conducting any interview, I did direct a number of questions and comments to each of the interviewees during our taped conversations, but in almost all cases you will not find my questions in the commentaries which you are about to read. I felt that to include my questions in a sort of dialogue form would only be an interruption to the reader's concentration. Besides, these highly interesting people did not need many questions or much coaching from me. Their memories are clear and poignant and vivid. In the editing process, I gently incorporated any of my few questions into their commentaries. After all, the spotlight in this book is shining upon the interviewees, not upon me, and that is as it should be.

In order to preserve the integrity of their comments, all interviewees were provided with the opportunity to review the final edited manuscript of his or her commentary for any corrections, and to clarify the accuracy of what was intended by the interviewee. Sometimes, in the process of adapting the spoken word on tape to the written word on paper, the possibility of deviation from the intended meaning can occur. The interviewees' final proofreading of the manuscript ensured an increased level of accuracy in the stories they wanted to tell, and it also guaranteed their approval of the final written version.

Preface

Fight on then by land and ships together. He among
    you who
meets his destiny of death by spear thrust or
    spear thrown,
let him die. It is with a sense of honor that he
    dies defending
his country. By his sacrifice his wife shall be
    saved and also his children.
His house and property will not be damaged,
    and the enemy Greeks
will go away in their ships far across the sea to
    the land of their fathers.

Homer, *The Iliad*
Book 15, lines 494–99
Ronald G. Perrier adaptation

In the above lines, the Trojan military leader Hector is speaking to his troops and urging them on to battle with the invading Greeks. In an attempt to rouse his troops to fight the enemy, Hector speaks about the nobility of fighting battles to protect the homeland. He says there is a sense of honor in fighting for one's country, even if one meets death in doing so. Although scholars are not certain, Homer's epic poem was probably written in the first half of the eighth century B.C.

Homer's ancient eloquence about the nature of war causes us to see backward and forward as to war's existence in all ages. The Ancient Greeks fought bloody battles, as did people before them and after them. Hardly a generation in human history has been spared from war's scourge—and war's felt necessity. In searching for a title for this book, I thought a line from Homer would give the book's contents a universal resonance. Thus, *A Sense of Honor* is the title I chose.

To paraphrase a thought from German philosopher Friedrich Nietzsche (1844–1900), life is lived forward but understood backward. At first glance this is an almost simplistic thought, but after some introspection it becomes rather profound. Most of us, when we are involved in or are witness to momentous events, never fully realize if the events are indeed significant. We are simply too much involved in the NOW of such events to consider that we may be living in an epoch of importance. Only later, upon reflection and with the perspective which time provides, do we see much more of the parts which make up the entire picture.

In this book you will find recollections of many people who were involved in one way or another with World War II. These people probably did not have any notion of the "importance" of the period at the time they were living it. Rather, they did what they felt they had to do at a time of national crisis. They did not think of themselves as heroes or as crusaders or in any other way as special or unique. But now, many years later, we recognize the greatness of those men and women. Life is lived forward but understood backward.

A good example of this phenomenon is Paul Tibbets, the pilot of the *Enola Gay*, a B-29 super fortress plane which, incidentally, was named after Mr. Tibbets' mother. The *Enola Gay* carried and dropped the atom bomb, code named "Little Boy," over Hiroshima, Japan, on August 6, 1945. In the spring of 2005, a CNN correspondent asked the 90-year-old Tibbets what it felt like to have had such a pivotal and heroic role at such a significant time in world history. Paul Tibbets simply replied, "I was not a hero. I was just asked to do a job and I did it."

Although Paul Tibbets and other soldiers may not have comprehended the full expansiveness of the war until many years later, even the least informed person was somewhat aware of the calamity of the war while it was happening. Its massiveness in terms of death, destruction, and geography caused people to see the encroaching God of War. Without doubt, when Americans were attacked on that infamous Sunday morning in December of 1941, most people knew that they had to become involved in some way. American pride and basic goodness had been besmirched that morning; and men, women, and children in extraordinary numbers came to their country's defense in a multitude of ways.

Why is a book of interviews of WWII veterans important? Quite obviously, it is necessary for future generations to know what these men and women did and why they did it. In their own words, up close and personal, these survivors explain in vivid detail their war-time activities. They speak of duty, of doing the right thing, of there being no alternative to getting involved in the defense of their country. In their actions they demonstrated valor and courage and a strong sense of survival against impossible odds. Their youthful exuberance led them on a path of adventure and danger which few of us can imagine.

My sincere hope is that the poignant stories you will find in this book will make history come alive for you and for all subsequent generations. Lest we forget.

Ronald G. Perrier
September 2005

Table of Contents

A Sense of Honor

Nearly 59 years after the end of World War II, the National World War II Memorial was dedicated in Washington, D.C., on Saturday, May 29, 2004. It honors all who served in the armed forces, those who died, and the millions of citizens on the home front who answered their nation's call to arms. Whether they were driven to answer the call from a perceived high moral purpose or from a sense of youthful excitement and bravado, it makes little difference. The call they answered ensured the survival of freedom and democracy in the world and protected the great nation they loved and honored.

The word "hero" comes from the Greek word *heros*, commonly thought to have meant "protector." Yet, I am certain none of the people whose words appear in *A Sense of Honor* would accept such an accolade as "hero." Exactly the opposite, for each insists they were merely doing what was expected of them as a citizen. Now, after many years of reflecting upon their individual contributions, they have chosen to share their experiences—some shared with modest reluctance, all with deep humility.

At first, World War II was proclaimed by many to be the war to end all wars. Instead, it became the most enormous human drama in history. If geographical vastness is used as the measure, it was truly the first "world" war, with combat operations going on simultaneously in virtually every time zone around the world. If the loss of human life is the measure, hopefully there will never be another war like it. Conservative estimates place the loss of civilian and military lives at 30 million (with the highest estimates ranging to an unimaginable 55 million lives). About 400,000 American lives were lost in this horrific conflict.

So, during the four-day celebration from May 27 through May 30, 2004, no one was surprised when hundreds of thousands of people gathered in the nation's capital. Billed as "A Tribute to a Generation," it included wartime reminiscences, reunions, big-band and swing music, WWII memorabilia and equipment displays, a religious service, military ceremonial units, and educational opportunities for all ages.

After two hours of pre-ceremony entertainment on that Saturday, at approximately 2:00 in the afternoon, a Marine bugler performed taps inside the memorial, and President George W. Bush was introduced. Knowing the majority of those sitting in the audience would remember Ernie Pyle as one of the world's outstanding reporters, often hailed as "America's most widely read war corresondent," the president stated:

> The soldiers' story was best told by the great Ernie Pyle, who shared their lives and died among them. In his book, *Here's Your War*, he described World War II as many veterans now remember it. "It's a picture," he wrote, "of tired and dirty soldiers who are alive and don't want to die; of long, darkened convoys in the middle of the night; of shocked, silent men wandering back down the hill from battle; of jeeps and petrol dumps and smelly bedding rolls and C-rations; and blown bridges and dead mules and hospital tents and shirt collars greasy black from months of wearing; and of laughter, too; and anger and wine and lovely flowers and constant cussing. All these it is composed of, and of graves and graves and graves."
>
> On this Memorial Day weekend, the graves will be visited and decorated with flowers and flags. Men whose step has slowed are thinking of boys they knew when they were boys together. And women who watched the train leave and the years pass can still see the handsome face of their young sweetheart. America will not forget them, either. At this place, at this memorial, we acknowledge a debt of long standing to an entire generation of Americans—those who died, those who fought and worked and grieved and went on. They saved our country, and thereby saved the liberty of mankind.

This book would be incomplete if we ignored the millions of innocent civilians who were affected by the injustices of war. Only three appear in this edition: a teenage Hawaiian boy who witnessed the infamous attack on Pearl Harbor; a Japanese-American perceived as a threat and incarcerated in an internment camp within the United States; and a German-born Jewish woman who miraculously survived the evil horrors of the largest and most efficient of the Nazi death camps—Auschwitz-Birkenau. Also here, to give a perspective of war in the present, 23-year-old identical twin brothers tell their stories about Afghanistan and Iraq, where each of them recently served.

Following are the stories of these citizen-soldiers who are now a part of an imperishable chapter in freedom's survival and the liberation of mankind. They fought, they sacrified, they protected, and they survived— all from a sense of honor.

Gary R. Dostal
Fort Wayne, Indiana
July 2005

Author's Note: Gary R. Dostal, a good friend of mine, is a retired college professor of speech communication whose avocational interest is World War II history. He graciously accepted my invitation to write an introductory essay for this book.

PART I

They Were Involved

Glen A. Smith
1944

Born: 1921

Present home: Minong, Wisconsin

Military history: Enlisted; entered service 1940

Branch of service: U.S. Navy and Army

Length of service: Six years Navy; 14 years Army

Highest rank: Chief Naval Officer in Navy
                  Master Sergeant in Army

Date/place of interview: August 10, 2003
                            Minong, Wisconsin

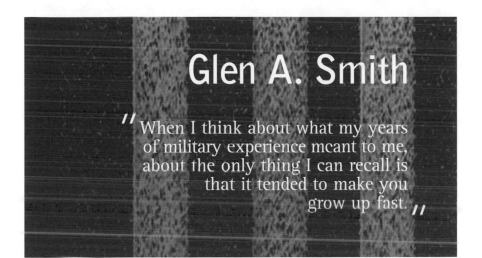

Glen A. Smith

"When I think about what my years of military experience meant to me, about the only thing I can recall is that it tended to make you grow up fast."

I was born in Trego, Wisconsin, in 1921, just about 14 miles from Minong. In 1922 we moved to Minong. I went through 12 years of school there and then enlisted in the Navy in 1940. I was going to go in the spring of 1940, but I was too little. My chest was about an inch and a half too small, so they wouldn't let me in. The Navy had strict rules about physique and fitness. So I spent that summer hoisting railroad ties—picking them up off the ground and raising them up like this *(motioning with arms)* and then throwing them over. Then I'd pick up the other end and flip it around. The boys at the ranger station there built me a trapeze, so I could work out on that, also.

By October I was in far better shape and passed the test, and they accepted me into the U.S. Navy. Since America wasn't at war yet in 1940, the reason I enlisted was probably economics. The wages in the Navy were really good back then—you got $21 a month! *(Laughter)* For a young man with a high school education, there wasn't much else for work around here. I couldn't see how I could go through four years of college because of lack of finances, you know? I thought I would get a year's head start earning money before thinking about college. Of course, I didn't know that Pearl Harbor was going to happen the next year. So what started as a way to earn money for college turned out to be a little over six years in the Navy! At the end of those six years, I was in Bellingham, Washington, putting the *Steamer Bay*, a Jeep aircraft carrier, in mothballs. For whatever reason, I had just a few months left to do, and they sent me to Japan. They put me on the USS *Piedmont* over there. My term of enlistment was up, and they had to send me back to the States. In the meantime, I was late getting back, so I actually didn't get out for two months and 22 days *after* my six years were up.

Actually, when I enlisted, the only enlistment you could accept was six years, so I knew going in it was going to be for that long. That was the minimum—nothing less back then. In other words, they wanted to hook you. They wanted to hook you good. It just so happened that I got in in 1940, and of course the war ended in '45 and I did not get out until '47. I suppose the Navy felt that after investing in all that training, they might as well get some use out of it.

When the Pearl Harbor attack happened on that Sunday morning, I was on the *Saratoga*, which was docked in San Diego, California. A little more than 72 hours later, we went to Pearl. The *"Sara"* was a classic carrier, and it was fast! It almost broke the record for steaming from stateside to Pearl Harbor.

I guess everybody was sad and confused and angry about the attack, but we figured we had a good ship under us. It was a sad deal pulling into Pearl Harbor and seeing all that destruction, just days after it happened. It was quite a shocker. You know, I have never gone back in later years to Pearl Harbor. I understand that a lot of Japanese visit the Arizona Memorial at Pearl. Weird, isn't it?

As I recall, as soon as the *"Sara"* got to Pearl, we were sent on our first mission. I can't remember what island we were going to go to, but about three days out of Pearl Harbor, a Japanese submarine torpedo hit us. That ended our career for a little while. We went back to Pearl, where they kind of patched the ship up, and then they sent us to the States to the shipyards in Bremerton, Washington. We were there for many months. What they did there was take off the eight-inch guns—the *Saratoga* was equipped with eight-inch guns—but a usual battleship had 16-inch guns. They were tremendous!

Once all of the repairs were finished, we headed back to Pearl. Not too many months later, we got hit again with a torpedo. This time, though, it didn't do nearly as much damage as the other one did. Then I thought, "Boy, we're going back to Bremerton, Washington!" Nope. The ship repair guys at Pearl Harbor got to work on the *"Sara"* right away, and in 30 days they had us out of repairs and on our way again. Most people today wonder how the Japanese subs could be in the water near Pearl Harbor without being detected. You see, back then they didn't have the detection equipment that they have now. It was pretty hard to find a sub. About the only way you could catch them is if they'd surface. You could spot them then. But if they were just cruising around in the water, it was pretty hard to find them. Of course, the destroyers had "Y" guns and all that stuff. They could do away with them if they knew where they were, but that is the thing—they didn't have the sophisticated stuff they have now to find them.

After the terrible destruction at Pearl Harbor, I felt anger for many years. It is probably a little anger, but it is not against the Japanese people. It is like with any country: It is the leaders who are responsible for the damn thing. The other thing that kind of galls me is that at the end of the war— after August of '45, when people who weren't a part of it or who weren't even there—would say, "You never should have dropped the A-bomb on those people!" I disagree wholeheartedly with that. They saved a ton of lives, and they saved many months of extended war by dropping those bombs. It was only a matter of days before the Japanese gave up.

Now, let's see.... I think I was on the *"Sara"* for a total of about three years. A fellow by the name of Henry Kaiser was building what they called Jeep carriers—CVEs (carrier vessel escorts)—up in Vancouver, Washington. He put one of those down the Columbia River *every week*! The Navy would commission them and away they would go, out to sea. So what they did was, they took skeleton crews off of carriers like the *Saratoga,* and I was on one of those crews. I was on the precommissioning detail. I was sent to Vancouver weeks ahead of the thing going down the river, putting all the gear and inventory type of stuff that needed to be put on there—spare parts and what have you. We sailed—the sailors that were there—in the precommissioning detail, and we got to sail down the Columbia River with a civilian crew. Then, of course, when we got down there, all the Navy personnel came on board. Kaiser built lots of them. Putting out one ship a week is just incredible, isn't it? It is almost like Henry Ford and his assembly-line production of the Model-T Ford, isn't it? Well, Kaiser had them all lined up there, and he just moved them down the line. Every time one would go down, the next one would move into its place. A lot of the stuff for building those ships was prefabricated, so that saved time. It's just like making airplanes. Look at the tremendous number of airplanes they manufactured at that time, too. Man, oh, man!

I was 19 years old when I went into the Navy. I didn't get married until after the war, so I never experienced any "Dear John" letters. But I had been around guys who got letters like that. Pretty sad. So I was a single 19-year-old kid from a little town in Wisconsin, and all of a sudden I was traveling halfway around the world and riding ships down the Columbia River in Washington State. It was a wonderful experience, if it hadn't been for war—a wonderful experience for growing.

"Join the Navy and see the world!" You got lots of travel in the Navy. You got lots of train rides that came out of Great Lakes Naval Station down there in Illinois. First thing you got was a nice, big train ride to San Diego by a Pullman car. When I first looked at the *Saratoga*, I couldn't believe the size of that thing. Oh, man! The full count of the personnel on the ship was about 3,000. Well, it was like a city. In fact, it was a very powerful piece of machinery because the *Saratoga* had 16 fire rooms and 16 boiler rooms. She furnished the city of Tacoma with electricity for about umpteen days—I forget how many. If something happened and there was a power outage in Tacoma, they just hooked the *Saratoga* up to the city power system and generated electricity for the whole city. It was a very powerful piece of equipment.

In terms of my rank in the Navy: Of course, you started out as a seaman. I was a Seaman 2nd, then in four years I made Chief Petty Officer. I was very lucky—I was in the right place at the right time for the promotions. I just went right up. Like I said, I was there a year before the influx, so I had a year's head start on most of the rest of the guys. I was in third class when those people started coming in. I was in first class when I went to the *Steamer Bay*. A year after I was on that ship, then I made chief. It worked out very well, and I was very happy.

One good thing about being on a ship: You didn't see many casualties. No. Very few were killed by the torpedoes. I saw some ships sunk in the Philippines. There were Jeep carriers—lots of them—and for whatever reason, we traded places with one. A kamikaze came out of the sky and hit the other one and sank it. The kamikazes were like the terrorist suicide bombers in Iraq and Israel today. The plane just dived right into the thing, loaded with fuel, bombs…whatever. The Japanese pilots didn't drop bombs or anything. They just— the kamikazes, the whole airplane—they just went into the boat below. That was a very close call. I figure I still don't know why we changed places with the guys on that other ship. We just sailed across the formation and shut up. It wasn't hours later when a kamikaze came up—maybe more than one, but….

You know, that reminds me: Do you remember those brothers from Iowa, the Sullivans? All five of those brothers were on the same ship in the Pacific, and they all died when Japanese kamikaze pilots hit their ship. Well, the military also learned from that during the war. Now they said, "Don't do it anymore. One brother is going on this ship, and the other is going on that ship." They would separate them so they all wouldn't get wiped out.

Saving Private Ryan and the John Wayne films are fine. But in reality, you are on duty seven days a week, 24 hours a day, and there is a lot of sweat and a lot of work being done that has nothing to do with the war. You are supplying people with clothing. You supply people with toilet articles. You are supplying them with food and all of this other stuff that has to go on, and nobody is shooting at anybody. You put in endless days at sea. The *"Sara"* was equipped for 60 days of supplies. Well, when you would stay 70 days, you know, the food was getting kind of short. In fact, it was down to beans and rice for about the last week. We would have beans and rice for breakfast, beans and rice for dinner, and beans and rice for supper. Not too much variety there! *(Laughter)* We did have coffee—we did have that. I mean, things like that nobody talks about. They don't make movies about those things because it would be pretty boring.

Yeah, it was pretty routine. That is the only thing—there was a lot of boredom. It seems that during the war they would put you to sea, and it is almost like they forgot about you. Then, of course, when you did hit someplace, it was all work because you had to unload the supply ship and such things—get ready to go again. It was all work and not much play, even when you were in port. For recreation they had movies. The *Steamer Bay* had what they called a "forward elevator," and they would put it down to the hangar deck and stretch a volleyball net across there. We did that almost every noon. That is, whenever the situation would allow it. Cards—yeah, there was lots of playing cards. I learned how to play bridge on the *Steamer Bay*. They were all sitting around playing cards, and they asked me to try it and I said, "Sure, I'll try it." It's a very intellectual game. You have to have lots of thought and lots of memory to play that card game. I haven't played any bridge since.

Well, anyway, I got out of the Navy. As I said, I had put in six years in the Navy, and when I got out things didn't work out too well in civilian life. Again, it was economics. I thought, "God, if I go back in, I've only got 14 years to go until I retire!" As luck would have it, years before that, if you got out of the military, you had to start all over again. If you put in six years and then got out and wanted to get back in, you would have to do another 20. They relinquished that a little bit—they said if you go back in within "X" number of years, your private service would count, and all you would have to do is 14 and you would be out—and that is what I did.

I tried to get back in the Navy, but they didn't want me. By that I mean they said, "Oh, yeah, you can get back in, but you have to start over again. We would have to drop you back to Seaman 2nd." I thought, oh, God! I wrote the Air Force a letter and I wrote the Army a letter, and the Army wrote back first. The recruiter said, "I bet I can get you in as Sergeant 1st Class." That was one rank below what I was in the Navy. I told him it was fine because it was a lot more than what the Navy was going to do for me. I went back into the military, but this time in the Army, and was sent to Fort Riley—and "luck of the Irish," I could type! They ran me through a typing school, and about three weeks later I was instructing typing. I stayed there for three years doing that. The thing kind of paid off. I stayed in the Army until 1963. I taught other things, too, besides typing. After I got through with Fort Riley, I went to Korea. My three years were up, so I had to re-enlist. As soon as I did, I was off to Korea. I spent 18 months over there. I was in a "port"—a transportation outfit that had 30-foot tides, if you can believe that. Water would be 30, and the tide would be 30 feet below that. The ships that were coming in had what they called a "tidal basin." The ships coming in had to come in at high tide. They had to go out at high tide, too. Of course, the tides would be going up and down as the seasons changed. It was a mess.

Anyway, I was there in Korea for a while, and then in between services I went to the Northrop Aeronautical Institute, where I became an aircraft mechanic. This one guy said to me, "Why don't you try for that helicopter outfit over there?" I said okay. I put in the paperwork and dang, they hooked me up to a helicopter outfit. I spent the rest of my 18 months up there. Then I came back to the States, and they sent me to Aberdeen Proving Grounds. Then they sent me from there down to Fort Gordon, Georgia. They didn't have much luck finding a place for me. I was working there when a chance to maintain atomic weapons came up in Albuquerque, New Mexico. I put in for that and dang, if they didn't ship me out there. I went to school there. After I graduated from all of the schools I could attend, they pulled me out and made me an instructor. I spent six years right there in Albuquerque, teaching maintenance, storage, and repair. My last six years were a really choice assignment.

I met my wife in the midst of all of this. We got married in 1947, after I got out of the service. She was enrolled in the nurses' cadet corps up at St. Luke's Hospital in Duluth, Minnesota. She graduated and shortly after that, we got married. And then we started having kids! *(Laughter)* Yeah, lots of them. Six of them. And grandkids, too. Let's see…we've got—I counted them here a little while ago—grandkids, we've got…oh, boy…five grandkids and one great-grandchild. You know, my kids and grandkids never talked much about me being in the military; but one of them, my son, before he went to college, was in the 82nd Airborne. He got quite a few jumps out of it, anyway.

It is a different situation with the young folks stationed in Iraq today. I was away from home for three years. I was gone three years before I was back on my first leave. Today, they are gone for three months and think it is overtime. Yeah. They tend to forget how things were back then. Well, nobody knew what morale was. They would come aboard and say, "You've got a morale problem!" We didn't know what the word meant. We were there to defend our country, and that is what we did. You didn't have much recourse. You didn't question authority, and you didn't ask why you were doing it.

When I think about what the many years of military experience meant to me, about the only thing I can recall is that it tended to make you grow up fast. I was 19 years old when I enlisted, but I felt I was much older than that as far as my environment was concerned and compared to most of the other people around me. I know I could hardly wait until I was 21 because then I could go out and get a beer. But as soon as I turned 21, they would quit asking how old you were. I think you grew up pretty fast.

When I finally got out of the service, I was very lucky again. My wife and I wound up here in Minong, Wisconsin, in 1963; and like I said, we had children, so the big house was exactly right for us. We didn't have this big kitchen then. We only had a little 8'x8' kitchen stuck on the end. Anyway, in '63 they were putting in sewers in town, so I went to work for the contractor who was installing the sewers. After that was done, I went to work for the telephone company for a short time and installed telephones. Then, after that, I went to work for Link Brothers, the company that sold the boats. It started out with one salesman, Bob Link, and me—and now it is a multimillion-dollar business. Then a fellow by the name of Jules Richards came up. He worked for the State Department of Natural Resources. He asked me if I would like to work for the DNR, and I said dang right, I would! He said that his boss, Mr. Dahlberg, had an opening in Spooner, Wisconsin, and he wanted to talk to me. I said to tell him that I would be in Mr. Dahlberg's office on Monday morning, and I was! *(Laughter)* We talked for about two hours, and finally he said that as soon as I could get released from Link Brothers Boat Company, I should come down and start to work down there in Spooner, and I said that was fine and dandy.

I put in 20 years at the DNR down there. Twenty years in the military, 20 years at the DNR, and 20 years retired, almost. And I was almost 20 when I entered the Navy. Lots of 20s! *(Laughter)*

Robert H. Wick
1943

Robert and Alice Wick
2005

Born: 1913

Present home: St. Cloud, Minnesota

Military history: Drafted; entered service 1942

Branch of service: U.S. Infantry

Length of service: Three years, eight months

Highest rank: Captain

Date/place of interview: November 10, 2004
St. Cloud, Minnesota

Also present: Mrs. Alice Wick

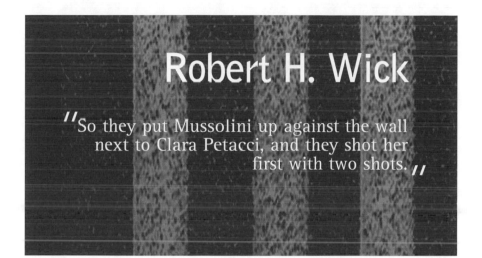

Robert H. Wick

"So they put Mussolini up against the wall next to Clara Petacci, and they shot her first with two shots."

B ack in the early 1940s, I was living in Newton, Iowa, at the time teaching at the high school. I was the director of debate activities there. I was going with a young woman, also a teacher, by the name of Alice Mead. We were not married but we were thinking about marriage, so I decided that I would enlist in the Army instead of waiting to be drafted. I talked with a few people who knew things about the Army, and I talked with the official in charge at the induction center. I told the official that I was probably not cut out for the type of things they wanted in a recruit, so I came home. Furthermore, I was bothered with near-sightedness, and I thought that they wouldn't let me enlist anyway. So Alice and I decided to get married, and about that same time I was drafted! We were married in April of 1942—and in July, the very next month, I was in the Army.

I went to Des Moines and stayed there for a day or two and then was transferred to Jefferson Barracks in Missouri, and there I was "processed." I was given a new change of clothes—the Army type. I had to complete a physical examination and was given all kinds of shots. I was also given a lot of written tests, including the so-called "intelligence" test. I did all right on the physical exam, and the Army clothes seemed to fit. The shoes were all right and seemed to fit, too. I did all right on the intelligence tests, as far as I could tell. It was very warm down in Missouri in July, over 100 degrees in the shade. I was there for a total of two or three *very hot* days, and then they sent me to Fort Carson, Colorado. I was there for only a few months for more basic training. Fort Carson was in the process of being built at that time, and I was one of the first people to be a soldier there.

Regarding basic training: I might say that we soldiers were not very well equipped at that time, as far as the Army was concerned. There were a lot of things that we should have had that we did not have. After all, this was less than a year after the U.S. had declared war on Japan in December of 1941. We didn't have the proper equipment. Furthermore, they did not have people who could type or do the payroll. So right away I had to get on a typewriter and take care of part of the payroll.

Before my basic training was over, I received a call that the colonel wanted to see me. I was rather frightened because I did not know what I had done wrong. He talked to me for a while and told me that they had looked at my credentials and that they were in need of officers in the infantry. He asked me if I would be interested in going to Fort Benning, Georgia. That was all kind of new to me, and I didn't know too much about it; but after a little deliberation and because he wanted to know right away, I told him that I would go. So from Fort Carson, Colorado, I went to Fort Benning in Georgia and was there for about 90 days.

You might be interested in knowing why I was selected by the colonel for the officer training program. You see, I not only had a bachelor's degree before I entered the service, but I also had my master's degree—and I had a few years of teaching experience in the high school in Newton, Iowa. I think that background impressed the colonel and was part of the reason why I was chosen to be a member of SIAM (Signal Information and Monitoring Company). In fact, *all* of us who were chosen for leadership positions had college degrees. Most draftees had only high school diplomas, and some had never finished high school.

The training for officers went all right for me, but it was tough going. It was 90 days of my life that I would not want to repeat. It was hard physically and it was hard mentally, but somehow I survived it. There were a total of 200 men in the officer training class, and 160 of us graduated. I was then commissioned there and sent to nearby Camp Wheeler in Macon, Georgia, as a part of the training battalion. It was a pretty good assignment for me because, by and large, I was a responsible person.

I stayed there for about a year, training infantry soldiers. I trained them in how to use and care for their weapons (the M-1 rifle). We would go out to the range, and I would show them how to fire and I taught them how to take care of their weapon. That was very important. You had to take good care of your rifle. It did not matter much what happened to you, but take care of that rifle! You would always have to keep it clean. That kind of training is what I did for one entire year. The soldiers would come in and be with us for about 12 weeks, and then they would be released—to where, I did not know. Most of them went overseas, I am sure.

After that one year at Camp Wheeler, I received a transfer and was sent to report to Fort Bragg, North Carolina, with the 100th Infantry Division. My time was over for training troops. I was at Fort Bragg only a couple of months, and it was a bad experience for me. I didn't particularly like it. The 100th Infantry Division was having trouble at that time getting efficient and organized in terms of their maneuvers. After a little while there—about two months—the colonel called me into his office. I was a bit alarmed about what was going to happen when he asked, "Would you like to stay here with the 100th Infantry Division, or would you like to be sent overseas immediately with 100 replacement officers?" From that point it was entirely my choice. I could not take a long time to deliberate. What should I do? That was one of the most drastic and speedy decisions that I have ever made. I am usually a person who takes a little time before I make a decision, but I gave it some careful consideration and finally concluded that it would be best to go overseas and be a replacement officer. I should mention that the 100th Infantry Division later on went into the Battle of the Bulge, and they had a rough time. Many of the men died.

We were at camp for about a week, making preparations to go overseas. When we did leave, we departed in the dead of night. I remember waking in the morning, and we were told to go to bed on the ship. We did not ask why. The Navy ship was named after William S. Black, who was Secretary of the Navy in the Woodrow Wilson administration. It wasn't exactly a new ship, and it took us about 12 days to get over there. This trip was a new experience for the other guys and me, of course. "Now hear this!" we heard on the microphone. "Now hear this!" We had to prepare immediately because there were submarines in the area, and they were a dangerous phenomenon at the time. We had protection with warships on the side of us and twice we had to put on life jackets, but we were never hit. One thing, I recall, bothered me a great deal. There was a terrible storm one night when we were in the middle of the Atlantic, and at about 10:00 that night it was my turn to keep watch on the upper deck. We had to be dressed in full gear. I was frightened because I had to hold on to the railing with one hand so that I would not be swept overboard. I do not know the reason why we had to keep watch in such dangerous weather conditions, but I think it was a matter of discipline—to see if we could take it.

There was another thing that happened when we were going overseas: I received notice from the captain of the ship that I was responsible for 200 men who were in the ship's hold. I never saw those men until much later, but still I was in charge. Apparently, at one time the men were playing some kind of card game, and a stabbing took place. I had to bring charges against the man who did the stabbing. I received the papers and filled them out; and then when the ship landed, the papers went over to someone else. I never found out what happened to that poor fellow.

We finally landed after 12 days at sea, and then we skirted the coast of northern Africa. The war was over in northern Africa by that time. We went through North Africa to southern Sicily through the Messina Straits up toward Italy. Naples had just fallen, so Naples was where we landed. I gave my 200 men some special instructions. I was warned that they need-ed to watch out for the young Italian boys who would sneak amongst the walking troops and steal their medical kits. In the meantime, there were MPs with clubs who tried to keep the little boys out. I told my men about this, but in spite of it some of them managed to lose their medical kits.

We marched then to a railroad station, and from the railroad station we went to Caserta, Italy. I do not know how many miles north, but it was just a few miles. We stayed there for a little while, and then we stayed in one of Mussolini's dairy barns. That strong smell is still a vivid part of my memory. I can remember very clearly that dairy barn smell just like it was yesterday. By and large, the men who I went over with, the 200 men I was supervising, went in various directions from there.

In the following two weeks, I did a little of this and a little of that. I was not quite assigned to do anything specific…no definite assignment. I then received a call from my higher-ranking supervisors that I would be sent a few miles north, and that is where I joined the group which was called

SIAM, which I mentioned earlier. What we had to do in SIAM was to learn a code. I was beginning to learn what my assignment would be, along with six other infantry officers. I might say that while I was learning the code, I received word that many of the men who were under my supervision as we crossed the Atlantic had become casualties. That did not mean that all of them were killed, but there were some who were seriously wounded, and some were killed mainly by sniper fire.

Now, back to learning the code. It was called the "One Time Pad System." I don't know where the name originated—but we had to learn, for instance, that XYZ meant "over the hill." Or ABC might mean something else. It was that kind of thing. It was sheer memorization. We were there in training for about 30 days. We would go to work at about 7:00 in the morning learning this stuff, and then we would have a little break now and then; and at about 6:00 at night, we would quit. This went on for those 30 days. When it was all over, the papers and everything were destroyed so there would be no record of any of this. Everything was in our heads. There were six officers being trained, and I was one of those six who went through this; plus, there were about 22 enlisted men. All of those enlisted men had done very well on the tests that they took. They had to have a minimum of 122 on the scale. They were all bright men. I don't recall what a top score was, but 122 was very high.

After that was accomplished, what would happen next was that each officer was issued a three-quarter ton truck, and in that truck we had radio equipment. Running the radio equipment was done by a radio operator and also, of course, by the driver of the vehicle. That was the way it worked. I really spent most of my time then, after we were prepared, not going beyond the battalion. We were not permitted to go much closer to the front line than the battalion went because they didn't want the equipment to get destroyed. We had pretty good luck. The reason for this type of equipment was that in a fluid situation, when the military was moving very fast, this did a lot of good. We could get the information back to General Mark Clark, who was in charge, and we could do what he wanted us to do with the information. I never spoke to General Clark on an individual basis, but I spoke with one of his aides. I am sure they sorted through all the information and told me only what I needed to know. I am not sure of that one way or another, however. We did this kind of information gathering for quite a while.

I changed places quite a bit. All of us changed. I would be with the South Africans for a while, and then I would be with the 34th Division for a while. I would be with the 92nd for a little while. I can't remember the names of all of them, but that is what we did most of the time. About that time I became sort of run down and weak. One day someone looked at me and said I looked yellow. "You look terrible. You must have hepatitis." They loaded me on a plane and sent me to a base hospital at Leghorn. I was there for a period of nearly three months. The war was still raging. Also, while I was in the hospital, one of the ward boys had diphtheria, and so a bunch of us got diphtheria. I didn't know if I was going to survive or not.

I need to tell you something else that is rather interesting. Benito Mussolini, as you know, was head of the Fascist party in Italy. It may seem like a digression that I am marking now, but it isn't. When I was an undergraduate at the Northern University of Iowa, I had a professor there by the name of Dr. Lambertson, and he didn't have very many students in his class. It was a public speaking/discussion class. He chose two of us to go before the Kiwanis Club in Cedar Falls, Iowa, and give a speech on the Italian Black Shirts.[1] They were a militaristic group headed by Mussolini. If I have the date correct, I believe that Mussolini finally took over the Italian government in 1922. That's a little background.

After I got out of the hospital, we learned that the Italians had surrendered to the Germans. When Mussolini was still in Italy, he was trying to escape by going into Austria. He was at the Gargnana area. It was there that somebody—a Communist partisan—caught him in a van trying to escape to Austria. They noticed his black boots. He had a German uniform on, Benito did, but it was the black boots that gave him away. So the partisans got ahold of him and arrested him and his mistress, Clara Petacci. She wanted to be with him, so somehow they made arrangements for her to join him there. They brought both of them to a villa near Milano, and they put him up against a wall. By the way, I learned this information from *Stars and Stripes*, which was our military newspaper. That is, this was not something I experienced first hand.

So they put Mussolini up against the wall next to Clara Petacci, and they shot her first with two shots. Then they opened up his shirt and hit him

---

1. See the endnote at the conclusion of this interview.

with two shots, and that killed him. As I said, I did not see the shooting; but the next day, I was sent by my commander on a mission to go to Milano. All at once, we ran into a fairly large group of people near an abandoned oil station. It was there that they were hanging the bodies of Benito Mussolini and his mistress, Clara Petacci, upside down! We were all standing there watching this as the bodies were hanging there. The atmosphere was electric! It was a bloody thing to see. One woman stepped out of the crowd and moved toward the bodies. I learned later that she had lost five sons in the war. She pulled out a revolver and pumped five bullets into Mussolini's body—one bullet for each of her dead sons. It was a mood that was very uncomfortable and shocking to experience. We just walked away; there was nothing we could do. That is my experience, tying it in with when I was in college.

The war ended in May of 1945. That was fine with us! After that time, when the Germans surrendered, I was in Verona. The German soldiers were surrendering en masse. They were weary looking. They were young. Some of them probably were not any older than 17 or 18 years old. That was the way they appeared, at least. These guys were just teenagers who were all worn out. We put up a big fence, and we were told by our superiors to take the weapons from the German captives and throw the weapons in a pile. That was my duty. Some others came along with trucks and carried the captured men away.

There was still some sniper fire, so we had to be very careful in the towns. I don't have any instances in mind where I witnessed any of that; I just learned that from *Stars and Stripes*. By the way, by that time I had made the rank of captain. I did not leave Verona until November. During that period of time, I went to Switzerland on a trip and also went to southern France and visited some of those coastal cities. In November I received notice that I was to be responsible for the transport of 800 soldiers to the Naples seaport. We had to load those 800 troops into railroad cars. You couldn't walk from one car to another because each car was a separate entity. I had someone to help me; he was an MD. When the train was ready to leave, I was in charge; but then, all of a sudden, I was *not* in charge anymore. I mean, how are you supposed to control 800 men on a train when you can't go from one car to another?

Just before the train was about to leave, a man was thrown out of one of the cars onto the platform. He had been stabbed in a fight. They threw the guy out…and there was the MD and me. We had to call the MPs to come in and help us get that guy to the hospital. In the meantime, the train pulled out of the station, and we were not on it. And I thought: Now I am in trouble. I am really in trouble!

So, what we did then was to get on an MP's Jeep, and we followed the train and flagged it down. It finally stopped and we got on, and we took that long, long trip from Naples to a town north of there. It was truly something else. You see what I mean? I was in charge, but not in charge!

The men would buy vino, the Italian drink they had all learned to love, and they would give the Italians not only the lira for the vino, but also the American money they had in their pockets. When they ran out of money, they would give the Italians some of their Army clothes. Some of our men, believe it or not, arrived without shoes! So that is an experience I will never forget.

As to whether I had been satisfactorily in charge of these men, I thought: Well, what is going to happen here? Maybe I will be put into the guard-house after all. Nothing happened at all, much to my surprise. I was discharged in February 1946 and then came home on the *Lake Champlain* aircraft carrier. I was finally through with supervising troops. I did not have any more duties to perform. The man guiding that aircraft carrier broke the record for speed coming home, and I arrived at Newport News, Virginia. The military decided that they wanted me to stay in the service and join the Army for a life career, but I was not very interested in that.

Now, let me tell you a little bit about the family. I did not indicate earlier that Alice and I had a daughter by the time I arrived home. She was born when I was overseas, and it was over one entire year before I first saw her. The day that she was born, I was in Pisa, Italy.[2] She was born on December 3, 1944. I learned about the birth of my daughter via a telegram from the Red Cross; it took about a week for the telegram to reach me. So I arrived home in Marshalltown, Iowa, which is where my wife Alice was living with her parents during the time I was overseas. Alice was there to meet me at the station, along with her father. It was in the dead of night, but I was so glad to have them there. I had been away from my wife for a long time.

---

2. See Part III of this book to view the letter which Dr. Wick wrote to his parents about his time in Pisa.

When I saw my daughter, Ann, the next morning, she had just awakened, and she didn't want to have anything to do with me. To her, I was a stranger intruding on her life. She was living with her grandparents and her mother and her young uncle, who was a few years younger than Alice. I was just this strange man! Finally, after about two weeks, she allowed me to hold her on my lap if her mother was nearby. That is the way I became acquainted with my daughter. She is now a very successful schoolteacher in the Edina, Minnesota, public school system.

(RGP—At this point, Mrs. Alice Wick joined us at the dining room table where the interview was taking place. During the interview, Alice had been busy in the kitchen. I then asked Dr. Wick for more background information.)

RGP: How often in your service were you granted a leave to come home?

Robert: Twice in all that time. I was gone a total of almost four years.

RGP: Did you and Alice correspond by letter?

Robert: Oh, yes. We wrote many letters to each other.

RGP: Did either of you save any of the letters?

Alice: I saved some of the letters, but I threw most of those things away. I am sorry now that I did, but I was so sick of the whole war situation. When Bob came home, I just wanted to forget as much of those awful war years as I could, so I threw those letters away. Bob still has the letters that he wrote his folks, though. We have some photographs of him from his war years, too. Could you use any of them for the book?

RGP: Oh, yes. That would be wonderful!

Dr. Wick, you did not enter the service until July of 1942, and that was several months after the Japanese attack on Pearl Harbor. Do you remember where you were when you heard the news that Pearl Harbor had been attacked?

Robert: Yes, I do. Alice and I were in church that day. We were visiting her folks that weekend. The radio was blasting the news out to us. That is when I first heard. A lot of people didn't even know where Pearl Harbor was. Of course, at that time most people didn't travel very much and weren't too familiar with places in the world. I did not travel much at all before my experience in the Army. I earned my master's degree in California and made several trips back and forth from Iowa for that, but that was about the extent of my travels. All of them had been in the United States. Most people in their lifetime did not travel more than 50 miles from home, but the war changed all of that.

Alice: I resigned from my teaching job and went with him after he received his commission in February 1943. We lived in Macon, Georgia, while he was at Camp Wheeler, and then we moved to Fayetteville, North Carolina, where he was at Fort Bragg. It was there that he was issued his overseas orders. I returned to Marshalltown, Iowa, to live with my parents. I was three months pregnant by that time.

Robert: Her parents deserve a lot of credit for taking her in because my pay was not that much. I do not remember exactly what it was, but it was small.

RGP: Would you care to comment on the differences between your experience in WWII and what is going on in Iraq right now? Also, do you think U.S. soldiers should be fighting in Iraq?

Robert: I do think, as far as equipment is concerned, that they are much better off today than they were in my era. I can't be too specific about it because I have not kept up with it, but I do know that a few years ago we took a trip to Louisiana and saw what the Air Force was doing, and I was just amazed. The second part of your question: Do we have a right to be there? Well, I guess I will just back up a bit and say that I did not object too much with our trying to get rid of Saddam Hussein. I think he needed to be kicked out of there. He had already murdered thousands of people. I do not give too much credit to the Bush administration who, I think, are not seriously thinking about the aftermath. I don't think they have given enough attention to what will happen after Iraq establishes its own democracy or to how long American troops will have to remain there.

(RGP—At this point, Alice Wick presented us with coffee and muffins.)

The Black Shirts were a powerful "protection squad" in Italy. The group's name was derived from the black shirts which they wore as a distinctive part of their uniform.

When Benito Mussolini came to power in 1922, thousands of Black Shirts welcomed him. Adolf Hitler was particularly interested in the Black Shirts' use of brute force to gain political power for Mussolini.

In Germany, the SA (*Strumabteilung* or Storm Troopers) had grown so large, numbering over two million members by 1933, that Hitler was uneasy about its size and strength, so he established a group of "armed escorts" who were totally dedicated to him. This group was called the SS (*Schutzstaffel* or Protection Squad).

Hitler wanted his SS men to be educated mentally and bodily so as to be the most highly trained National Socialists. Probably due to his admiration for Mussolini's Black Shirts, Hitler made brown shirts a distinctive part of the SS uniform.

Jacob "Jack" Rinsema
(with wife Jean)
1945

Born: 1917

Present home: Bloomington, Minnesota

Military history: Enlisted; entered service 1942

Branch of service: U.S. Navy – Seabees

Length of service: Three years, five months

Highest rank: Carpenter

Date/place of interview: November 15, 2004
Bloomington, Minnesota

Jacob "Jack" Rinsema

"That was our job, to build up these bases, but at the same time it was dangerous because we were also exposed to the Japanese air raids."

Maybe it would be best for me to start this interview with when I first heard about the Japanese attack on our naval base at Pearl Harbor.[1]

On Sunday afternoon, December 7, 1941, while we were in church, our pastor announced to the congregation that in the early hours of that same morning, Japan had cruelly initiated a deadly attack on our naval base in Honolulu. I was 24 years old at the time. The Japanese launched about 200 planes from several aircraft carriers and left our naval base, plus many Navy fighting vessels, in shambles. About 3,000 service people died. All the Navy battleships stationed at Pearl Harbor had been destroyed, except for one. What a sad day in our history. This could only mean one thing—*total war* against Japan, Germany, and Italy.

That attack motivated me and so many other people to do something to defend our country. We were strictly patriotic. We wanted to fight for our country against another country that was so infested with evil forces. Rather than wait until I was drafted, I thought I would enlist and join the service when I wanted to. I joined the Navy. Even then I did not get into

---

1. Mr. Rinsema wrote a short personal history called "The Life and Times of Jacob Rinsema." I am grateful to him for permitting me to quote from that source as a supplement to his taped interview.

the part of the Navy that I had wanted to. I went into the Seabees, a construction battalion.[2]

In May of 1942, I drove to Chicago and enlisted in the U.S. Navy and was taken into service on June 19, 1942. My first stop was at boot camp in Norfolk, Virginia. The second stop was at Quonset Point, Rhode Island. The third move was across the U.S. to Yerba Buena—or, as it was commonly called, Goat Island, an island located in the San Francisco Bay. It served as an anchor for the Oakland Bay Bridge. The first span of the bridge was from Oakland to the island; the second span was from the island to San Francisco. That was the location of the 1939 San Francisco World's Fair, and some of the gaily colored buildings still survived and were being occupied by the Navy. It was during our three-week stay at Goat Island that eight of us decided to take a ferry boat to San Francisco and enjoy a T-bone steak dinner as a farewell to the U.S. and to have a last fling for who knew how long before we would return to U.S. soil, if at all. From that place we hauled anchor and went south to Port Huneme, California, where we loaded more equipment and men. After a few days there, we again hoisted anchor. In September—three months after I enlisted—we were headed for who knew where or for how long. *We* certainly didn't!

We left in a two-ship convoy. Ours was the Dutch ship called the *Somelsdyk*. The other ship was also of foreign origin, a Danish vessel. After many days of looking only at the blue waters of the huge ocean and the second ship and the faces of 1,100 fellow Seabees, we finally arrived at Noumea, New Caledonia, which was an island governed by the French. There we lay at anchor for about four weeks. We had liberty to go ashore quite frequently. Finally, our orders came through to weigh anchor and strike out in a northerly direction. After two days, we arrived in the New Hebrides Islands and dropped anchor at the island of Esperito Santos, a British protectorate. We arrived to see the bay cluttered with debris. Two days earlier, the troop transport ship *Calvin Coolidge*, a large ocean liner, had hit a Japanese-planted mine. Miraculously, not a life was lost because help was so immediately available, but debris from that accident was everywhere.

---

2. The Seabees were one of the construction battalions in the U.S. Navy which built naval aviation bases and facilities. The word "Seabees" is an alteration of CB, the initial letters of "construction battalion." Thus, CBs became known as the Seabees.

We lay at anchor there for two weeks, awaiting further instructions, which finally came through. One of our two ships was to leave and prepare a base of operations on Guadalcanal. At the time, that island was not completely dominated by the Marines. The Japanese offered strong opposition and harassment. The first ship with an advance party was to land and unload at Koli Point. Two weeks later, the second ship arrived at Koli Point because the first Marine Raider Batallion had cleared the area of the Japanese, and it was now safe to proceed. The advance ship soon rejoined us and established a beach camp at Koli Point. Because of my experience with lumber, I was put in charge of all the lumber and plywood supplies, which didn't amount to a whole lot. Our purpose was to build air fields, power lines, roads, and whatever needed to be built for the Army and the Marine Corps. That was our job—to build up those bases—but at the same time it was dangerous because we were also exposed to the Japanese air raids. I think we had at least 300 raids. Of course, they weren't always that close. The Japs had to fly high because the Marine Corps could hit them with the anti-aircraft guns if they were lower. The Japanese were not very accurate.

After three weeks, it was decided for safety precautions that we would move our entire operations two miles inland along the Malibu River. In my outfit, there were a little over 1,000 men. So move we did—everything but the lumber supplies. I was told to stay with the lumber until it could be taken to the new location. I didn't relish staying at the beach camp in my tent alone, but orders were that I remain at my post, so I did. I had a poorly constructed table made out of tree branches, and on it I stored my sea bag and other supplies, including my aluminum mess gear and cup. I dragged my sleeping cot to the center of the tent and, with my loaded rifle, I tried to sleep. Along about midnight, when it was totally dark, my table made of tree saplings decided to collapse. I sat suddenly bolt upright on my cot with my rifle trained right on the spot, awaiting further noise— should it be a mouse, a cockroach, or a Japanese. My rifle was prepared to speak and meet the challenge. Of course, nothing happened. Daylight revealed that it was only the collapsed table. Nonetheless, I made it clear to the lieutenant that there would be no more nights alone at the beach in my tent, even at the risk of a court martial. That was the scariest experience of the whole war for me.

Since we weren't operating as fighting soldiers, we did not need as much in the way of basic training as other recruits did. In fact, I think it was about three months from the time that I entered service to the time that we were in Guadalcanal. That didn't allow much time for training. Even the training we did have was poor because the whole war was new, and supplies and supervisors were not in place yet. Sometimes training was very quick, and it was called "90 Day Wonders." But it was mainly the officers who got basic training in 90 days. The officers already had an education from going to college, and the Navy did not take very many people for officers who didn't have a college eduction. They sent them right to military school and gave them training with other officers, and then they were sent right into the activity.

Anyway, back at the new camp, we had a sawmill set up. Then I had my hands full handling all the green lumber they cut in the jungle. I had help, however, because all of this green lumber had to be stacked and slatted to air dry to keep it from molding. We had crews of men cut trees from the jungle, mostly mahogany and beetle nut trees. We had crews clearing the jungle for roads and airfield construction. We also had crews building telephone communications and crews who did nothing but spray fuel oil on swamps and streams to control mosquitoes—a very necessary operation. About 95 percent of our men were infected with malaria. Personally, I sustained 17 bouts with malaria before it finally subsided. We had landed there in November of 1942, and a year later we were told that we were going home. That was because so many men in my outfit were contaminated with malaria. Our daily activities, aside from the air raids and being shot at, were to build landing strips and that kind of thing. We also built docks on the ocean to unload ships, and we built bridges to cross the rivers. Whatever had to be built, we were there to do it. Labor is what it was. Heavy labor. That is what it was.

I became a carpenter once I was out of the service. When I was in the Seabees, I was so young that I did not know too much. I was put in charge at a lumber yard at Guadalcanal. The sawmill that we had was brought with us from the States. We had men who had been trained in using it because that is what they had done in their civilian lives. They set that sawmill up at one end, and we cut up millions of pieces of lumber for everyone's use: Army, Navy, and Marines. We had crews that would go into the jungle and cut down trees and take logs from out of the forest and load them up onto the trucks and haul them down to the sawmill. I was put in charge of the lumber after it was cut. As I mentioned before, the lumber was as green as green could be, so we had to strip it so it wouldn't rot. Then that lumber went off to the Army, the Navy, and the Marines—whoever needed it. They didn't have to come with a checkbook; they just came and got the lumber. *(Laughter)*

The outfit that I was in, the 14th Seabees, was in a camp built in the jungle there. It was a very modern camp, as camps went. We had mess halls and recreation halls. Everybody had a plank deck in their tent. We lived quite well; but earth tremors, floods, and humidity were a part of our existence. Everybody had to have a foxhole outside of their tent. Because our camp was located on one end of the airfield that we were constructing, we got a lot of "attention" from Japanese planes. However, as I said earlier, the Japanese flyers were not very accurate—they had to fly very high because the Marines enjoyed giving them a "warm welcome" with anti-aircraft batteries.

At different times the Japanese tried to retake possession of Guadalcanal. During that time, they had second thoughts about the strategic value of the island. They assembled a large task force somewhere north of us with many ships and about 40,000 troops. That proved to be a last-ditch attempt to retake the island. Our reconnaissance, however, discovered a large task force approaching the canal. Every man on the island was alerted and assigned a position. Our position was to guard along the Malibu River. All night long we could hear the big guns exchanging fire, but by morning it was evident that a great battle had been won. Three Japanese ships were run onto the beach in order to give their troops a chance to escape to land. It was estimated that many did not get ashore; but with no food or arms, they were doomed anyway. They fled to the mountainous area, and the Marines quickly dispatched those who didn't die of starvation. It was reported that most of their ships, including their fighting ships, were destroyed. Later, one of my buddies and I went to see the rusting hulks of those Japanese ships. I still have pictures of them in my WWII album. But, as I said, we had to have foxholes right near our tents. We had to make very sure where every foxhole was—that was an order issued from headquarters. Every tent needed to have an adequate foxhole—either a community foxhole which held five men up by the tent, or you had to dig one foxhole for yourself. The guys I was with built a community foxhole, but the guys in the tent next to us opted to dig their own individual foxholes.

This one guy—his name was Jake Addington—he was a nut from Alabama, you know, and he just procrastinated and did not dig a foxhole. Another guy in Jake's tent—his name was Robert Baraby—was from New York, and he had a deep New York accent, too. He dug a foxhole for himself. One night we had a particularly strong attack. Everybody headed for their holes. Jake and Bob were both in the habit of sleeping in the nude. Most of the guys slept in the nude because it was so hot there.

When the air raid sounded, both guys didn't take time to dress. They just put on their helmets and rushed out of the tent. Since Jake hadn't dug a hole of his own, he jumped into Bob's hole. When Bob came to his hole, he saw it was occupied by Jake! It was a rare comedy to see Bob wearing nothing but his steel helmet on a clear, moonlit night, exchanging coarse words with Jake about who had a right to be in the hole. It was even funnier because of Jake's southern drawl and Bob's New York accent. *(Laughter)*

There really was a lot of humor in war. Comical incidents were quite frequent. One night we had an earth tremor that was quite scary. No damage occurred. It wasn't that bad. The following night, two guys in our neighboring tent decided to have some fun with another of their buddies, whose name was Elmo Lee Smith. When Elmo was out taking his evening shower, those guys tied a rope to his bunk and ran it to their bunk. Later, when it got real quiet, one guy reached down, grabbed ahold of the rope, and started shaking Elmo's bunk. Elmo jumped up and yelled. It was one of those times when you just had to be there to thoroughly enjoy the results.

About this time, a buddy named Alex Toquinny ("Frenchie") and I found a discarded water pump in the Navy dump. We fashioned a wood-turning lathe from this pump. We got blocks of mahogany wood and were able to make some very nice fruit bowls. Other guys would see what we had made and told us how beautiful the bowls were and asked us to make bowls for them. We would tell them that they could use the lathe and we would show them how to do it, but that they would value the bowls far more if they made them themselves.

My best buddy, Frank Ross, made a beautiful, extra-large fruit bowl, polished it with a wax solution, made a wooden box for it, and sent it home to the States—or so he thought. About a week later, he was told a package awaited him at the post office. When we went over to pick up the package, he was given the box he had sent home 10 days earlier. The ship that was carrying our outgoing mail was bombed and had sunk in our harbor, and the box was picked up from the water with other debris by Navy boats. One corner of the box was burned through, and part of the bowl had been charred, too. He was consoled when we told him that he had acquired a very unique war trophy or souvenir and had a good story to tell.

In October of 1943, the scuttlebutt (Navy slang for rumor) said that our battalion was to be on alert—meaning, be prepared to expect something. We were told that by a certain date we had to be packed and assembled to leave the island. We all thought, without a doubt, that we would move toward the hot spots again. After much of the usual Navy confusion, we boarded a liberty ship. After we were seagoing, an announcement was made over the PA system that we would indeed be going home. A rowdy cheering resulted, you may be assured. This early departure was because of the unusually large percentage of us suffering from malaria attacks.

After several days we arrived at Pearl Harbor. Some evidence of the bombing was still around, but most was cleared away. The sunken battleships are still cluttering the harbor today. While lying at anchor, we were given permission to go ashore. Several of us took a trolley and headed to Waikiki Beach. At that time, there were only three hotels on the beach. Today, there are hotels as far as the eye can see. After four days, we again hauled anchor and headed east. It was on the trip between Pearl Harbor and San Francisco that we experienced a violent storm. We were ordered to stay below until the storm abated. The waves were so violent that the ship shuddered. I truly feared for our welfare, and I know I was not the only one. We also heard the news over the PA that a liberty ship, like the one we were on, had been broken in half by the same storm. By morning the storm had ended, and the sun made its appearance again.

Arriving in San Francisco in November of 1943 was another thrill. It was announced that there would be no cheering as we passed under the Golden Gate Bridge, but at that point we could toss our caps in the air. We docked at berth number six. The Red Cross and Salvation Army bands were on hand to give us a warm reception. The harbor was teeming with fighting ships and submarines, and sailors were everywhere. We were immediately put on waiting buses and driven about 35 miles inland to Camp Parks, which would be my home for the next year and a half. Everyone was in high spirits and thankful to be home. The next order of business was to take leave time to see our dear ones. Thank God for sparing the entire battalion, with only the loss of two men.

The first stop of my 30-day leave was in New Holland, South Dakota, to visit with the young lady with whom I had been exchanging letters for a year and a half. Also, for the first time, I was going to meet her mother, brothers, and sisters. What a joyous week of celebrating. Jean had arranged for a substitute teacher to teach her classes and had agreed to accompany me to Indiana. Two cars filled with her relatives drove to Chicago to welcome me back. Even now, at 87, I weep while thinking about this. The Lord is indeed a precious Lord. He watched over all of us during those trying times. Jean and I stayed with my parents for the next three weeks. But, alas, those weeks came to an end, and I had to leave. The plan was that Jean would travel with me as far as Omaha. Then she would go north, back to New Holland, and I would continue west to Camp Parks. Things did not go according to our plans, however. Halfway to Omaha, I suffered a violent attack of malaria. The conductor wired ahead to Omaha, where an Army ambulance took me to an Army hospital, where I remained for 10 days to recuperate.[3] After 10 days, we continued our trip as planned. It was a good period of rest, relaxing, and sharing, and I was so happy to have Jean with me.

Then it was back to Navy business. The next several months were rather uneventful until May 1944 came. We had planned that when the school year was completed, Jean would come to California, and we would be joined in holy matrimony. All of those plans were realized. We were married on May 23, 1944, in the Alameda Christian Reformed Church. The church also had a Christian school. Since the teacher was leaving, Jean was asked to fill the spot, which she did. The friends we met at that time are still friends to this very day, although many have gone to be with the Lord.

After one year in California, I was assigned to a new battalion and was soon to leave for Alaska. I was again sent to Port Hueneme, California, to await boarding our ship, which was being loaded but not yet ready. While waiting for several weeks, I had leave and drove 450 miles to Alameda for weekends with Jean. It was on one of these trips, while passing through a small town, that I noticed celebrations everywhere. People were shouting:

---

3. See Part III of this book for the letter which Jack wrote from Omaha to his brother.

"The war is over! The war is over!" What a day of rejoicing!

As I think back to my time on Guadalcanal, I realize how many close friends I made there. After all, we were living together 24 hours a day. There have been several reunions of my 14th Seabee outfit since the war, but I have never been to one myself. They usually have them down in Texas; but due to my circumstances, I could never get away to go down there. You see, my wife was hurt in an automobile accident right after the war, and she became crippled as a result. Furthermore, at age 46, I was stricken with a brain tumor, and I was out for quite a while. I am still suffering from the results of it, but I can walk pretty well. My wife, Jean, passed away in 2001. We were married 53 years. That is her picture over there on the wall *(pointing)*. She was a wonderful woman, and she truly loved the Lord.

You know, I still keep in touch by letter with some of the guys I was with on Guadalcanal, but most of them are dead now. Also, you kind of lose touch after a while. I was a pretty religious kid growing up. My family was very religious, also. I don't ever remember a time when my folks and siblings did not attend church regularly. You'd think that being in the war would have added to my religious beliefs, but it did not contribute anything to my faith, which was very strong already. The war was such an evil place, and there were lots of guys who swore and talked filthy and told dirty stories and all of that. It really was not that nice of an environment for me to be in. It was a thousand miles from nowhere, and I felt a lot of homesickness. But a reasonable person could understand that when you are out there, you might just as well make the best of it because you were not going to go back until someone sent you back. You were there for the duration, you might say.

I have already talked about my wonderful wife Jean. We also had three fine daughters. Two of them became teachers, and the third one worked in the insurance business. And I have several grandchildren and great-grandchildren. I have a very nice-looking family, as you can see *(pointing to photographs)*, and I certainly am very proud of all of them.

By the way: Did I tell you that after I was discharged from the Navy, after the war ended, that I went into upholstery work? I learned the upholstery trade, and I stuck with that for about four years. But then I decided that I wanted to go back to carpentry work. I realized that I liked working with lumber more than cloth. I never enjoyed upholstery work very much. There is nothing like the smell of lumber. I made a lot of things in Guadalcanal. I will show you one thing that I did. *(He hands over a beautiful wooden bowl.)* That is teakwood. And I have another thing here that I carved. I think you can see the carving on it. I made that with a pocketknife and a wood chisel. It's a wonderful little box with all kinds of ornate flowers and leaves and that sort of thing, you see? And do you notice what is carved across the box? It says Jean: J-E-A-N. That is my wife. I made that for her when I was in the Navy. This is a Japanese medical kit, and this thing is a very interesting piece—a necklace for Jean. There is only one in the world like that. I made it from beetle nut and the dried seeds of native weeds. We cut a lot of beetle nut and mahogany trees up there. They had a nut on them that looked something like a chestnut.

Well, this is probably enough from me. Maybe sometime when you come back for another visit, I can show you more things. Your putting this book together is a great service to me and my family and to everyone who has lived since WWII. Now, today's readers will see first-hand what some of us went through. Of course, I was only one of about 16 million people in uniform who were involved in one way or another. In WWII, we sat on Guadalcanal and followed the actions of the other forces as they hopped from island to island—and on many of those islands, anywhere from 25,000 to 50,000 lives were lost. Very sad.

Ralph P. Fredrickson
1943

Born: 1921

Present home: Lake Shore, Minnesota

Military history: Drafted; entered service 1942

Branch of service: U.S. Army

Length of service: Three years, three months

Highest rank: Sergeant

Date/place of interview: July 3, 2003
Lake Shore, Minnesota

Note: Mr. Fredrickson died suddenly on July 26, 2003.

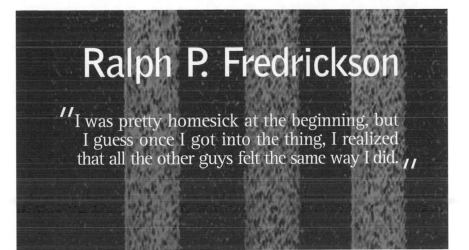

Ralph P. Fredrickson

"I was pretty homesick at the beginning, but I guess once I got into the thing, I realized that all the other guys felt the same way I did."

To start out, I thought you might like to see a few things I've saved from the 1940s. Here are some propaganda leaflets, which the Germans dropped on camps where American soldiers were stationed in Europe. Those leaflets were intended to make us lonely for home and sad that we weren't with our friends and loved ones. Here's one showing a young lady dancing and partying with a bunch of guys at a bar. The message reads: "Hey you, American Soldiers! While you are far away from home trying to defeat us Germans—WHICH YOU NEVER WILL DO—your wives and girlfriends are partying with guys who are draft dodgers. Your women have forgotten you already!"

Here is a Safe Conduct Certificate signed by Dwight D. Eisenhower, which the American military dropped on Germany. Its purpose was to urge the German people and German soldiers to capitulate and stop supporting Hitler's war efforts. This is my wife Carol's ration book.[1] I never had a ration book because military people did not need to, but she did.

When I was home on furlough, I did not need any ration stamps. I could fill up the car with gasoline and drive as much as I wanted to and all that

---

1. In these books were stamps which you had to have in order to buy certain things that were in short supply, like coffee, sugar, gas, and other supplies. See Part III of this book for reproductions of a ration book.

kind of stuff because I was a service man. Looks to me like my wife has a lot of these stamps left over. I wonder if they are still good? *(Laughter)*

I was drafted in 1942. The draft was fairly new, but it was necessary after the Japanese attack on Pearl Harbor on December 7, 1941. I was drafted on the 11th of August 1942, and they sent me home for about two weeks. I reported for active duty on the 24th of August. I felt nervous about leaving home. I was just 21 years old and had never been away from home before, but I guess that I felt that everyone my age had to go and get the war over with. I had no reservations about that at all. I felt that it was my service to my country.

I went to Missouri for basic training. Basic was only about three months at that time. While I was there, I experienced the first of a lot of invitations from civilians. You know, to parties and "other entertainment" for servicemen and so forth. *(Laughter)* There were lots of parties and dances that churches and social groups put on for us. *(Laughter)* Yep! Then, of course, the USO had entertainment and social functions for us, too.[2]

It was all so strange to me. As I said, I had never traveled really very much alone. I guess the farthest away from home I had ever traveled was from my home in Faribault up to Minneapolis to the University of Minnesota. I was at the university for one year before I was drafted. That was not enough to exempt me, even though I was taking engineering classes.

I was pretty homesick at the beginning, but I once I got into the thing, I got involved in a lot of other stuff, and I realized that all the other guys felt the same way I did. After three months of basic training, I was shipped out of Missouri to California. I was stationed at a training center in the Mojave Desert. That is where I got some experience in desert living. It was pretty hot. It was so dry and dusty that it affected my lungs, and I got strep throat and a high fever. While I was there, I was going to apply for OTS (Officer Training School), but another program came along called ASTP (Army Specialized Training Program). They said that this was where they were going to get their future officers. Then I got orders to proceed to Salt Lake City for an assignment at a college. Later they sent me to Carnegie Tech in Pittsburgh. Before that, they sent me to the University

2. For more information about the USO, see the endnote at the conclusion of the interview with Jane A. (Meyer) Elsen later in this section.

of Kentucky in Lexington. For a guy from Faribault, Minnesota, who had never traveled, I was sure seeing a lot of the country!

I went to the University of Kentucky for three months, and that is where I took special survey course work. It was after that that I went to Carnegie Tech; and then after being there for nine months, they decided that they needed more bodies in the combat area, so they sent me for assignment to the 358th Steel Artillery of the 95th Infantry Division in Harrisburg, Pennsylvania. When I was first assigned to that division, I received further training with the fuel artillery battalion. Then the 95th Infantry Division was alerted for overseas shipment. One of the requirements they had was that if you hadn't had a furlough for quite a while, you should go home on a furlough before you left. So I went on a furlough for 10 days, and then I was back. The place of embarkation was Camp Miles Standish near Boston Harbor in Massachusetts. We got on board the *Mariposa*, which was kind of a luxury liner that they had converted into a troop transport, and they put a bunch of us in there and we went to England. That was in 1944.

Kind of an interesting sidelight: When the 358th returned from overseas a year later, we came back on the same ship, the *Mariposa*. As we entered Boston Harbor, there was a tugboat preceding our ship, and it had a big banner which we could all see: "Welcome Home 358th! Job Well Done!" That was a very emotional moment for us.

The battalion arrived and arranged its affairs under ETO—the European Theatre of Operations. There we received our equipment and embarked on an LST (landing ship tank) convoy, which is exactly the same ship that was used for the D-Day invasion on June 6, 1944. So we landed at Omaha Beach. If you have ever seen the movie *Saving Private Ryan*, that is exactly what we did. The LSTs went to shore, but not under enemy fire. We landed then on the 11th of September at the site of the historic landing at Omaha Beach. Three months prior to that was the D-Day invasion.

I am sure that *Saving Private Ryan* was filmed on Omaha Beach because I recognized the same things in that film. Like right at the end of the beach—maybe 100 yards of beach—there is a cliff straight up. A road was up there at the top of that cliff, and during the landing German soldiers occupied that road above the cliff. That is why the Germans could kill so many American soldiers as they landed on the beach down below.

You know, I never found out what the "D" in D-Day stood for. I mean "V-E" meant Victory in Europe and "V-J" meant Victory in Japan. But the "D" in D-Day—I just don't know.[3]

It was very emotional for us to be landing on the same beach where so many of our fellow soldiers had died just three months earlier. We drove past the cemetery with all the crosses in it. We drove inland into Normandy, stayed there for a few days, and then we moved by motor convoy several more miles inland. That was where we experienced our first combat action. We were in support of the infantry several miles inland. This was in October of '44. I was only 23 years old, and I was facing a life-and-death situation. It was very emotional and scary.

On the way up, they had posted men at various points to make sure we had made the right turns. I remember being out there. You could hear the explosion of the field artillery and all that. I knew what I was headed for, and I knew it was not a game. One thing, though: I never did see any of my buddies get wounded or killed. That was because we were not in the combat zone yet. Being the field artillery, we were probably 1,000 yards to a mile behind the infantry. I was in the service section of the field artillery. By being in the service section, we traveled up as close as we could come to the infantry to pick out the field positions for the next firing positions. It would be the infantry that would take any fire. They would have got it—they were out in front there. On a couple of occasions, we got up close enough so that we could see some direct fire from the German field artillery. We proceeded across France, and on Thanksgiving we were at the Maginot line.[4] The Maginot line was a line of defense the French had put up to stop the German advances, but it did *not* stop them.

The Germans went through, and then we went in to the Maginot line to kick them out of there. It was there, while we were surveying for new gun

---

3. The "D" means "designated" and was used by the military as a secretive labeling for the date of a surprise attack. Often an "H" would follow the "D"—"H" being the hour of the planned attack. Apparently, the use of "D" for designated surprise attacks was fairly common in military planning, but for some reason D-Day has remained as the label for the Normandy invasion on June 6, 1944.

---

4. André Maginot (1877–1932) was a French politician who was Minister of War from 1922–24 and 1928–32. He proposed a line of fortification along France's border with Germany, and it became known as the Maginot line. In an era of mobile and air warfare, however, fixed fortifications were impractical and outmoded. The German army overtook the Maginot line in 1940.

positions, that we got up fairly close. In our section, as we were making a survey, we saw white flags being thrown from a group of Germans who wanted to surrender, so we took five prisoners. That was my first contact with German soldiers, the enemy.

The German soldiers were much younger than we were because by that time in the war, Hitler was drafting kids as young as 15 or 16 years old. They were just scared, teenage kids. I remember one of those young German soldiers in particular. Of course, we were always interested in picking up souvenirs. That kid had a wristwatch, and I said, "Give it to me!" He held it out, and he said it was "kaput"—it was not running any-more. I suppose he kept it because it was a present that he got from his mother when he graduated from high school or something. But I took that watch from him. To this day, I still feel guilty that I took it away from that kid. It didn't do me any good—the watch didn't even work! Those kids didn't speak any English, and we didn't speak any German. We learned some German words, though. Like I knew what "kaput" meant.

We could write letters home as often as we wanted to, but we turned the letters in to one of the officers who was the censor officer. I heard that my family and friends got some letters that were censored and parts were blacked out. We were not allowed to say anything about where we were "now," but later we could tell about where we had been. I do not remem-ber exactly how much time had to pass—either a month or two weeks or whatever—but after that we could tell people where we had been. I'm sure it was frustrating for people back home to get censored letters from me and they had no specific idea of where I was or anything.

There were four of us kids in my family   an older brother and two sisters. I was the youngest. My brother was in the service, too. He was in a photo group in the South Pacific. His photo group was not in a combat area. It was a photo reconnaissance that he was in. Neither one of my sisters went in the service, but a lot of women did join—nurses, clerks, and even pilots.

You're probably wondering how I can remember so many details from 60 years ago. Well, you see, I have this combat diary, and that is how I can remind myself about some of these things. I can remember real clearly some of the things that happened to me as a 23-year-old kid when I was in the service because it was the most profound time of my life. But I have a hard time remembering what happened 10 days ago! *(Laughter)*

All the education I got in the Army was extremely valuable. After the war, under the GI Bill, I went back to the University of Minnesota, and they appraised my educational background and gave me a certain amount of credits for the work I had done at the University of Kentucky and Carnegie Tech. I followed a regular engineering curriculum at Carnegie Tech, and almost all of those credits transferred to the University of Minnesota. At the University of Minnesota (although I only had one year as a freshman before I was drafted), I went back and entered as a junior. I got a lot of credit for my experience in the Army—and that education was at some of the best schools in the nation. I got my degree in 1948, a Bachelor of Civil Engineering.

As I listen to the news these days and hear reports about the war in Iraq, I often compare what's going on now with what was happening 60 years ago. One similarity is that in this war, they are going after a person who was exactly like Adolf Hitler. During my time, we had Adolf Hitler to contend with and to defeat. For that reason, I feel that we did the right thing. We did the right thing because a generation ago, we had to get rid of Adolf Hitler. This time it is Saddam Hussein. You know, Hitler and Roosevelt came to power within months of each other, and they also died within months of each other about a dozen years later. At least Roosevelt died a hero, and Hitler apparently did himself in.

Before I was drafted, I was in love with a wonderful girl. She is sitting right out there on the patio—my wife Carol. Yep!

When I was first drafted and went to Fort Snelling, Carol came with my father and mother to bid me farewell. But things happen when one is absent, and she met another guy. She got married, eventually. When I came home I got married, too. Carol's first husband died. Without going into a lot of detail, my first wife and I divorced, and Carol and I ended up getting married 20 years ago. Even though I knew her way back when, before I was drafted, it took a long time before we got to be with each other! *(Laughter)*

That war *did* interfere with a lot of our private lives. Yes, it did! It took three years and 11 months out of my life. My life was not my own. War can sure interrupt lives. My opinion is that it boils down to being at the right place at the right time. Or the wrong place at the right time. In other words, if I had been assigned to a unit or if the 95th Division had been picked out for the landing at Normandy, who knows what would have happened to me? Also, our division was the second division to be sent back to the States on what they called redeployment. The war in Europe ended in May and I was home before the Fourth of July, so I got home quickly. But soon after I got home, we received our orders to proceed to Camp Shelby, Mississippi, for overseas deployment.

Fortunately, the U.S. dropped the atomic bombs on Japan in August. I know that there are some people who think we shouldn't have dropped the bombs. But of course, the bombing kept me home—and the war ended right then. The atomic bombs were dropped on August 6 on Hiroshima and on August 9 on Nagasaki. In fact, I think that the second one was dropped after I was at Camp Shelby, Mississippi. Prior to that time, our general said, "We are going overseas...." So we just got ready for it. But then they dropped the second bomb, and everything got canceled.

I have always had the opinion that it saved a lot of the Japanese people's lives—those bombs, I mean. I know there were a lot of innocent civilians who were killed; but if we had invaded Japan, we would have lost a lot more of our soldiers and even more Japanese civilians.

I've been referring to this little booklet now and then. *(Holding it up)* It's a little history of my battalion. I get a kick out of this ending, here: "Thus ended the first participation in a war against an enemy of the United States of the 358th Fuel Artillery Battalion...." It goes on to say what we did, and at the end is says, "There may be another job for the 358th to do in its country's service against an enemy before it reverts permanently to reserve or inactive status...." You see, what's interesting about that last sentence is that this booklet was written before the war with Japan had ended. At that point nobody knew how much longer the war would go on, and nobody knew about the plan to drop the atomic bombs on Japan.

Kenneth J. Porwoll
1941

Born: 1920

Present home: St. Paul, Minnesota

Military history: Minnesota National Guard, Brainerd;
inducted into service 1941

Branch of service: U.S. Army – Light Armored Tank Division

Length of service: Five years, five months (including three years,
six months held as a POW by the Japanese)

Highest rank: Staff Sergeant

Date/place of interview: March 14, 2005
St. Paul, Minnesota

Kenneth J. Porwoll

" The Bataan March was a 100-mile trip. We did 60 miles of walking, and for the rest we rode on a train, squeezed into boxcars. "

My service in the military dates back to the late 1930s. I was raised in Brainerd, Minnesota, and my teenage years were spent during the Great Depression. Those were rough times for everybody, and we all knew what poverty was. But we also knew what good friendships were all about, and I had many friends. We all had grown up together.

Most of us, though, did not have much money. If you had fairly good clothes to wear for school or for parties, you were very lucky. Anyway, when I was about 19 years old, the National Guard in Brainerd had parties. My buddies and I heard that the Guard was going to have a New Year's Eve party, and it was going to be the biggest social event in town. It cost $25 to go to it. Who could afford that? None of us had that kind of money. But if we joined the Guard, we would get in free—*and* we would get a nice new uniform to wear. And we could meet girls! *(Laughter)* Or you could take two of them to the party, if you wanted!

My buddies and I started talking about joining the Guard. After all, we didn't think we would ever be involved in a war. That was the last thing we thought would ever happen. I mean, this was the late 1930s, and most Americans felt that we would never be directly involved in any military way with what was going on in Europe and elsewhere. Boy, we were soon to find out that that idea was wrong. So about a dozen of us guys signed up for the Guard at the same time, and we had a great time at that New Year's Eve party.

Another reason for joining up was that we also thought it was a macho thing to be in a tank outfit and learn to drive a tank. I remember the first time I was on a highway with a tank. The sergeant was saying that I needed to shift it into high gear, but I wasn't able to do it. He told me to use two hands; and when I did that, I broke the shift lever. He told me that I was done, and he made me shut the tank off and get out of it. Even though that happened, they kept me anyway. *(Laughter)*

For many years, I didn't want to talk about my experiences in the war; and then all of a sudden, I *did* want to talk about it. I think there were a couple of reasons for wanting to discuss these things. One reason was my long hospitalization, when I had a lot of time to think and reflect. When I came home from the service at the end of July 1946, I spent a year in the hospital and then two more years confined in a back brace. I was really limited in my activities. I came home from the war with tuberculosis of the spine. It had degenerated a couple of the vertebrae in the spine, so I lost my support. It began to pinch the nerves and made everything very uncomfortable. The Army sent me down to Santa Fe, New Mexico, where they were doing spine surgery and treatment. There were 63 of us in the ward. Only half of us felt better after the surgery. That is how touchy spine surgery was back in those days. Now I have come to brag about being one of the first men who had this new thing that they developed where they take the infant cells—today it is called stem cell research. They took an inch and a half off my hipbone, and then they fashioned new vertebrae in the lumbar spine area. That is what fixed me up.

I lay there for about a year in a plaster cast. I couldn't even clean myself after having a bowel movement. The nurses had to do that. It got to be quite a process. When I got out of there and got home two years later, I had formed an abscess on the fusion area. I was back in the hospital again for another nine months.

After that, I felt so good that I went to play golf, but that agitated my condition. I got so that I couldn't even walk. The length of bone in there was irritating the little guy below it so much that it formed a lot of calcium around it and shut the nerves off to my legs. The doctors had to go back in there and remove all of that arthritic buildup. Then, finally, I felt good. I stayed away from golf after that. *(Laughter)*

But there is another reason why I decided to talk about my WWII experiences: What happened is that I met Iris Chang. She is the woman who wrote the book *The Rape of Nanking*.[1] She was in town a few years ago, talking about her book, so my wife Mary Ellen and I went to listen to her in Minneapolis. Afterwards, I went to introduce myself to her. She asked me how many times I had talked about my experiences. I said that I talked about them very little, and she became upset with me. She really read me the riot act. She said that the Japanese were going to get away with the whole thing if we didn't speak up. That is why she wrote her book— because her folks lived in Nanking, and she wrote about what the Japanese had done to them. The Japanese denied many of the things that had happened in Nanking. She lived in Japan for three years so that she could get a real understanding of those events, and then she wrote her book. She told me that if I didn't talk about what happened, then I was stupid. I told her that I would do it and that I would keep doing it until I could do it without all of the emotion and choking and all of the other things. So that's what I am doing now. I am talking about what went on and what I went through.

The other thing that helped me tell my story was that there were 20 of us from Brainerd who came home. We would get together on a regular basis and talk about the war.

I was held prisoner in Japan until the bombing of Hiroshima and Nagasaki, after which Japan surrendered. Truman was right to order those bombings. He was right—100 percent right. The Japanese were training their school kids and old women to fight with bamboo spears. They were going to defend the beaches. Nonsense! There was a segment of the Japanese army that espoused the thinking that it would be wonderful if everybody in Japan was killed in the war. How glorious that would be for Japan! That would be their supreme sacrifice.

---

1. Iris Chang's book *The Rape of Nanking: The Forgotten Holocaust of World War II* (1997) is the first English-language history ever written about the Japanese army's 1937 conquest of China's capital city and the massacre of many of its inhabitants. Chang, a freelance journalist, describes the circumstances under which the Japanese killed a quarter of a million Chinese, nearly all of them civilian combatants, during the first few months of their occupation of the city.

I spent one and a half years in the Philippines and two years in Japan as a POW. The food was terrible and limited. Most of us POWs weighed way under 100 pounds. The food was very scarce. In the Philippines, the torture of POWs was really, really bad. The orders were that if you didn't work, then you wouldn't get fed. Then it turned out that if you were sick and the doctor would say that you were unable to work, you would get half rations and die. One of the details in the Philippines was working on a 100-acre farm with hoes and pickaxes to clear the area and plow the soil. When harvest time came, the Japanese got the whole farm of food. The only thing the soldiers got was a little bit of food while they worked the farm. The Japanese army's orders were that they were to live off the land that they took. If they took over land from someone else, then they were responsible for making that land their own. In Japan, that was the same way.

Our first POW camp was Camp O'Donnell. It was kind of a strange thing. We came off of a starvation diet there in Bataan. The last fighting was done with less than a third of a ration per day, per man. It got to the point where it took two men to do a one-man job. If you needed to dig a foxhole, you would never get it done by yourself because you were so weak. The march was eight days for me, without any food and hardly any water. When I got to Camp O'Donnell, they served lugao, which is rice boiled to a loose consistency—kind of like oatmeal, like wallpaper paste, almost. That is what it tasted like, too. A lot of those guys would take a spoonful of it and get it down, only to throw it up again. They would do that three or four times and say that it wasn't fit for human consumption, but it was the only thing they had to eat. Many of them would not eat it, so they died.

The Bataan march was a 100-mile trip. We did 60 miles of walking; and for the rest, we rode on a train in crowded boxcars. The Japanese would allow you to take water from streams where there were dead people lying in the water. I did that one time. I had to fill my canteen because I only had a little water left, and I had a small bottle of iodine. I poured the majority of the iodine into the water and didn't drink it for a while to see if the iodine would work to kill the germs and bacteria. By the time I drank the water, it tasted very weird because it had too much iodine in it. I reached a point during that walk when I didn't have any water. I thought I was going to die on that march. The Japanese had told us that if we went to the roadside well to get water, we would be killed. I thought: Hey, I may as well die happy by going to the well. So I went to an artesian well and took a drink and filled my canteen. I turned around and started walking back in the line. The other guys looked at me and started to run towards the well. Every one of them who ran to the well got shot.

The thing about the march was that after a while, dehydration set in. I learned after I came home that our brain tells our body to take water from the blood in order to keep our vital organs viable. Because of that, the blood gets thicker and doesn't flow as easily. At the same time, the brain also gets deprived of oxygen, and you get kind of goofy. Maybe I was in one of those goofy spells when I decided that I might as well die standing rather than die lying in a ditch. Our marching orders were that if you couldn't walk, then you would die. You weren't supposed to get help from any of the other guys, either. You know, the Japanese lost so many soldiers on Bataan that they had to call home for resupply. Lots of people probably hate to hear that America surrendered, but our generals surrendered us. MacArthur was down in Australia, and he said that we needed to get our guys together for a counterattack. Well, we didn't even have enough energy to carry our rifles, let alone attack!

There were Filipinos with us on the march. There were Filipino scouts who got good training from American officers. Much of the regular Philippine army had never fired a rifle or a gun. They came out of the rice paddies, and they couldn't wear shoes because their feet were too wide. They had always been barefoot. Many times we would ask them where they were going, and they told us they were going off to find their friend— but they were actually looking for food. If you didn't feed them, they didn't stay.

The Filipinos had tremendous casualties, but they sure raised hell with the Japanese! When it came time to defend that front line around Bataan, the barbwire disappeared under dead Japanese soldiers. After a week, the Filipinos had to move back because of the stench. When they did get food, they couldn't eat it. We are talking well over 40,000 Filipinos and about 12,000 Americans. They claim that there were over 17,000 who were on Bataan who never showed up in prison camps. Those poor Filipinos! The Japanese soldiers would shoot them in bunches of six, seven, or eight. When the Japanese got into our hospital area, the Filipinos who were in there were so afraid of them that they felt they had to get out of bed and obey the commands. Even if they were missing a leg or an arm, they left the hospital. They thought they could navigate on their own, but of course they didn't make it.

I have another story about my being on the march with four other guys with whom I had gone to high school in Brainerd. We hung out together and thought that maybe we could help each other. On the same day that we started walking, the biggest guy—his name was Jim—was hit with a malaria attack. His fever went up to 105 or more, and he was disoriented. We took turns, one on either side of him, guiding him down the road. After an hour of this, his fever turned to a chill and his knees buckled, and he couldn't hold his own weight. He knew that the order was that if you couldn't walk, you'd die. He told us to turn him loose and leave him behind because he knew that we wouldn't make it if we had to carry him with us. We argued with him a little bit, but we realized that he was right. I felt so bad that I started apologizing to him. I went to high school and grade school with him. I told him that I felt so bad that our friendship had to come to this conclusion. He told me to forget it and that he would find another way. I thought to myself: That's the proof that he hadn't given up—he was looking for tomorrow. We let him slide in the ditch. As sick as he was, he was thinking about the welfare of his friends. We never mentioned his name again for the rest of the eight days that it took us to finish that walk. In fact, we all kind of separated. We didn't like one another too well after that experience of abandoning our friend Jim. When I went to get water at the well, I came back and looked for the other fellas. They wouldn't drink my water. They told me that I had stolen it, so I had to drink it. I almost poured it on the ground. But I couldn't do that, so I passed it around to some other guys who were walking with me.

The Japanese would pull an American soldier out of the line and start yelling at and beating him. While four or five Japanese were doing that, the others would say to the soldiers who had been walking with him to go and help their buddy. The first day, when four or five guys would go to help, they all got beaten to death. I had to keep telling myself that I wanted to live—and that kept me from going out to help someone. But each time you *don't* go out there, you die a little bit on the inside. That gets to be pretty heavy. The only way to get out of that is to ask, "God, where are you? What are you going to do about this?" An hour after I asked that, a little voice in my head said, "Ken, if you want to get to the end of this road, you will have to walk it. So pay attention to what you need to do."

That was good advice, because before the end of the 60 miles, you were so tired and so fatigued that you had to think about how to walk.

When we got into little barrios along the way where the fighting hadn't been going on for some time, the Filipino women had moved back into their homes. They lined up cans of water along the road and packets of rice and fruit for us. The Japanese decided that they didn't like that, so they kicked the cans over and chased the women off. When the Japanese turned their backs, the women threw the packages to us. When the Japanese turned back to the women, they didn't know who had thrown the packages because all of those women's heads were down. We passed through three different towns where the Filipino women were doing this for us, and the Japanese soldiers were trying to prevent them from doing it. At one point there was a woman standing in the window of her home, and she raised her hand to throw out a package. A Japanese soldier next to me raised his rifle and shot her out of the window.

We got into San Fernando, into a barbed-wire area. The second morning I woke up there in the sunshine. I was so achy and tired. I rolled over and was looking into the eyes of that Jim who had malaria and who we had dropped in the ditch. This was our buddy from Brainerd. I asked him what he was doing there, and he said that he was lying in the dirt, like I was. Very funny! I asked him how he got there, and he told me that he had walked there, just like I did. I told him to stop competing and tell me what had really happened. He told me that when he went into the ditch, he looked up ahead and saw a culvert. He crawled into it and slept off the malaria attack. During the second day, when another group of Americans was coming down the road, he joined them. Imagine! We all thought he had died. How he got to lie next to me that night, I have no idea. Whether I picked that spot or whether he picked that spot, I have no idea. The other three guys showed up, too. We all felt pretty good about our reunion.

One of the guys said that the Filipinos were bringing food up to the gate and that the Japanese were putting it into a barrack's bag. One guy said that he was really hungry and that part of the food belonged to him—and he was going to go and get his share. He told us that any of us were welcome to come and help him. If we didn't help him, then he was going to do it alone. We told him that we were with him. The plan was to go the next day at noon, when the Japanese soldiers disappeared. They went for lunch someplace. Only two of them stayed there. The plan was that one of us would go and get the bag and throw it to another one of us, and he would fend off any Japanese who would try to stop us. One of us was supposed to make a scene—like we were starting a fight at the water spigot, which was right at the entrance of the little area where the Japanese were. My job was to stop the first Japanese soldier who would come out and put a football block on him. Our two men went in and were racing out with this barracks bag between them. It wasn't too long after that when a Filipino went in there. He started screaming to the Japanese that a bag had been stolen. They came racing after our guys, and I hit the first one in the knees. He went into the group at the water spigot. As I rolled over, the second one was coming through, and I tripped him. He fell on top of the first one. I pushed Americans on top of them, and I pulled their rifles out and threw them over the fence.

As I looked down, I saw two of my buddies give the "high five" sign, so I told the others that we were done and that it was time to go. There were about six Americans on top of the Japanese, and they were really struggling for their lives down there. It was funny. Then the Japanese couldn't find their rifles when they got up, and they probably wondered if they were on the short end of the stick because their officer would have killed them if they had lost their rifles to Americans. Eventually they found their rifles, and they simmered down enough to say that they had had enough. However, they did come back later that night with a squad of 30. They checked every man in the compound to see if they were eating. This was four hours afterwards! *(Laughter)* They never found anyone eating. The food was long gone.

After we got the bag of food, I went back to Jim, who was in the dirt and beginning to have another malaria attack. I gave him a cake of sugar. The Filipinos harvested sugar cane. They would take the juice from harvesting the sugar cane and boil it. As the scum floated to the top, they would skim it off and plop it on the ground and later feed it to their horses. Jim was complaining. I told him to shut up and eat the cake. I told him that if he didn't shut up, I was going to get a Japanese guard and show him who stole the damned bag of food! *(Laughter)* So all of us guys from Brainerd were back together again.

The next day or so, they marched us to the railroad yard. We were happy that we were going to get a ride. No more walking! In this jovial spirit, we walked into a railroad yard with boxcars, and they started putting us into the boxcars. They tried to shut the door, but there were so many of us men that they couldn't get the doors closed. So they took their rifle butts and hammered us until they squeezed us in far enough for them to shut the door. This was all happening in the tropic sun, in a steel boxcar. We had 40 miles to go, but it took four hours to get there. Men died standing up. There was no room for any of us to fall down. When we got to the little city of Capas, they opened the doors. Live men crawled out and fell to the ground, and dead men fell to the floor of the boxcar.

Things never seemed to get better. In the city of Capas, the Filipino women had food and water for us along the road. This time, the Japanese guards were easy. They told us to help ourselves, but we weren't allowed to stop. That wasn't a problem. We would just walk along and grab a can of water or a package of rice or something. We walked for about six miles. Jim told us again that he couldn't make it. He said that he was going to fall out. We kept telling him that he only had a few miles left to walk, but he told us that he couldn't make it. He fell out, but he was able to get on one of the little taxi carts from the villagers. As he and the cart passed by, he waved at us and asked how the walk was. *(Laughter)*

When we got to Camp O'Donnell, we waited for the commandant to smoke his cigarette and drink his tea. His first words to us were that he hated us Americans and hated our people. He told us not to think about going home because we were going to be his slaves and that our people would be his slaves, also. He told us that if we didn't work for the Japanese war effort, then we weren't going to get fed. He said it over and over for two hours.

Many were dying in that place, and there weren't enough men to bury the dead. Then the Japanese said that anybody who went on burial detail would get extra rations. People accepted; but many of those who carried the cadavers to the burial ground were so exhausted that they fell over once they got to the holes, and the guards would kick them over and bury them alive in the holes along with the dead. The men I was with decided that we had to get out of there. If we stayed there for two more weeks, we would be dead. When a work detail came up, we all volunteered. Fortunately, it was a bridge-building detail, and we got assigned to a Japanese engineer company. The Japanese officer in charge of that detail understood that if you wanted men to work 12 hours a day, you had to feed them. So he fed us the same as he fed his troops. The Filipinos would give us fruit and stuff along the way, too. I have to give the Filipinos a big hand. They were loyal to us all the way through the march to the end.

The first bridge that we worked on was going to be over a large gorge, so scaffolding had to be built all the way up. While we were there working on that, there were other American prisoners of war in the mountains, either cutting down trees or getting them ready to come down to use as pieces of the bridge. In the midst of this activity, I got yellow jaundice. With that disease, you get so weak that you don't feel like doing anything. I turned in for sick call, and an officer gave me the option of going back to that terrible camp or staying with him and doing light duty. I jumped at the chance to do light duty. By light duty, I had to carry water from a well two blocks away for the Japanese guards to use in the kitchen and bathroom. The second time that I went to the well, there was a package of brown sugar with a little note attached to it that said that I should take three teaspoons of it a day in order to help with my yellow jaundice. I couldn't believe that someone out there cared whether I lived or died. The Filipinos were on my side! Each time I went to the well, there was something else for me. There was not always a note, but there was always something to eat. I made that detail in pretty good shape, then.

Anyway, we built that bridge without metal or nails or bolts or screws. When we left there, we were loaded up in a Japanese truck, and we drove right across the bridge. It didn't wiggle or creak or fall down. We put it together like Lincoln Logs. The second bridge that we built was in flood country, and we had to pound pilings into the river bottom. All of the men had to work together so they wouldn't have the rope come snaking and hitting one of them on the sides. After a while, you started to get smarter about what you were going to do—especially if you were too sick to do that work, like I was. I was watching a Japanese soldier as he chiseled a lot of different designs onto a large post. Apparently, it was an inventory system, marking the number and name of the bridge. I tapped him on the shoulder and told him that I could do that. He handed me the chisel and the hammer and told me to show him. I chiseled a little bit and realized that I had found myself a job sitting down.

Those of us who were Catholics were always asking the Japanese to allow us to go to Mass on Sunday morning, but they wouldn't let us do it because they didn't have enough guards to watch us. In order to remedy the situation, we *all* went! The Japanese, the Filipinos, and the Americans all went to Mass together. Then the Filipinos fed us afterwards at church. I think that was another reason why the Japanese did it: They, too, were on a rationed diet. What a layout of food they had at the church! They had roasted pigs and chickens as well as fruit and other things. As we left the area, there was a nun passing out another piece of fried chicken for the road. Along with the chicken, we also got a rosary. When we got back to the camp, the Jewish guys asked us what the rosary was, and we told them.

After that camp, we were moved to Camp Cabanatuan. Another work detail was at a copra factory. It was there that I came down with dinghy fever. Dinghy fever is different from malaria because it gets into your bones and makes it so that you cannot function. Every bone in your body aches. The Filipino doctor told the Japanese captain that I was unfit to work and that I needed to stay in the factory and eat coconut, which was a kind of cure for the fever. At the time, anything that was edible was welcomed. You had to be careful of the coconut, though, because it was really oily—and you could have problems the other way as well. That is how I lived through that one.

When we were being transported down to another camp, we were in the back of Japanese trucks. We would go through these little villages, and the Filipinos threw food to us. There was one Filipino who was eyeing the Japanese guard, and when the guard was looking the other way, he took a coconut and heaved it up and hit the guard in the head, knocking him out. When the poor guy came to, he didn't know what had happened. They told him that he had fallen over and had hit his head on the truck. *(Laughter)* It was at that camp that they decided to make a hundred-acre farm to feed the Japanese army. While I was there, I was on a detail to build a dam to catch water.

Well, my whole ordeal as a POW held by the Japanese lasted for three and a half years. I guess my Catholic faith helped me through many of the really rough times. You recall when we had to abandon our friend Jim in the ditch because he couldn't walk any longer? Well, at that time and at many other "low" times on the march, I asked God, "Where are you?" I thought God did not know we existed. Later, when I found Jim, I apologized to God for my smart mouth. I was sorry, because God really *was* there and *did* care. I kind of repeated that throughout my days. I think that's what kept me going.

One of our guys who was on the march told us that he just wanted to die. His name was John. He was in the camp and was sick and weak and losing hope. We were all at a very low point. The Japanese put John into the "zero ward," where everything you possessed was up for grabs by the stronger guys with a strong sense of wanting to live. There was not enough of anything to go around, so you usually ended up naked, lying on split bamboo in a hut. Another guy gave John half of a blanket. That guy was a complete stranger to John, yet he gave him that gift. A week went by and we hadn't heard if John had died, so some of us went back to his ward to see him. There he was, sitting with that half of a blanket around him. We asked him if he was feeling better, and he said, "Not really." But he was happy that the other man had given him his most precious possession. It prompted John to wonder, within himself, if he wanted to live. He decided that he *did* want to live. After John came home, he went to college, got married, and had kids. All because someone had given him part of an old blanket.

Another story I know is about this man who lived in Aitkin, Minnesota. During the war, the "hell ship" taking him to Japan had been torpedoed. He and four others made a raft from flotsam. He was the last survivor left on their raft. The only thing he lived on were the little fish that flopped up on the boards of the raft. There weren't too many, but they were enough to keep him alive for three days. The Japanese found him and tied him up on the deck, in the sun. But he survived that torture, too, and came home as well.

On my ship going from the Philippines to Japan, we had 700 Americans on board. Half of them were locked in each of the two holds. They were so crowded that there wasn't enough room to sit or lie down. The toilet was only a washtub in the middle. There was screaming and hollering all of the time. There was one man who screamed constantly, but his screaming was different from the others. We had a doctor in the hold with us, and he went to see what that guy's problem was. The doctor found out that his appendix was about to burst. The doctor asked him if he would be willing to let him operate if he was able to get surgery equipment. The guy, who was in great pain, said yes. A little while later, a jackknife, needle, and button thread came down. The doctor said he needed light, so they put a 60-watt bulb on an extension cord and lowered it down. Four men held the guy down while the doctor took his appendix out, without any anesthesia.

After you reach a certain point in pain, you black out—and that guy did. The doctor returned the jackknife and needle to the Japanese officer. Two days later, the Japanese officer asked how that guy was doing. He had lived.

Sometimes the crowded confinement was just too much for some guys, and they went crazy. When that happened, someone had to be killed in order to protect the other people in the hold. Strange as it might seem, a sense of humor is what brought most men out of it. That is why we named the guards "Mickey Mouse" or "Speedo." It was something to laugh at. "Mickey Mouse" was a little guard with a big ego and big ears. Of course, the Japanese knew nothing about American cartoon characters, so they took these names in good nature. That guard was always lording over the men and beating them up. The guys told him that he was a *big* shot. He was just like Mickey Mouse: a big and important movie star. All went well and everyone had a good laugh, until the day when he was abusing a prisoner. That POW had had all that he could take and told the guard that Mickey Mouse was a damned rat! That really fired him up. No one dared call the guard Mickey Mouse again—but we'd had our chuckles.

In the Philippines, what bothered me was that POWs were killed without putting up any resistance. That really bothered me. I always felt that if someone wanted my life, they would have to pay a price for it.

One day, I was working on a rock-carrying detail. We had to move rocks from one pile to another. As we walked to and fro, I noticed there was a corral of steers, and they had a large water trough. I thought that if a dumb animal could have all of that water, then human beings should be able to have as much as they wanted, too. I walked over to the corral and rolled in and dropped into the trough. I soaked up the water and as I did, the bulls started to get nervous. I had to get out of there before I started to draw more attention, so I rolled back out of the corral, and one of the guards spotted me. He ran at me with his bayonet, and I knew that I had to get to him before he got his bayonet onto his rifle and got to me. I ran at him with two rocks, and when I got up to him I yelled at him and gestured about what I was going to do with the rocks, and he understood. I backed away from him, and he put his bayonet down. We were isolated. There was nobody else around, and no other Japanese were witnessing him. It worked out fine.

When we were held prisoners in Japan, at noontime we would go out from the buildings and sit in the sun and relax. Once, as I sat against the building, I looked inside an open door and saw a lot of junk. I went inside and came across some grass mats, and I lay down and fell asleep. I didn't know how long I was asleep, but I was awakened suddenly by a Japanese soldier with a rifle. I don't know how I got up off the ground or how I got ahold of him, but when I came to realize what I was doing, I had his rifle under his chin. I tried to fire the gun, but I couldn't get it to fire. It dawned on me that he had the safety on, so I held him with one hand while I searched for the safety—but I didn't know where it was. I just decided to smile and say, "Ah-so." He softened up a little bit, and I released the pressure on his chin and slowly lowered the gun. I was able to get out the door, but I jumped to the side in case he wanted to shoot me. He didn't, though. Strange!

I went right back to the work site and positioned myself so that I could watch the door of that building from that direction. Time went by, and the Japanese solder didn't come out. I began to wonder if maybe I had shot a hole in his head, but I didn't recall any gunfire. I looked at my clothes and didn't see any blood. I kept thinking that I had to have done something to him because he didn't come out of the door. I was so concerned. So I went back there. I went slowly and quietly alongside the building, and I heard him snoring inside! Then it dawned on me that I had taken his sleeping spot, and he had awakened me to get me out of there! *(Laughter)* You can train yourself to be automatic about different things.

When we were in Japan, we had two sets of guards. Wherever you were working, the guards were up there to see that the job was done right. At that time, we were in an area of Japan where it was cold. In fact, the Winter Olympics were held in that area a few years ago. At the end of our work shift, we had buckets of warm water, so I washed up. Once, when I was done, a guard started beating on me. I found out from another person that the reason why he was beating on me was because he thought that I hadn't been working since I had a clean face!

You know, despite all of the cruelty and torture which the Japanese guards inflicted on us POWs during my three and a half years in captivity, I do not hate the Japanese people. My attitude about them changed long ago. Some people, for many years, wouldn't eat rice because it was Japanese. That is dumb. If hatred does that to you, then it is no good for you. It can kill you. I got to a point where I felt sorry for the Japanese, and I just pretty much got rid of the hate.

I have never been back to Japan since the war. I have talked to a couple of fellas who have been back there. When we POWs would walk back to camp in the winter, it was really cold. Often we saw a house up on the hill. We saw a warm, yellow glow and assumed that a family lived there—all safe, secure, and warm. We would wish that we could be in that house. This one guy I know had joined the Merchant Marines. Years later, he said that he was going to go back there and find that house. That was one of the things that carried him through: thinking of the comfort of that house. It got him over all the discomforts that he was going through. When he visited Japan many years after the war was over, he hired a taxi and told the driver where to go. They finally arrived at that house. He went up to it, knocked on the door, and told the people there that he just had to talk to them. He was invited in and was served tea. Somewhere along in the conversation, he was asked where he was in 1943. He said that he was there in that town and had seen their house as he walked back to the POW camp. Immediately, everything was shut down, and he was asked to leave the house. Too bad. You see? Carrying hate for all those years is not good.

As I've said, I hold no grudge against the Japanese. That was then, and now it is all in the past.

Melvin O. Vietor
(with wife Leona)
1942

Born: 1915

Present home: Rural Stillwater, Minnesota

Military history: Drafted; entered service 1941

Branch of service: U.S. Army

Length of service: Four years, three months

Highest rank: Medical Aid

Date/place of interview: June 24, 2003
                                                Stillwater, Minnesota

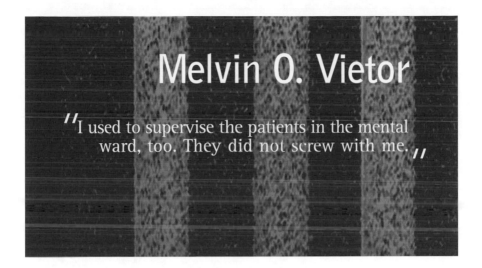

Melvin O. Vietor

"I used to supervise the patients in the mental ward, too. They did not screw with me."

We were a select few, you might say. We were drafted, another boy and me. Well, they drafted the other boy first, but he had an infectious eye, so they rejected him and they took me the next month. I told my dad I could get out of it, but I said, "I'll put my year in and get it done with." Well, it turned out to be *five* years because of Pearl Harbor on December 7.

I went into the service in September and had my basic training. Then I went down and did my exams at Camp Grant, where I trained as a mechanic for six weeks. Then there was an opening at an Army hospital in Illinois, and they said, "Well, you guys have got a choice. You can either work in the kitchen or work in the medics. They need help in the medics." I did not like the idea of the kitchen—that's pots and pans—so I thought, well, I'll try the medics. So I went to the medics. I was there probably about a month when the war with Japan was declared on December 8.

Then I wanted out, but they said, "Oh, no—you're froze!" They said, "We will give you our schooling. What do you want?" They gave me a list, so I said I'd take orthopedics. I was in orthopedics for about three months. Then they started having trouble in the mental ward at that same hospital, and they said, "Tiny, you go down there and help them out for a couple weeks." Well—a couple of weeks turned into four and a half years.

See, what it really amounted to is this: When they invaded Germany, they would fly the mental cases back to New York, and then they flew them in to us at the hospital in Illinois. We kept them until they got a little stabilized and then shipped them to the base nearest to their home. Say you were from Louisiana: We would take you back to your camp in Louisiana. If you were from Fort Snelling, we would take you back to Fort Snelling. We would get them after the third or fourth day after they were wounded or had emotional problems.

I was 26 when I was drafted, so that made me quite a bit older than those young 18- or 19- or 20-year-old kids who were in the war. You see, I was one of the old ones. I always had met the planes that came from the battlefields, so I would take care of the boys and patch them up. We would bring them to the wards and screen them out. Of course, some of them had really bad wounds and would never walk again. How could you tell a person something like that? "You are never going to walk again. Your spine is gone." Well, it's pretty tough telling young kids news like that. We would patch them up as best we could.

The biggest joke was they would come in to the ward and I would say, "What do you want to eat?" And they would say, "Whoa! This is the Army! Don't we just get what the Army wants to feed us?" I'd say, "What do you want to eat? You want steak and eggs? You'll have steak and eggs." See, the guy in the kitchen and I had a pretty good relationship. I would write all of these wounded soldiers' food orders down, and I would take that to the kitchen and they'd make this great food and I'd bring it up to these young kids. They'd say, "This is never the usual way in the Army." They always remembered me for that. I always took the kids into consideration.

I had it good, in a way, but I thought I was going to be there for only two months. I mean, it was pretty bad. You know, a dumb farmer like me getting into something like that. You see, I was the ward master there, and I took care of the oxygen and stuff—and the ammonia ward, too. We had some awful cases to deal with. It was a battle in those wards every day.

Well, you saw a lot of pain and amputation and death. It wasn't all roses. Since I was one of the older ones—I was 26—whenever they had a shipment or anything, I had to go out and put those supplies and materials in the right wards and everything like that. I was at that field for five years, so I knew every damned angle there was. Also, since I was older, I tell you—them kids, some of them—it was pitiful. They were kids, and one in particular kept crying for his mom and all that. He was about 18 years old and had never been away from home before. So I had to go and be a soothing dad or like an older brother to those kids. When it was time for one of them to be released from the hospital, I was the one who used to take patients from all over the United States by train. When I was on the train with those kids, I always had a private compartment behind the doctor.

I used to supervise the patients in the mental ward, too. There was this old doctor—he used to get me mad! They would leave me alone with him all the time. The doctors were supposed to be helping me, but he would just leave me alone with the patients all of the time. But I knew the patients, and they knew me. They did not screw with me. You know, I had one little guy in the mental ward—cockier than hell! Well, one time I took him to the bathroom, and we had a "little understanding"—if you know what I mean! (*Laughter*) He came out of the bathroom a little less cocky. I gave him a toothbrush to clean all the cracks in the floor, and I had him doing that. You know, from that day on, I ran the ward. Before that, the patients thought that they could run it. I'm a big guy and, well, that is where I got even. There weren't any of those guys I couldn't handle.

Once time they sent me out over to the prison ward to get a big, colored guy and take him back to the mental ward. He was way over 200 pounds. I said to the other guards, "Who is gonna help me?" They said, "We ain't going in there with you. You are reliable—they sent *you* there to get him." I always carried a towel in the van. That colored guy came at me. I put the towel around his neck, and I stepped back and choked him out. We laid him on the floor, and I had to do it two more times before he understood that I was in charge. Boy, he got on his knees and said, "Good Lord, I've seen the light! I see the light, good Lord!" I had him in the ward for about six weeks. Every time he would get a little unruly, the nurses there told him, "We'll call in Tiny." Then he would say, "I see the Lord! I see the Lord!" Now you may think that was mean, but if you didn't have control of those disturbed people, they didn't respect you.

A lot of them should have never been in the service in the first place. There were about 25 to 50 percent of them just bucking for a discharge, but the ones who had been in POW camps in Japan were in rough shape.

The Japanese never gave them any sleep. Those were the guys I liked to take care of because in six weeks they would show great improvement. We could turn them loose in about six weeks and put them in an open ward. We had up to 25 to 30 people in that ward.

I really didn't hear back from many of the guys I took care of after the war was over. I guess they were just glad to be out of it and happy to be back home to start their lives over. They probably just wanted to forget all the bad stuff that they went through in the war. I *did* hear back from the parents of one of the kids I took care of because they appreciated what I did for their son—because I took care of their boy and everything. They even made clothes for my kids and sent them as gifts. That was pretty nice.

One day we got a new nurse in the open mental ward who came from some religious outfit. She was too trusting of those guys. I had a real bad patient once. I put him in the ward, but I did not give him a chair—all he got was a mattress and blankets, at first, because I did not know what he was going to do. Well, this nurse came on duty one night and said, "Why doesn't he have a chair?" So they gave him a chair and silverware and everything. Right away he went and broke up the chair, broke down the door, and started throwing stuff around. He went and broke the door down and everything else. So I came in and there was that guy, parading around with a part of the broken chair and yelling that he was going to kill every son-of-a-bitch in the place. So the nurse said to me, "Here's your boy. He's all yours!"—and then she ran out of the ward. I looked at this guy a little bit and said, "You better get back to bed!" He said, "No! I am gonna kill you!" But he went back into the room, and the nurse peeked in the door and said, "What are you going to do?" I said, "I'm not going in there. Call the fire department." So she called them, and they blasted him out of the room with a fire hose into the hallway. When they hit him in the hallway, I went down the stream of water and jumped on top of him. The old doctor came in about that time and said, "Tiny! You are going to kill him!" I said, "I think he needs it!" *(Laughter)*

I broke my thumb in the fight with that guy that night. We kept him about a week. We were like a halfway house, you might say. Then he was going to go to a complete mental ward. We took him out there in an ambulance; we had him sedated pretty heavily when we left. The trip took about six hours, or something like that. When we finally got there, the guy started coming to, and the old doctor was scared and did not want anything to do with him. We took him to the mental hospital there, and I was with him. We got him registered and everything. God, I no more than walked out the door before he was raising hell. So I turned around and went back in and got real close to him to threaten him, and he said, "Tiny, I'll be good!" Then they took him to his ward. You know, I went there three or four months later; I took some patients there. And that same guy, when I walked in, he said to the other patients, "Don't ever fuck with that guy!" *(Laughter)*

Charles M. Nolte
1943

Born: 1923

Present home: Minneapolis, Minnesota

Military history: Enlisted; entered service 1943

Branch of service: Naval Air Corps

Length of service: Two years

Highest rank: Seaman 1st Class

Date/place of interview: September 5, 2003
Minneapolis, Minnesota

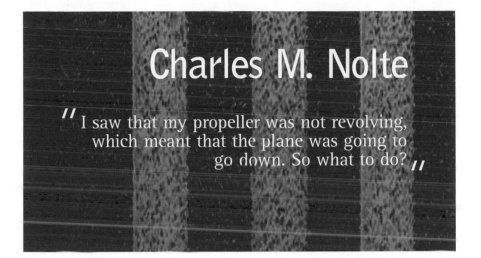

Charles M. Nolte

" I saw that my propeller was not revolving, which meant that the plane was going to go down. So what to do? "

I would have probably been in the Navy for quite a bit longer, except that I got a medical discharge. I was in the Naval Air Corps most of the time that I was in the service, but before I even started my rather dim military career, I was very interested in history from a very early age. So much so that I used to save newspapers—headline newspapers—even back when the Wallis Simpson/Duke of Windsor situation was going on. I saved all those papers before they yellowed and drifted away. I was particularly interested in English history. Maybe that is because my father majored in history at Yale University under Charles Seymour, who was then the president of Yale and one of the greatest historians of the twentieth century. So history—even when I was eight, nine, 10, 11—I was *very* interested in history. I knew all about the rise of Fascism and all of American history, and I followed those interests.

I knew the war was coming because my father told both my brother and me most explicitly. On one occasion—it was immediately after we heard Churchill speaking from Britain in one of those great speeches just after 1939, just after the war began and when it looked its darkest for Britain— my father, with red eyes, turned to both my brother Richard and myself and said that there was going to be a war and that we were going to be in it and probably killed. This was, for a 16-year-old kid, not what you wanted to hear.

Another thing that had happened by the time I was 16 was that I already knew I wanted to be in the theatre. Of course, I was already dealing with my sexual ambiguity at that time, too. I thought that I was the only person in the hemisphere who had this particular problem of homosexuality. Also, my older brother had a very symbiotic relationship with my father and knew he was extremely bright and knew everything about everything. Next to that incandescent older brother, I thought of myself as a very dim bulb. Naturally I wanted to emulate him, so when he decided that he was going to go into the Naval Air Corps, of course that is what I decided that I would do, as well.

By the time of 1941, December 7, I was already out of high school. I graduated from high school that June in 1941 and worked at the Old Log Theatre in Minnetonka and was in one of the very first productions they had there. I then went to the University of Minnesota in September of 1941 as a freshman. My dad was working there and was soon to become dean of the Extension Division, so I could live at home and ride in and out from Lake Minnetonka with him. But on the occasion of *that* day— December 7—of course we all remembered where we were when the news came. The next day my dad and I went to the university as usual. It was a Monday morning, and we would always stop in his office at what is now today the Nolte Center for Continuing Education. In the main foyer in the lounge, hundreds of students, professors, and other people occupied all of the chairs. Most of us were sprawled on the carpet, and we were listening to the radio at one end. We heard Roosevelt, and he began his famous statement that December 7 was the "day that would live in infamy." Later, as I walked across campus on my way to Scott Hall (the home of the theatre department at that time), I realized that we were going to go to war. Everyone knew it, and everyone also knew that it was a patriotic thing to enlist or to help in some other way.

I can't imagine anybody not wanting to go to that war. All of the kids who I was working with in plays at the university—freshmen, sophomores, and juniors—they all had a plan immediately. In fact, one really skinny guy named Bob was determined to get in the service, but he was so thin! They couldn't take him. He beefed up by eating a ton of bananas the day before he went in for his physical. *(Laughter)* Everybody was going to go to war despite the fact that most of us in the University Theatre were determined that we were going to be *big stars* in the American theatre! This was long,

long before television or even when motion pictures had that impact, so going into the live theatre was where actors went.

I knew that I was going to go into the service, and my brother immediately enlisted; and when the time came when I reached the age of 19, I did enlist. Everybody enlisted! It took a long time for them to call people up— particularly for a particular corps, like the Naval Air Corps. They couldn't process all of us enlisters until '43. They had so many thousands and thousands of kids who were enlisting. That particular branch of the service was unique in the sense that you had to learn to fly, but they didn't have any planes.

I knew right from the time I enlisted that I was marked because I had never taken any science in college. I knew nothing about physics or chemistry or any branch of that. I knew I was going to have a severe disadvantage. My brother, on the other hand, could sail through those science courses.

He was two years ahead of me, so of course when I was actually called up, he was already flying out of Pensacola. I had to follow in his footsteps every single step of the way, starting out in Northfield, Minnesota, at St. Olaf College, which was where preflight training was set up. I think it was at that time that I realized that I had severe emotional problems about this whole experience.

Those were the darkest days of the war. The Battle of Britain was on, and London was bombed. Battles were also raging in the South Pacific. Of course, being an avid history buff, I had followed every inch of the war's progress through the newspapers and in books. Every night we listened to H.V. Kaltenborn. Most of the reporters were actually overseas giving their radio broadcasts, and that was so important to everybody back home. Yet in those preflight classes at St. Olaf, I felt a sense of inadequacy, even though I was physically adequate for the endeavor.

One of the most damaging episodes in my entire life took place at St. Olaf College. It was gorgeous in the autumn on that campus. It was so beautiful. The whole world was on the brink of war—but there, outside, you saw beautiful oak trees on that wonderful campus. One day I was sitting there in a class, and we had this damned test. I can't even remember what the subject was. The professor said to the class, "I am very proud of you boys. Just think of it—60 students in this class, and only one failed!" I could feel the blood rising. I am sure everyone could see. Of course, it was me. I realized that I had a *lot* of work to do! This was a far cry from appearing on stage in *Saint Joan* at the University Theatre, which I could do with a modicum of effort. I also knew that I was the only one of 60 guys in that class at St. Olaf who was in love with the other 59! *(Laughter)* It was difficult to concentrate on the course content. With looking out the window at all of the beautiful autumn weather and looking around the classroom— well, there were just too many distractions! *(Laughter)*

Anyhow, I managed to get through preflight training at St. Olaf. I brought my grades up, so they didn't wash me out. I somehow managed to pull my grades up enough so that I could go next to Le Mars, Iowa, for flight training. It would be my first time getting into an airplane. I managed to get through that, but then we graduated into the "yellow perils," which were biplanes. You had to wear goggles, sit in an open cockpit with your flight instructor sitting in the seat behind you, but you were actually flying the plane. I managed to get through learning how to fly.

I rather enjoyed flying. It seemed simpler because it was Iowa down there below you—totally flat. So if you had to land unexpectedly, it would not be any problem. One time, while flying solo, I suddenly was confronted with a great problem! Looking out ahead of me was a dead propeller stick. Do you know what a dead stick is? It is when the front propeller has stopped. We are talking a *long* time before jet planes. So there I was, looking at it, and I saw that the propeller was not revolving—which meant that the plane was going to go down. So what to do? Well, actually, it was a lovely day, and I somehow did not think that I was going to be killed. I thought: Well, we can go down lazily, like a leaf. You could do that because those planes were very light. And so I managed to glide down, leisurely, and found a cornfield, a stubble field. All of the corn had been sheared off by that late in the autumn, and I made a pleasant landing. I didn't think it was necessary to bail out. I dragged my straps from the parachute across the field to a farmhouse nearby, and I went into their kitchen and asked to use their phone. They told me I could use the phone, so I called the base and said that the plane and I were intact, but there was a dead stick in front. Of course, after that, I fancied myself as a great hero. *(Laughter)*

Anyway, I still have all of those records that tell you how well you did on each flight. I managed to get through, and I became an accredited flyer. Shortly after that I was sent to Iowa City. Now we are getting into the bigger stuff. Now there are hundreds of us, all soon to become accredited as pilots. From there you would go to Pensacola, and you would really be flying the big planes in the Naval Air Corps.

Since there were so many of us and the program was so rushed, the military took over many of the colleges all over the country. We had to do a lot of our exercising in a college swimming pool. They were using that pool so frequently, without changing the water, that it rapidly became a cesspool. This was a long time before we found out how to keep swimming pools clean. That is what exactly happened. I contracted a strange infectious disease which they used to call "cat fever"—which was a common thing— and I was sent over to sickbay, because the first thing that happens with that disorder is that you become totally blocked up with mucus and your temperature rises. This was long before penicillin, and they didn't have antibiotics yet. They really did not know how to treat it.

The upshot of all of this was that while I was in the hospital at Iowa City, the infection moved from my nose and one by one into each sinus cavity. Ultimately, although I was in the sickbay there for about three months, I think, they had no definite solution to my problem. The doctors would come in and bring suction pumps to try to drain my sinus cavities. At one point they pierced one of my sinus cavities and tried to suck the puss out. Of course, later it just came right back.

By that point, my father became quite alarmed back in Minneapolis because I had never been sick a day in my life, and I was a pretty good physical specimen. I had gone from 165 pounds—which was what I weighed when I went into the service—down to 125 pounds. My dad became quite alarmed. He got in contact with a doctor he knew in Iowa City and asked what was going on. That doctor, Dr. Washburn, then took a more active interest in my particular case because I think my father threatened to write President Roosevelt! *(Laughter)*

Well, they said that they didn't know what was going on, but the infection was now in my sphenoid sinus cavity. Most doctors should have known that if your sinuses are infected, you might come down with meningitis. At that point they really became quite alarmed. They sent me to the Great Lakes Naval Hospital outside of Chicago. I spent about six months there where, presumably, the care was much more accurate and complete.

By that time in 1944, we were getting to the point of the D-Day invasion on June 6. I remember that every morning I got the Chicago *Tribune*. I was following the war very carefully, although I was not a part of it. I felt very sad because I was bothered by not being involved. I used to look in the Chicago *Tribune* every day, and right on the front page they had maps of Nazi Germany. It was black in the middle, and the other countries were in blue or gray or whatever. You could see the two forces, the Russians on the east and the Americans and British on the west, slowly coming closer and closer. The Russians were also getting closer and closer as they moved west. It was very exciting to watch all of that.

Well, at last I was considered well enough to be released, and I was given passes to go into Chicago. That is when I happened to see one of the first performances of *The Glass Menagerie* by Tennessee Williams at the little theatre near the opera house in Chicago. I was fortunate to see that play in its original form.

Finally they sent me for reassignment to the Great Lakes Naval Training Station, which was right next to the hospital. There I was assigned to a bunk in a cavernous place where there were four-high bunks—thousands of rows of them. I thought, "What the hell am I doing? Where am I going to go? What are they going to do with me?" I think they thought I was going to be an oceanographer or perhaps a meteorologist. I knew by that time that the war was winding down, so I wasn't going to have to face any action with the Japanese part of the war. I kept wandering around the naval training station, day after day. Nobody told me what to do. I was in limbo. Imagine floating around and the whole world around you is in a state of chaotic catastrophe. I felt like a zombie just existing with no purpose in that huge naval establishment. Nobody was checking on me or telling me what to do.

That huge ward held thousands of guys, many with serious casualties. It was all sad and terrible, yet there wasn't much bitterness or anger from those kids. There was some bitching about the military, but that was the usual kind of behavior from 18- or 20-year-old kids. I didn't make many friends there because I was a non-person. The other guys had seen action, and many were wounded. I wasn't doing anything. I wasn't going any-where. It struck me as so bizarre: I had this passionate interest in the war, yet I had no ability to do anything about it. There I was: a little, useless cog in a vast machine.

Finally, in exasperation, after a month or two of that, I went back to the naval hospital and went back to my ward, and the first person who saw me was Lieutenant Commander Washburn, my doctor. He said, "What in the hell are you doing here?" I said, "Well, I am waiting for my reassignment." He said, "Your reassignment? We gave you your medical discharge three months ago!" My discharge papers had been lost behind a cabinet somewhere. Boy, you never saw a process quicker than what happened then! Within a day I had my medical discharge and my 30 percent disability status, and I was out of the service.

The minute I got home, I was very, very anxious to get on with my life and do something. My God, here I had wasted three years! I could fly a plane, but I hadn't contributed anything. By then the GI Bill had been signed by President Roosevelt, so with the GI Bill and with my 30 percent disability, I had a certain maneuverability. My dad could never have afforded sending me to college. I mean, my God! The only way that my brother got to go to college at Yale was because he was a Rhodes scholar, and that paid for his tuition.

There I was, without even being accepted at Yale and with nothing to prove that I could get into Yale. I had only one year at the University of Minnesota, taking mainly theatre courses that I knew Yale wouldn't accept as legitimate because they didn't have an undergraduate theatre department. So I took the bus—against the violent objections of my father and my mother—to New Haven, and I went into the registrar's office at Yale and I said, "I am here." I was the second GI back at Yale, and they knew my brother because he had a very distinguished career there. They knew my father because he, too, had a very distinguished career at Yale. They just said, "So, you are here." I was passionate about getting back into the theatre, but I couldn't as an undergraduate; but once I got enrolled at Yale, I was like a dynamo. The sinus infection had cleared up, but I still had the 30 percent disability, which provided me with a lot of money back then. Although I am listed in the class of '47, I was actually in the class of '46 because I got out of Yale in a year and a half.

When I finished at Yale, I went straight down to New York, and within a month I had a job at Theatre Incorporated and became associated with

Alan Schneider, who directed me in my first play in New York. Soon I was cast in a play at the American Negro Theatre on 126th Street with Julie Harris. It was a play that she and I had done together at Yale.

By that time the war was over. So *my* war experience is probably not the same sort of thing as most of the other people interviewed for this book. Perhaps my experience falls into the category of "background" and not direct involvement. I was certainly aware of the casualty lists—everyone was. But you see, the casualty lists did not mean as much then compared to those we might have now. The newspapers were not ready and anxious to pull out all of the death figures. In fact, *Life* magazine, until late in the war, did not show the bodies of American soldiers. They just simply would not do it. For example, nobody had any idea of the horrendous casualties the Russian army had suffered. But in my case, I felt that I had a new lease on life—I had avoided getting killed in the war. That is why I pursued my education at Yale with such vigor.

My brother also never served overseas. He was down in Pensacola, and he would have gone overseas if the war had gone on longer. But then there was Truman and the atom bomb. Everything happened differently, and quickly.

There is always a lot of discussion as to whether or not we should have dropped the bomb on Japan. There is no question that that was the right thing to do. Absolutely! It seems to me so stupid to say, "Well, we killed 58,000 people at Hiroshima, but we would have killed at least 580,000 if we *hadn't* done it!" What logic is that? Everybody knew that to attack the mainland of Japan—even if they bombarded it days in advance—we all would have had horrendous casualties. Truman didn't waste one moment's thought on that. I do not think that anybody who actually lived through the Second World War would say, "We never should have done that." We would have used that bomb on the battlefield if we hadn't been able to stop that war. That is a no-brainer.

You know, this is the first time in many, many years that I have thought about all of this. I do have a lot of material in my journals about this, of course. I think the reason why it had such a profound effect on my life is the fact that I was a failure in the war in that I didn't get to serve, to fight or do anything like that—which I probably wouldn't have been good at, anyway. But my medical problems caused such a change in my whole physical being, going from 165 pounds down to 110 and getting out of the service like that as a wraith. That is why I took a set of barbell weights to Yale with me. From that point of view, the war focused me and motivated me. Already I had been motivated to be in the theatre from the time I was in late grade school, but the wartime experience is what caused me to get my act together. And, as I said earlier, in those days the only place for an aspiring actor to go was New York.

I had been to New York only once, and I knew that was where I wanted to be. Imagine going to New York in the middle of the war and in one week seeing the third performance of Thornton Wilder's *The Skin of Our Teeth* with Katherine Cornell and Judith Anderson. I saw Ruth Gordon in Anton Chekhov's *The Three Sisters*. That is when the theatre meant something wonderful. I had to keep emphasizing to my students, when I taught theatre, that television did not always exist! That has made such a difference. When I started my acting career in New York, there were no Off-Broadway or Off-Off-Broadway theatres. There was only one Broadway—that was it. Imagine being in *Antony and Cleopatra* and *Caesar and Cleopatra*—I was in both of them. Both of them have casts of about 30 people, and you cannot economically afford to do that anymore.

I got my Actors Equity card in 1947.[1] About the time I did *Antony and Cleopatra*, among the other young actors my age appearing for the first time on Broadway were Charlton Heston—who was my roommate for a while—Eli Wallach, Tony Randall, and Maureen Stapleton. They were all in that play with Katherine Cornell, who at the time was the leading actress of the American stage. You start out that way, and then you are starting at the top.

---

1. Actors Equity Association, the professional actor and stage manager union, was founded in 1913 to protect its members against the severe mistreatment that permeated the industry at that time. Actors and stage managers must develop a qualitative and quantitative résumé of experience before they are eligible to apply for their Equity card and thus become members. Today, the membership of Actors Equity numbers approximately 43,000.

James S. O'Brien
1951

Born: 1922

Present home: Stillwater, Minnesota

Military history: Enlisted; entered service 1941

Branch of service: Infantry (Career Soldier)

Length of service: 40 years

Highest rank: Major General

Date/place of interview: July 16, 2003
Stillwater, Minnesota

Jean "Deke" DeCurtins
1945

Born: 1918

Present home: Stillwater, Minnesota

Military history: Enlisted; entered service 1941

Branch of service: U.S. Army

Length of service: Nearly four years

Highest rank: Private 1st Class

Date/place of interview: July 16, 2003
Stillwater, Minnesota

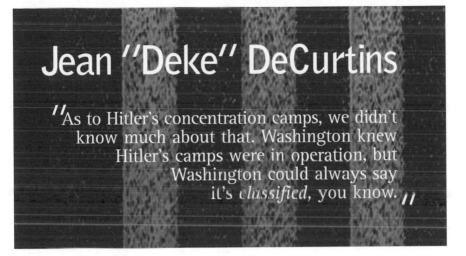

Jean "Deke" DeCurtins

"As to Hitler's concentration camps, we didn't know much about that. Washington knew Hitler's camps were in operation, but Washington could always say it's classified, you know."

Deke: We were the first troops to go to Northern Ireland. Even though Ireland was a free state, it was still part of England, part of the British Isles. That is why we trained there—because it was English, and the U.S. had been giving lots of military equipment and supplies to support England long before we got into the war after the attack on Pearl Harbor on December 7.

Jim: We spent about six months in Ireland—right, Deke?

Deke: About seven or eight months.

Jim: Seven or eight months. Then they put a call out for people who wanted to go back to OCS (Officer Candidate School). I was one of those guys who was selected. So they sent me back to OCS, and I just kind of literally kept bouncing around the States. So anyway, when the news came about Pearl Harbor, they wanted us right away. Nobody even knew where Pearl Harbor was. *(Laughter)*

Deke: They rushed all the troops to the seaports because they expected an invasion on the United States.

Jim: We were practicing shooting at airplanes at a camp down in Florida.

Deke: They actually did spot a submarine off the coast of Washington, a

Japanese sub. When they invaded Africa, that is when they sent us down there to Africa. We saw more of the world than I ever thought I would. But then the whole thing most people don't remember is that the Depression was on for 10 years before the war, and nobody went anyplace. Except those young guys who went to the CCC (Civilian Conservation Corps) camps.

I tried to get into CCC camp, but I only had one brother, so I couldn't qualify for that. You had to be almost on welfare to get in. Well, there was no welfare then, but you had to have four or five brothers and sisters, and you had to be in bad financial shape. My dad had a barber shop all the time, so he was working. He wasn't making much money, but he was working—unlike a lot of people.

Anyway, we went down to North Africa. The front was about—I don't know—700 or 800 miles away. We did a little training there. We were always short one battalion because they were guarding Eisenhower at Algiers, so we were always in the secondary position. The big German general down there was Rommell. The British were coming up from Egypt around that way, and we were coming the other way. They were pinning the Germans—Montgomery was the big general with the English—and they were kind of squeezing the Germans towards Tunis. It took maybe six months before they finally squeezed them out. Of course, Rommell—they threw him back to Germany. In the meantime, they were strengthening the forces in Italy and Sicily because they knew that was the next front. This was all Winston Churchill's idea, not the Americans'. The Americans thought they could go over there and invade right away. Well, they ended up getting slaughtered. So they put the pressure on Sicily. That took about 30 days. That was in July 1943. Then we went over to Italy in September. They started out right at the bottom of the boot and worked their way up. *(Pause)*

Mussolini was there, but the Germans were running the show by then. They had all the defense lines all the way up to Lionhead—about five lines there across Italy. You see, the mountains run right straight up Italy, so all they had to do was to defend all the passes.

Jim: And climb up the mountains.

Deke: Yeah.

Jim: How the hell the Americans ever lived to climb up those hills, I will never figure it out.

Deke: All you could take was a Jeep, no tanks. That is why they pulled Patton and that first armored out of there—you couldn't use tanks there, but they used field artillery. *(Pause)*

There was a WWI vet who used to come over to the filling station in Stillwater, our hometown, where we hung out. He used to say to us guys there—we were about 18 years old then—he'd say, "You guys are gonna last about two minutes up there." Well, he was right, sort of. We put a machine gun up, and outside of two minutes we were knocked out of action. We were both hit.

Oh, yeah. I got hit right in the hand. I was gone for about three months. I was gone until the end of the war in North Africa—two months because my hand was kind of paralyzed. Then I went back to the hospital, and they had all these guys from the 1st Infantry Division back there. Yes, I spent a lot of time in the hospital after being wounded two times and having my feet frozen. But despite the hospitalizations, my service record was very active. I was directly involved in several battles and engagements in many places in Europe. Those guys from the 1st Infantry Division were real tough guys, but when I came back later to that hospital, all of those guys were gone. Some were wounded, some were "z-eyed"—sent to the zone of interior—some had been transferred. That's the way the war goes. There is just so much cannon fodder. It is just like one of those guys over there in Iraq who said, "Geez, I didn't think we were expendable." Well, you are! Damn right you're expendable! You don't mean anything!

Well, you see—it was in yesterday's paper—it said that the Pentagon is making the same mistake this time as they did before. When those guys in the first Gulf war came back, they complained about ailments—you know, breathing problems and stuff in their blood and everything. It took them about three years before Congress and the Veterans Administration went to the Pentagon and raised hell with them. That's because the Pentagon figured that it's their money, and they weren't gonna put any money out for those guys over there who had these ailments.

It was just like me, Jim. I never told you this—about the last time I went to the Vets Hospital at Fort Snelling, Minnesota, because I had shrapnel in my hand. I wanted to get reclassified as far as pension was concerned. They told me, "You don't qualify enough for Social Security. That would be age 75. That is the limit." They said, "Since you are 85 and you get up every day and you can eat and nobody has to take care of you and you drive your car around—what are you hollering about?" That is the answer you get these days. Well, I get this call, and he says, "Were you satisfied?" I say, "Yeah. I know." I know they wouldn't give me anything, so I said that's the end of it. He says, "I'll get you another appointment." I say, "No. Don't bother."

I went over with two guys—-they knew their way around, see? One was a Marine, and the other guy was his brother. When you are like me, 85 years old, going over to Fort Snelling, that isn't a joy ride, as far as I'm concerned. So these guys, they knew their way around. They told me to go up there and meet this guy and that guy. These guys had been going back and forth—they didn't get anywhere, and neither did I. It was just like when I was sitting there in the living room, watching the TV screen, and I thought: All those guys in Iraq are waving their flags now; wait until 50 years from now—they won't be waving flags. On the other hand, I never felt used by the military because there were 15 million people in the service then. Everybody in town was in the service. If you had come back to Stillwater, nobody would have been here.

One thing that you guys don't remember is that war was declared in England in 1939. In other words, all of the Englishmen were gone for about three years. When American GIs went over there to England, those English women went crazy for them. The GIs all had fancy uniforms and all kinds of money. Did you ever hear that phrase: "Americans are over here—overdressed, overpaid, overloved, and oversexed"? *(Laughter)*

I saw a lot of battlefield action, a lot of death. You see, I was in a heavy machine-gun outfit, so we came in right behind the infantry. We were always behind them—right behind the front-line infantry. One time—it was 4:00 in the morning when it started breaking day—I put my gun down and started walking around, and I saw these guys all lying there. They were lying there with their bodies on the sidewalk and their heads in the gutter. I thought, Christ—I have seen tired guys, but I have never seen them that tired! *(Laughter)* There they were, all dead. The shell that had exploded in the middle of the road had killed everyone on each side of the road, I was about 22 then. That's pretty young to see so much death and dying. By that time that was in Italy I had already seen action in Africa.

I guess people always wonder how soldiers "unlearn" the killing instinct they learned in boot camp and on the battlefield. There is a story about Mrs. Franklin D. Roosevelt. She wanted to send all of us guys away for six weeks before we shipped home and after we were discharged so we could learn manners and civilian life again. She wanted it, but it never went through.

Jim: Once they got back home, these ex-GIs were all wilder than hell. I don't know what the hell that was all about.

Deke: Well, lots of returning GIs went out drinking almost every night. One thing about it: Most of us guys were all single then. They never took anybody who was married; they never drafted them. You could get out of the service. Remember that, Jim?

Jim: Yeah. In November of '41, just before Pearl Harbor, you had to have five kids and be over 28 and married before you were deferred. Wasn't that it? That is why I feel sorry for these kids today—these guys in Iraq. I bet they have no idea. I bet 80 percent of those guys are married.

Deke: Not only that there will be a lot of widows. Another thing is that those women, they have to carry the load alone back home. You know, that means that there will be a lot of divorces. There were a lot of "Dear John" letters back when we were in the service.

Jim: I was seeing a girl down in Hudson, Wisconsin, when I was 18. When I came home—it was probably the middle of the year—I was floored when she told me that she had just married another guy.

Do you know something, Deke? All of the guys who went into service from Stillwater—I don't think any were killed.

Deke: One guy got killed. He was a draftee in our outfit.

Jim: But he didn't go with us?

Deke: No. You know, these days they don't dare have a draft because that keeps public opinion out of that. Everybody who is in the service these days—everyone who gets killed or anything—they can always say that person volunteered. That is the way that goes.

Jim: Well, actually, we started picking draftees back in '41.

Deke: Yeah. You got draftees in, but they took guys over 35. Then, when they went to Ireland, any guy who was over 35 got weeded out. After that, we kept getting the guys who were younger and younger. When we got to Italy—well, Christ, we had guys in there who were 20 years old who were drafted. They were just going through the guys layer by layer. Just like today—the guys who are 32 years old and can't stand army life. But those guys who have been in it for a long time, they are used to it. They have enough grade—sergeant or above—that they don't generally have to do all that hiking and marching. Those guys over there in Iraq aren't doing more than they have to because the temperature is 100 degrees.

Jim: You know what really gets me? Deke and I are pretty much the same height. We used to carry packs back and forth for days. I wonder if those young kids over there in Iraq now can carry a pack for any long period of time.

Deke: Another thing is that when you go to the front, all you take is one blanket and a raincoat. You got what you would consider a "light pack." All of your heavy stuff was back there in the kitchen. Those guys serving in that dry heat in Iraq should be rotated. Even an older guy like me knows the army situation. They may have been over there for only 10 months, but that intense heat captures your strength a lot more than like when we were in Italy or someplace with a milder climate.

Jim: In some wars after WWII, many soldiers wondered why they were fighting. Back in '41, we didn't ever have to ask why. We just went. There was no question about it.

Deke: We had seen all those pictures of Hitler and all that stuff. England, Germany, and those countries were two years into the war before we ever got in there. Remember going to the movies in Ireland and seeing all those Russian battle pictures? Then you had some idea of what was going to happen. As to Hitler's concentration camps, we didn't know much about that. Washington knew about them, but not many people were aware that Hitler's camps were in operation. Washington could always say it's "classified," you know. It is just like today. They let you know only what they want you to hear. All we knew then was that lots of people disappeared someplace, but we didn't know about the camps. It was public knowledge that Hitler didn't like the Jews and was after them, but nobody knew what had happened to them.

Jim: Just a brief thing: Deke, here—he goes to the library all the time. I don't think there is a book there that he hasn't read.

Deke: Yeah. I read everything. You know, we gave a speech at a school not long ago, and we didn't have any problems. Those kids asked lots of questions, but they didn't stump us at anything. Maybe I should be a professor someplace. *(Laughter)*

I never give the war in the Pacific a second thought because I was never there. I had enough to think about over in Italy, Germany, and North Africa. That did not bother me at all. But the Pacific—it was like a totally different war.

Jim: And fighting in the jungle—I would not like that.

Deke: There's a lot of humor in the Army, too!

Jim: Yeah. There was a lot of humor.

Deke: If you've ever read Ernie Pyle's books, they were good books during that time—and Bill Mauldin's cartoons. Pyle was at the front. I mean, if you just stay at regimental headquarters, you are going to miss a lot. That is where a lot of people went, and they didn't get much farther than regimental headquarters, so they missed really knowing about the war from direct experience.

How true are Hollywood movies to the real war? Well, the last film I saw, *Saving Private Ryan*, was the most realistic of all the war movies I have ever seen.

Jim: Another one is the film that came out earlier with Robert Mitchum— *The Story of G.I. Joe*. That was a good movie. And that one that came out before the war was over, *The Fighting Sullivans*, about those five brothers from Iowa who all died on the same ship. That was emotional.

Deke: They say that the first half hour of *Saving Private Ryan* is probably the most realistic of all the movies.

Jim: Yes, it was! Real good!

Deke: The reason they had Eisenhower go back there on the anniversary of D-Day was just to film it and explain everything for history. Ronald Reagan went back there later for the fortieth anniversary, I think. Clinton went back there for the fiftieth, I think.

Jim: Yeah.

Deke: As for the D-Day invasion, they figured they would lose. I think they predicted 20,000 casualties, but they lost 9,000.

Jim: One time an elementary school teacher called me up and asked me if I'd give a speech about WWII and Korea. I told them that I don't give speeches. Well, then this teacher said that they had to get someone to talk about those things and he knew I was the best, and they just wanted to ask a couple of questions and that it would only take about 10 minutes. I said okay, there is nothing wrong with that.

Well, then the teacher asked me why we dropped those bombs on Hiroshima and all that. It was no mistake, I told him—even though we dropped two, we should have dropped 102. Then we wouldn't have had to go back. The original plan was to invade Japan, but Truman thought too many lives on both sides would be lost. So he decided to bomb Hiroshima and Nagasaki.

Harry Truman—there's a guy we could use in Iraq right now. And also General MacArthur. He just took ahold of that country and turned it into a grave mound.

Deke: One thing about MacArthur: He ran the civilian part as well as he ran the general part. He was pretty well respected, but he went too far as far as Truman was concerned. MacArthur just tried to supercede. He ran the war the way he wanted to, and when Truman told him what to do, he wouldn't do it. It was as simple as that.

Jim: You know, with a general who has four stars, you are not going to tell him what to do, even if he is president. What does a president know about military matters? Good old Harry was a down-to-earth sort of guy. We used to call him "Old Joe," and he loved to have a little shot of whiskey every night with his wife Bess. He ran around with Sam Rayburn from Texas, and Rayburn felt the same way. They used to be in the White House every night together until about four in the morning, playing poker. Imagine doing that now!

Deke: Well, I'll tell you. After seeing Clinton and Nixon and the rest of them guys, I figure anybody can be president.

Jim: I am in favor of what Bush is doing now, but I hope he isn't over-stepping his bounds.

Deke: I tell you, the next 12 months are going to be the big deciding point for him. If they keep dropping a soldier off every day, then there is going to be a lot of public opinion there. You know, I was at the library yesterday, and a woman said that she was going to be glad to see the Democrats coming in again! The Democrats and Republicans have this game going: If it isn't us, it's them; if it isn't them, it's us. It is the same game, back and forth. The thing they don't want is an Independent in there because an Independent would pull the rug from under them. They've had this game going for the last 25 years. Just like right there now, under Medicare: They say that if they *both* don't vote for it, then they can blame the other party. Yeah. And they know that there is always another election coming up. That's all they do is worry about the next election.

Jim: As far as my relationship with the Army is concerned, I started out in WWII, and I stayed with it a long time.

Deke: You stayed in it for 40 years, didn't you, Jim?

Jim: Yeah. I reached the rank of major general, and when I left in July of 1979, the retirement money was pretty good. It put five kids through college! *(Laughter)*

I got called out in '51 with the National Guard. We went to Korea then. That was still an operation in regiment, so we went across enemy lines. Although I went on inspections and could go back to a safe area at night, there really wasn't anything dangerous, other than taking artillery. I was in Korea for only about a year.

Well, you can see that Deke and I have some very clear memories of things that happened to us 60 or more years ago. And that is pretty good for a couple of guys in their 80s, huh? *(Laughter)*

Jane A. (Meyer) Elsen
1943

Born: 1922

Present home: Plymouth, Minnesota

Military history: Enlisted; entered service 1943

Branch of service: U.S. Marines

Length of service: Two years, two months

Highest rank: Staff Sergeant

Date/place of interview: August 13, 2003
                          Plymouth, Minnesota

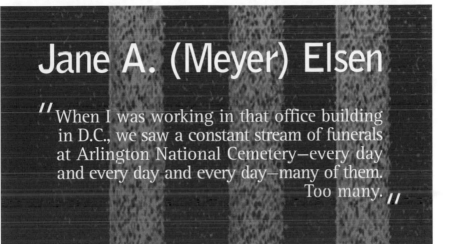

Jane A. (Meyer) Elsen

"When I was working in that office building in D.C., we saw a constant stream of funerals at Arlington National Cemetery—every day and every day and every day—many of them. Too many."

Well, first of all, most people went into the Army, but I was never in the Army. I was in the Marine Corps. I was just finishing college at the University of North Dakota in Grand Forks the last year and a half when December 7, 1941, happened and the war started. The guys on campus were drafted or they enlisted. You'd notice that this guy would be gone, then another and then two more would be gone, and so on.

It was a general understanding that if you were called up or even enlisted and you were within a semester from graduation, you could finish up all your classes over the weekend and graduate. In my case I had not quite reached the last semester. There were a lot of weekend graduations. Finally, to meet the demand, even if the student had a whole year left, they just let them graduate. That was a reasonable thing to do. Most of them were "drafted," so to speak, and their only choice was: "You are going to go where you want to go"—whether it was the Army, Navy, Marines, or Coast Guard. They all just left "head over tea kettle," and the campus changed.

Instead of the previous situation of having a more men than women, all of a sudden it was all women, and Army squads and Navy squads were taking classes together. They used the campus a lot for military classes. I had a little over a year to finish when the Army needed people, but I thought, "No. I will try to finish school first." Then the Navy wanted people, and then I heard about the Marine Corps. So I thought, "You know, I think I might like that." Grand Forks was a nice, small university town of 30,000. I think the percentage of young men in the town was next to nothing. My parents had three sons—one entered the Marine Corps just before the war started—and so that was kind of a natural thing for me. I just wanted to go someplace and do something. Grand Forks was fine, but it was just all women and old men. There was a popular song lyric at the time: "They're either too young or too old." *(Laughter)* I wanted to go someplace and do something. It was also a very patriotic town. It was a very "white" town. We did not have any "diverse opinions." After Pearl Harbor, everyone supported the war. There was this "feeling" in '41 and '42. So I just think it was kind of a combination of things. I decided, "Well, my brother was a Marine and he's not here, so I'll go and I can find something to do." I knew I would end up in an office because I had graduated in accounting and business administration. I thought that it did not sound too bad.

The military didn't have a special name for women in the Marines. The Navy called women WAVES, the Army called women WACS, and the Coast Guard called them SPARS. But the Marines were just the Marines—the Women Marines. They never shortened it, but there was a common contraction: the "WRs"—women reserves. It was never official. We had no nickname. There were relatively few of us. I think the WACS had about 500,000 women, the WAVES had 250,000, and we had 24,000. The Marines were a little more "picky" about who got in. They didn't want just anyone under 19, and they didn't take any blacks. I didn't even notice that—really! There were no blacks in the Marines. I am sure there are now, but at that time there weren't.

I think the blacks had difficulties being accepted in the men's Army and Navy. I don't know if it was ever understood. I grew up where we didn't have any blacks, so I did not miss them or notice that there weren't any in the Marines. We had one black man in my hometown who was a porter at the Elks Club. I didn't notice it when I was first stationed in Washington. Once a bus that I was on stopped when it hit the edge of Virginia, and I said, "Why are we stopping? There isn't a stop sign here." There were two blacks sitting in the front of the bus, and they were told they had to go sit in the rear. The Navy annex building in D.C. where I worked had lots of blacks—women and men. They were all mixed in Washington, D.C., but they weren't in Virginia. I was kind of shocked. I had never seen or thought about segregation before. At the time, I really didn't think a thing about it. However, I was really shocked when those two black men had to go to the back of the bus. That was the law, and the drivers enforced it.

As to the training I had to go through: It was six weeks of boot camp, but that was more classes on history than anything else. We learned how to march in Saturday parades and all that stuff—like, this is how you carry a flag. They had quite a few history courses on the Navy and the Marines, too. We did learn how to shoot a rifle, but it was more fun and games than anything else. If we did not hit the target, it was okay. We learned how to use the gas masks, but everybody knew that we were not going to be put out on a battlefield. We were not being trained for that. They did offer some electrician courses and some aircraft courses, but those were special. For the most part, we just stayed six weeks in North Carolina and waited for our uniforms to come. *(Laughter)* We did call it "boot camp," though.

When that was over, they gave you a choice as to where you would be assigned, but you didn't necessarily get there. You'd say, "1-2-3." I think what was open at the time was California, Washington, D.C., and New York. I put down California as my first choice and Washington as my second. I ended up in Washington, which was Marine Corps headquarters. I thought I would end up in an office someplace, and I was right. I did accounting. I was an accountant. After a while, they opened up a uniform shop, and that is where I spent most of my time. It was a good job, but there wasn't much to do. The days were long, and we worked six days a week and only had Sundays off. Finally they decided that it didn't work well for women and said that we could pick a day off; and if we arranged it with our office supervisor, then we could have one day off a month—to go get a haircut and that sort of thing.

For the most part I would say that the work weeks were kind of long. I wasn't used to working on Saturday. I had never done that in my life. Nobody was oppressed or anything, and we didn't have very many men directly assigned to the base, but they were close by. I certainly saw more men there than I had back home. *(Laughter)* In Washington, D.C., the men were in and out a lot—rather quick rotations. You didn't have a chance to make very close friends with anybody because they would come and go. The only ones who stayed were a few married men, and the military tried not to send them overseas if they had children. So some of them were around. There were lots of places to go for entertainment. The city would just heave with Navy, Army, and Marine Corps guys, but they were always in transition. But D.C. didn't lack people. It didn't lack men. Unlike back home in North Dakota! *(Laughter)*

I met my husband about a year after the war ended. He came to the University of North Dakota, where I was teaching. I was coordinating veterans' enrollment, and I taught for about three years in the accounting department. He enrolled and showed up in my class—or showed up over in the accounting department and eventually enrolled in my class—but the class was full, so I gave him to someone else. He came into the office where I was helping sign up people, and I noticed him. He was from Chicago. We weren't busy in the office at the time, so he and I just started to talk. He worked in the bookstore downstairs, so we just kept running into each other. It was just one of those things. I noticed him and he noticed me. Kind of romantic and sweet, huh? *(Laughter)* I lived in town and had a home in town, so we had a place where we could go where nobody knew we were together. Faculty and students weren't supposed to date, even if we were about the same age. Unlike when I enlisted, the campus was overrun with men. Oh, just oodles of them! All about my age, too!

The GI Bill was one of the best things the country ever did. Universities accommodated them without too much difficulty because the state universities, like the University of North Dakota, had relatively low tuition. But those people on the GI Bill had everything paid for by the government. They were paid considerably more than a regular student needed. I enrolled in grad school and paid almost nothing. I went to the airport and learned how to fly. That was fun! I had already been to college, so I wanted to try something else. Besides, I didn't qualify to draw any GI Bill benefits for anything other than just school. The rest of them got a stipend, but I was working, so I did not get a stipend. So I took my GI Bill of Rights to the airport, and there were quite a few guys who did the same thing. They had dreams of a vocation, but mine was strictly an avocation—just get a private license or a commercial license or a flight instructor's license, get married, and move out of town. *(Laughter)* There were very few women in the flight program, and I expected to get some ridicule or ribbing from the guys. But for the most part, I didn't. The guys were really, really nice. Now, they had gone to ground school and had picked up a little bit, you know, because they all had more or less some affiliation with aviation. I didn't know which way was north...and I didn't mind asking. *(Laughter)*

The instructor and his wife became really good friends of mine. He said, "Your being in the class just made it so much easier because you weren't afraid to ask any questions—dumb or intelligent." The guys were afraid to ask questions. It was a macho thing, I guess, but I really didn't care because I really *didn't* know which way was north. I told you that I am directionally dyslexic! *(Laughter)* So that was one of the fun things that came out of it. Then I met my husband because he was using his GI Bill to go to school. He transferred from St. Cloud State, where he went to college for his first two years.

They did everything that they could for the veterans to get them enrolled. It was the VA that helped my husband. They had these tests that they gave to help students decide what career path to follow. He scored so well because he was so well read and well traveled. He had no trouble scoring high on those tests, and they told him he could take most anything he wanted to. But he had not earned his high school diploma. The guy at the VA told him that they were so busy that he should just go and enroll in the college courses he wanted—it would be at least a semester before they would catch up with him. They didn't catch him until the end of the second semester. By that time he had gotten very good grades, and the registrar told him that he had created an awful problem for him.

The registrar asked him if he had had any high school, and my husband told him that he had had one year in Chicago. He asked him if he remembered the name and address of the school, and he told him that it was right there on the sheet. The registrar told him that he was hesitant about going to the board of education to get a waiver, but he was willing to try that first. The good news about all of this is that my husband became a lawyer. He just didn't want to waste his time by going to high school. He was very well educated. People who read and travel usually are.

I should get back to telling you more about my time in the Marines. In D.C., I worked in a very big building filled with civilians, Marines, and sailors. They were all in administrative work. The base where I lived was just three or four blocks from that building. At work we could look out the window and see Arlington Cemetery. Soon several of my friends were transferred out, and so I asked to go to California. I spent the last six or seven months out there. I always did office work. I think I did one night of guard duty once. That is the worst thing that can happen to anybody. Terribly boring! The nights were so long. I only got stuck with that once, though. I never got stuck with mess duty because there were people who really liked working the mess hall a lot. The food was very good. We had really wonderful cooks. We had the same food allowances as the men did. Therefore, we had very many fresh vegetables and that sort of thing.

There was no hardship, really, connected with this. You didn't get home as often as you would like, though. We had 30 days of furlough a year, so you could get home twice a year. But sometimes you really couldn't get a big enough stretch, so you would save it up and get a couple of days here and a weekend there to go someplace. I got home just about once a year. That wasn't a lot, but most people weren't going anyplace. The reason they weren't getting anywhere was because people didn't have gasoline, and there were very few cars. If you worked for the government you could get extra gas, but most people rode the buses a lot. My parents had ration books for coffee, sugar, and gas—all of the necessities. That wasn't a real hardship. Nobody was going hungry; they were just making sure that people weren't piling it up.

There is no doubt in my mind that President Franklin D. Roosevelt was probably about as good a person as we could have had for that time. People had confidence in him, and he wasn't a bad politician. He got us out of the Depression, and then World War II started up. The day that he died—April 12, 1945, I believe it was—everything was so simple then, in retrospect. Most people in Washington knew about his death long before it ever got on the radio. There was no TV at that time, either. Before they got it out on the radio or in the newspapers, it was common knowledge in Washington because everybody had secretaries. All the secretaries had access to phone conversations. If there ever were a *highly* confidential conversation between any generals, they would ask the secretary to leave the room. Otherwise, the secretaries knew everything. Of course they did. They had work to do, so they didn't sit there and listen all of the time, but they certainly knew to listen when they wanted to listen. There was really no such thing as a secret in Washington.

The news media respected the privacy of people in power. They never reported FDR's affair with his lady friend. The news people also had an unwritten code that they would never show FDR in a wheelchair or on his crutches or being helped out of a car. Today they would be all over him. Secretaries and other people who had access to sensitive information had a great respect for any knowledge that they had. You knew to be careful about where you discussed it and that sort of thing. When you went into a bar, you were very strongly criticized if you talked about where you worked or any type of matter that was going on because there were no secrets in the service. Everybody knew everything, and they didn't even have the technology that we have today. Even if you told a secretary to leave the office, she would pick up on the information later on.

Look at this photograph of Roosevelt's funeral procession. *(Holds up an 8"x10" aerial photograph showing Roosevelt's coffin, preceded by three platoons of soldiers)* This is a picture of FDR's funeral procession from the train station to the Capitol. You know, the reason I got that photo is because a friend of mine thought I should have it since I am in it. That's me *(pointing)*—the fourth one back, in that platoon. It was a sad day, but I was proud to be marching not too many feet ahead of the caisson that carried his coffin.

When I was working in that office building in D.C., we saw a constant stream of funerals at Arlington National Cemetery. Every day and every day and every day—many of them. Too many. The funerals upset us quite a bit at first; but after a while, we kind of ignored them because otherwise you couldn't stand it. There was always an air in the morning when the officer would come in and turn on the lights and wake everybody up. Everybody would look to see if she was carrying a yellow telegram, because the only telegrams that were not telephoned in were death notices. So if she had a telegraph notice, it was never the telegram itself—it was just a notice that there was a telegram in the office, and you had to go and get it. You would always look for that. When she didn't have any yellow slips in her hand, then it wouldn't be too bad. The radios went on— BOOM! Did we lose any ships during the night? When she had nothing and there weren't any ships missing or destroyed, then it wasn't going to be too bad of a day. But there was always this little air of apprehension.

I noticed it again after 9/11 and the World Trade Center attacks in 2001. Same feeling: You wake up in the morning and turn on the news to see if anything has happened. And the D.C. snipers in 2002—every day we would listen to see if they had shot any other innocent people. For me, it's exactly the same feeling. Some of those casualties on those yellow slips of paper were relatives of some people I was working with. Absolutely. We would have casualties in the families and friends who had died. It was always hard because in a squad of 78 people, you were bound to have these things happen. But to find out about those horrors the first thing in the morning—that was terrible. There were certainly incidents that would come in during different parts of the day, but the ones that piled up over the night seemed worse. Sometimes the officer would come in with three slips for three people in one squad room. There were injuries or something wrong with someone someplace. And oh, how we supported the people in our squad at such times! Oh, yeah. The support-group bond is different in a military situation. The bond that you build is strong. No place else do you ever work, eat, sleep, and all those things in the same place with the same friends, day in and day out.

We did have a good time. I have to say that I was so glad I was not old enough to be an officer, because we thought that officers never had very much fun at all. They probably did in their own way; but on the other hand, they were old, you know—almost 30! *(Laughter)* I was only 20 at the time. Of course, so were the soldiers. They were 19- or 20-year-old kids who were getting slaughtered out there. Most of the soldiers we saw were just kids, because the others just didn't hang out in the same places. The hotels always had rooms with parties or dances going on. The USO[1] did a really good job—particularly in California, in L.A. The actors and actresses came around at regular intervals. Bob Hope and Bing Crosby came to the base three times while I was there—always with a bottle in each hand. Their capacity was amazing! *(Laughter)*

When Bob Hope died a short time ago, I felt sad because I had worked for special services, which had put on those USO performances. I could go backstage and look whenever I wanted to. The performers never came backstage; they were doing shows *on* stage. Great performers. Such a good time! You can't manufacture having a good time. When they worked together, it was wonderful! There was no script...no nothing! They would just sing a song, do a dance, talk to the guys—and they seemed to genuinely enjoy entertaining the troops. They were thoroughly enjoyed by the troops, too. Those stars also visited wounded soldiers in the hospitals, too.

---

1. For information about the USO, see the endnote at the conclusion of this interview.

When you can have an impact on somebody's life that much, it is like watching a child light up when you bring him an ice-cream cone. To have that kind of impact—and they did—you can't do it if you don't enjoy it. And many of the big stars worked at the Stage-Door Canteen. They served coffee and doughnuts. I saw Dinah Shore once. Many, many stars just stopped in. They would come for a couple of hours and talk and laugh for a while and leave. They worked hard at it. I have to say that they did their part for the war effort. And those beautiful ladies would dance with young men who had never been far away from home before.

I wonder if our overpaid show business people today would ever give so tirelessly of themselves? I am afraid not. We don't have the unity now that we had at that time. We never will again. I don't think we have that kind of unity. They can talk diversity, but it takes generations and generations before it really mingles.

I know one thing about the war: The North and South in the USA disappeared. Lots of soldiers from the North married women from the South, and vice versa. That cultural gulf kind of disappeared after the war. They were slow mixing the blacks with the whites, however. In retrospect, I wonder how could they have been so slow? It was such a different time. But the marriages between the Northerners and the Southerners just broke down a lot of biases. They really did. When the soldiers went south, they met girls; and when the soldiers went north, they met young women, too. But mostly it was north going south. Then they came back and tended to settle in the south. You have so many Northerners, and they become part of the family. You just can't have the same animosity. "Damn Yankee" dissipated a lot. I had friends who lived down there, and they married Northerners. People said, "You married a Northerner?" and that was the end of it because pretty soon he was a part of the group. There really was not any cultural difference to speak of.

By the way, speaking of marriage: If you were a married woman, you could still enlist, but only if you had no children. WWII broke down the barriers of married women working. It was never the same. The University of North Dakota had a rule about that time: You could not hire a married woman, whether she had children or not. When you got married, they wouldn't hire you. I can remember when I was still there, the business manager asked me to type up a letter asking the board for a waiver to hire a married woman because he needed more help in the office. At the time, they didn't have any married teachers, and that caused a serious teacher shortage, so they had to bend the rule during the war. But the women had just temporary assignments, I guess. It was very strict before the war, but after the war they never went back to it. It never was the same again.

During the war there was the "Rosie the Riveter" movement, where women worked outside the home to keep the economy moving while the men were fighting overseas. The women *stayed* in the factories. It even accelerated, I think, because people started having lots of children right after the war. Then there was "the Pill," and with smaller families women started working more. There really wasn't enough to do at home. One or two kids, and then they all go off to school. I never worked outside the home, but I ran a small business from home. We had four children. I was plain busy all of the time! I was never bored, because my husband was involved in community affairs and all kinds of stuff, and I could always help him with his business.

I was discharged from the Marines in December of 1945. About four months earlier, we dropped the atomic bomb on Hiroshima and Nagasaki. The reaction was, "This is it! We will be out of here soon!" You could almost see it coming, with Germany falling, so to speak, and Japan. That was the final thing. We knew it was going to wind down fast. That must have been a very difficult decision for President Truman, because there are still a lot of people today who think it was wrong to bomb Japan. But a lot of people think it was right. What was it that Truman used to say? "If you can't stand the heat, then get out of the kitchen!" Most people realize that if we had *not* dropped the bombs on Japan, there would have been so many more deaths on both sides. That is true. That is something that helped Truman's decision, I am sure. How do you know how many more deaths there would have been? It must have been a very difficult decision. But that was the wind-down to the war. Suddenly everyone was counting out how many months they had been in the service and how many points they had. Did they have enough to get out by Christmas? And I did! I was home for Christmas. Yes.

As for marriage: My husband and I didn't get married until 1950. We went together for about a year—but, you see, I hadn't even met him until 1948 or '49. I was teaching, and I was flying out at the airport. I was refereeing basketball games. In other words, I was having a high old time as a single woman after the war! It was nice and pleasant. Some people think that we were given a pension; but no, there was no pension unless you stayed in the service for 20 years. Of course, there was a pension if you were dis abled. I wasn't disabled. So the only benefit would be the GI Bill if you went to school. I do not know of anything else. We had some insurance that we had for a while, but then we cashed in those policies.

I think the situation is quite different today. Now, everybody who comes out thinks they have a pension coming—but some of those people in World War II were in service for six years. It was ugly on the ground, and the food was horrid! They weren't hungry; but most of the time they were thirsty, and some of the time they were slightly uncomfortable in the cold and often uncomfortable in the heat. Soldiers in WWII put up with this for as many as six years—and still they got out and picked up the pieces, got settled in their lives at home, got married and had kids, but still collected nothing! They just went home and picked up the pieces. They came back with less whining. The guys who were over in the Gulf for six months or over in Iraq for six or seven months think they've had it so rough. The soldiers in the 1940s did it for years! I am sure that it shortened some of their lives, too.

There are so many emotional problems as a leftover of the war experience. I can understand that. But I don't think we had nearly as many after WWII as we do these days. I think emotional problems are a little bit like what my mother used to say. I had asked her once: "I hear people are having all these problems during menopause. Did you have problems during menopause?" She answered, "Not really. But then I didn't know what problems I was supposed to have." *(Laughter)* I think these people come back now expecting to have some reactions or something. I don't think that most of us did. Or if we did, we didn't have a name for it—like post-traumatic stress syndrome. Everybody seemed to be too busy. There were jobs or they were going to school or they were getting married or they were having kids. They were busy! As far as their commitment to the war: For the most part, when Pearl Harbor was attacked, it was *our* people being attacked. That made everybody say, "I have a reason for going to fight this war." It was a much more united country and a much more self-sufficient country then. You would hear farmers say more than anyone else, "Well, it doesn't look like we are going to have a good crop this year, but I AM NOT ASKING THE GOVERNMENT FOR HELP! THEY'RE NOT COMING IN HERE!" That was the prevailing thing: "I will take care of myself!" You just made do.

I had a lot of friends who were going to the university who were living in basements. The furnace was over there, and they were living over here. They were plain old basements—a husband and a wife, and pretty soon a kid down in the cellar there. And they didn't really feel sorry for themselves. They were proud of it. Saying things like, "My wife is working part time over here." But there wasn't any place to stay after the war. They put up huts on campus, and the business manager really hated to see them coming. He said, "I wish I could put up a 'go away date' as soon as they put them up." But they were cheap, quick housing, and they were called "temporary" —and yet they stayed and were used for bookstores or storage. It was often many, many years later before those ugly, "temporary" buildings were finally torn down.

Even after all of these years, there are four women whom I have seen off and on ever since we got out. Every three or four years, the four of us will get together. Everybody has gone on in their own way, had different lives and new lives. We don't spend a lot of time talking about the war or anything else. I did go back—it must have been about four years ago now— to Washington, D.C., for the dedication of the Women's War Memorial at the entrance to Arlington Cemetery.

The entrance is kind of dedicated to women in service from all wars. There were thousands of women there. I have a friend in Washington, so I stayed with her. Thousands of people came back, and I was so surprised to see so many of them in wheelchairs. Yet they all came back for that. I went because I thought primarily that the four of us were getting together again. I was surprised to see the big group as organized as it was. What they did was, they put together a computer program and got pictures from all over—any picture they could get their hands on. A picture and date, that was all—names and dates. It is still there and growing, I guess. I haven't been back since.

You know, most of us who were involved in the war had never been more than a few miles from home. But that all changed when we were sent to distant places. I remember especially people with southern accents—I can never spend enough time down there! Bostonians had their accents, too. There were people who had a miserable time during the war, I am sure; but most of us, day in and day out, if you had sustenance, you'd find something to laugh about. You pick up the pieces. I remember reading a book about a prisoner in a Russian camp and how he survived in the awful conditions of that camp. Every day there would be one little thing. Even if it was as simple as mopping the floor and waiting until he heard the scratch of someone's boots before he threw out the extra water so the commandant got his boots wet. Little things like that.

Hardship? In my case, I never felt any hardship. People who had lost sons—and my folks certainly knew about that—were devastated by the loss of one son. I could have gone to Pearl Harbor, but I didn't go because I had one brother in Europe and another brother who had died. My parents would have worried about me taking a boat over there because it was for the duration. If you got to Pearl Harbor, you would stay there. You weren't going to come back until after the war. I knew it would be kind of boring. There wouldn't have been a lot going on. Nothing coming in and nothing going out, to speak of. In retrospect, however, I would have liked to have gone.

I'd like to add a little interesting thing about President Truman. Shortly after Truman came into office, after the death of FDR, I was in a bank in Washington, D.C., one day with some friends. Somebody wanted to cash a money order or something like that. While we were standing there, someone came in and said, "All you people here have to stay right here because we have been told it is a matter of security!" A car pulled up, and about half a dozen Secret Service men and Truman walked into the bank. And someone said, "He's getting his safe deposit box." And I thought: safe deposit box? Somebody said, "Yeah. I think it is papers. He put some papers in there, and he has to sign for them to get them out." I thought that would never be done today. Imagine! The president of the United States had to go *in person* to sign for them himself because they were secret documents or something or other. A few minutes later Truman came out with his little briefcase and waved to everybody in the bank. I wonder if the bank officers asked him for his ID? *(Laughter)* That would never, ever happen today. But Truman personally came and signed because those were the bank rules. He was a friendly man who liked meeting people, and he did wave to all of us; but there were probably 12 or 14 people in the bank, and I am sure he didn't want to take the time to go around and shake everyone's hand. But he did wave, and he ran his own errands. We thought that was funny.

The USO was formed in response to a 1941 request from President Franklin D. Roosevelt, who determined it would be best if private organizations handled the on-leave recreation of the rapidly growing U.S. Armed Forces. Roosevelt's call to action led six civilian agencies to pool their resources and form a new organization, the USO (United Service Organizations), whose purpose was to coordinate civilian war efforts so that such services were not duplicated or overlooked. The six civilian agencies were the Salvation Army, the YMCA, the YWCA, National Catholic Community Services, National Travelers Aid Association, and the National Jewish Welfare Board.

Throughout WWII, the USO was the channel for community-based participation in the war effort, and USO centers were established to become the GIs' "Home Away from Home." Between 1940 and 1944, U.S. troops grew from 50,000 to 12 million, and their need for a variety of services grew accordingly. USO facilities were quickly opened in such unlikely places as churches, log cabins, museums, barns, beach and yacht clubs, railroad sleeping cars, and storefronts. At its high point in 1944, the USO had clubs in over 3,000 communities.

USO programs were as varied as the places that housed them. While most aimed primarily to provide off-duty recreation for the mostly male and fairly young service personnel, some were designed for women in uniform, while others provided child daycare for military wives. USOs could be many things to many people: a lively place to dance and meet people; a place to see movies or find religious counsel; a place to talk or write letters; or, of course, the place to go for free coffee and doughnuts.

The USO truly made history when it came to entertaining the troops. From 1941 to 1947, USO Camp Shows presented an amazing 428,421 performances. In 1945, curtains were rising 700 times a day all over the world to audiences as large as 15,000 and as small as 20 on some posts. Over 7,000 entertainers, from the biggest movie stars to unknown vaudevillians—brave "soldiers in greasepaint"—traveled overseas. Some never returned, having fallen beside the fighting men or in plane crashes.

By the war's end, the USO could claim that more than 1.5 million volunteers had worked on its behalf.

Leonard D. Zylla
(with wife Gertrude)
1942

Born: 1916

Present home: St. Cloud, Minnesota

Military history: Drafted; entered service 1942

Branch of service: Signal Corps; later in U.S. Air Force

Length of service: Nearly four years

Highest rank: Technician 4th Class, Grade 4

Date/place of interview: September 8, 2003
                              St. Cloud, Minnesota

Also present: Mr. Wade Kampa, Mr. Zylla's grandson

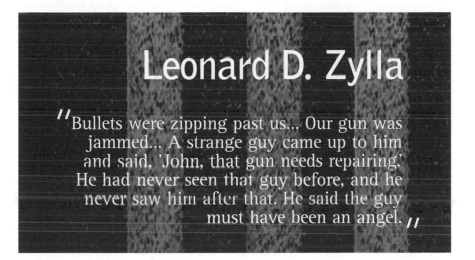

Leonard D. Zylla

"Bullets were zipping past us... Our gun was
jammed... A strange guy came up to him
and said, 'John, that gun needs repairing.'
He had never seen that guy before, and he
never saw him after that. He said the guy
must have been an angel."

Y ou know, many of us vets didn't want to talk about the war for
many years. As far as I know, I don't think they even talked to
their wives or families about it, either. I don't know. But we as a
group never talked after a battle was over. We never talked to each other
about the battle. After the battle, we were evacuated that same day and
went to our main base. I don't remember if it was two days or three weeks
later that they sent us to a place for recuperation. We were still together as
a group, but we never met or talked about it at all. I think we wanted to
suppress it. We didn't want to believe what was happening. At that time it
was very traumatic.

We were not a combat unit. We were not trained for fighting. It was all
new to us and very surprising, too. So we just kept quiet about it—then,
and for many years to come. That is what happened to me. I mean, my battalion had a reunion a few years ago in Nashville, and I don't know how
many fellows from my unit were there—10 or 12 of us and our wives.
Then our wives listened to us. The wives couldn't believe what we were
talking about. They were amazed, and we were amazed. Of course, "Big
Mouth" me said somebody ought to tape it. *(Laughter)* I wrote to all of the
fellas whose addresses I had, and I asked each one what happened. They
gave their details of what happened in their particular foxhole. Up to that
point, the only thing I knew is what happened in *our* particular foxhole—
nothing else about the others.

About 45 years after the war, my daughter Janice and I compiled this document *(holding it up)*. It's called "Memories of the Fifth Platoon, 565th Signal Aircraft Warning Battalion in Sausapor, New Guinea," and it is a compilation of the experiences of the surviving members of my battalion in New Guinea. You'll notice in it that the other guys refer to me in it as "Preacher." *(Laughter)* Well, I sort of carried my religion—I wouldn't say my religion, but my thoughts—and I would try not to swear. I wanted to act Christian. I sort of chided any guy—after all, we were only 52 guys—I sort of chided one if they swore, and so forth. Then they nicknamed me "Preacher," "Bishop" and stuff like that. When we would have a chaplain come, if it was a Protestant chaplain, I would try to get all of the boys to go to their services. The same thing would happen with the Catholic chaplain. I would say to them, "Come on, come on, you guys, go to services!" Of course, I didn't have too much luck with that until after the war was over.

After the war was over, we were on an island, recuperating. I'm a Catholic. The first opportunity we had to go to confession, every one of the Catholic boys lined up to go to confession. Every one of them! I can't say anything about the Protestant boys because I don't know, but I know all of the Catholic boys did. What did we have to confess? Well, you have your personal sins—what you have done wrong—and I, as a Catholic, believed that if I did something wrong, then I had to tell my priest what I did wrong, and of course he gave absolution and resolved the sin. A lot of those boys probably had been to confession, but I know some hadn't been for years, and some of them weren't church-going people. They did go after that, though. Have you heard the slogan: "There are no atheists in foxholes"? *(Laughter)* That just happened to be the case. I don't know what *they* did, but I prayed. I prayed that night very, very much. My patron saint was St. Michael the Archangel. I prayed to him. I am sure it all helped.

There was something very strange that happened one night when we were attacked. We had two anti-aircraft guns; and when we heard we were going to be attacked, we put them in the foxholes with us. That is the only protection we had—one gun on each end. Ours was on one end and the other was three-fourths of the way down. Well, I know what happened to our gun. It jammed, and we—the three of us who were firing that gun—we knew nothing about it. We had never fired a gun like that before in our lives. We didn't know anything about how to fire it. One guy was on the trigger, and because the gun was water-cooled, we had to keep it in the water to keep it cool and loading. It jammed, and we knew nothing about it. So I ran out from foxhole to foxhole, trying to find Sergeant Dole, our first sergeant. I finally found him and told him that the enemy soldiers were getting closer and closer. After our machine gun stopped working, you could hear those guys in the bushes loading and trying to shoot our lights out. I told him to hurry up, and he knocked me to the ground and asked me if I wanted to live. I was running and he knew how to crawl, so he knocked me to the ground and told me to get down.

Bullets were zipping past us. Somehow Sergeant Dole got our gun going. The only thing I didn't know was that the other gun had stopped working, too. I knew nothing about it until 20 years later. One guy by the name of John had been sent to gunnery school, so he knew how to repair guns. He wasn't in the foxhole with the machine gun; he was in another foxhole. Our gun was jammed, but of course John didn't know it. A strange guy went up to him and said, "John, that gun needs repairing." He had never seen that guy before, and he never saw him after that. We were only 52 guys and we knew everyone in our unit, but this guy who gave us the advice to repair the gun was not one of us. So John goes and repairs the gun, and he tells us what he went through. He thought the gun would be too hot to repair, but he did get it repaired. He said, "That guy must have been an angel, because I had never seen him before and I never saw him after that!" Of course, they got the gun repaired and they held the enemy off. It is really amazing, isn't it? Like I said, I didn't say he was an angel, but John did! I don't know if John was a religious man or what. But it is one of those things that you cannot explain.

When we were in the Army, they put us on radar. Even they didn't know what we were in. They had us in signal corps, they had us in the Army, and finally they put us in the Air Force, which is where we belonged in the first place because our job was to detect enemy planes and report by radio to the airbase that enemy planes were coming. Then they would send the alert, and so forth. So we were out in the field, away from our headquarters. They did put us into the Air Force at the end of the war, but up until that time we were called signal corps. We operated in New Guinea, and the battle kept moving. When that ended, we were shifted to Sausapor— that is on the western end of New Guinea Island. Of course, we didn't come in on the invasion; we came in three or four days after. When our troops landed at Sausapor, they found that it was too shallow. They pulled back 12 miles to the base there where they built a fighter squad, but they didn't say anything to us, so we landed there. There we were—our main base was 12 miles east of us, with nothing west of us except a Japanese stronghold of 100,000 men. We were the buffer. Theoretically, they should have pulled us out of there for safety's sake. We had highly sophisticated radar that the Japanese didn't have. We also had a code machine. If it had fallen into enemy hands, it would have been a disaster. But there we were, all by ourselves. We had one platoon of infantry, then us, then the main base. We had one group of platoon people—probably 15 members.

There were an estimated 250 Japanese soldiers who were hiding in the jungle. They didn't dare go out on the ocean because our planes would have spotted them. By the grace of God, there were some New Guinea natives—I would say about 15. It was a family of natives. They came to where we were and said, "Japanese coming! Japanese coming!" I don't know if they said Japanese or not. We fed them for about a day or so, but they would not stay. We radioed our main base and told them the Japanese were coming on. They didn't believe us. Our first lieutenant said that we were going to build big foxholes right on the edge of the jungle. We dug our pillboxes facing the jungle, and then we put up lights facing the jungle. We were ready, but we really weren't. In about a week, you could get pretty lax—nothing happened. But we still had guard duty—24-hour guards.

Believe it or not, we had very poor food during the time we were there. The military leaders did not care about us as a platoon. They were very, very greedy. They had food on the main base, but we only had rations. One day they sent over a boatload of fresh meat—steaks! We hadn't seen steaks since we left Australia. We had no place to put the steaks because we only had so much room. So we wound up passing them out to everyone. That night we were playing cards in my tent, and about 9:00 the lieutenant came in and said, "Len, part of the lights are out." I said "Yeah," and he said, "We should fix them!" I told him it was raining out, but he said we needed to fix them right away. He told me he would go with me, so I put on my poncho and brought out my flashlight, and we went out and fixed the lights.

Dummy me! Part of the power for the lights was on. I grabbed the wrong wire in the dark and cut it—and the wire held me. I couldn't move. I was frozen. The lieutenant backed away. I said a prayer, the wire came off, and I got the lights repaired.

Twenty feet away from us, in the jungle, the Japanese were dug in. We didn't know it at the time. They were ready, and their order was for 12:00. The Japanese followed orders very specifically. You and I, when "lights out" was called, we would have snuck around; but the Japanese didn't! They just waited. Their orders were for 12:00. Anyway, we got the lights fixed up and were talking about steaks again, so I went back to the tent. The card game had busted up, so we decided to go have a steak. We helped ourselves and made some more steaks.

Imagine those Japanese—they hadn't had anything to eat for over six months, and the aroma must have driven them crazy. After eating the steaks, we went back to sleep. Our guard there, every once in a while, would shoot his gun, and we'd yell, "Cut it out! We want to sleep!" He told us that he saw something moving in the trees out there, and we thought there were wild pigs or some animals. We went back to sleep—it was about a quarter to 12:00—and then there were shots coming back from the jungle. So what did we do? We started to open up and all the other guys, presumably, jumped into their foxholes, and we all started firing at random. We didn't see any targets; we just shot. We could hear the Japanese cock their guns, and they were trying to knock our lights out. And then the gun jammed. While I was gone it was quiet in our foxhole, and a few of the guys heard some noise. One guy in our group had a grenade. See, they weren't issued to us, but those guys stole what they could steal. He threw this hand grenade at a noise, and it stopped. Well, that is another story. In the morning, when the daylight infantry came in, there were three dead Japanese with their machine guns pointed at us. See how the Lord was with us?

We didn't find out until the next day that on the other end of the line, our power plant guy was there, and he did all of the firing. He couldn't see anything, so he just got on top of the power van and watched with the lights. When he saw a log moving, he would shoot at the log, and then it would start moving again. Finally, just before it reached our camp, it stopped moving. Presumably, he got them.

How did we know what the Japanese were preparing for? Well one of the Japanese was a lieutenant—I forget his name. He made a diary of it, and we found it later. How did we find out about this? Well, this was probably...I don't know...one of our fellows was working in Washington, and he had access to all of those files. So he looked at the files, and there was all this information on how the Japanese were planning what they were going to do. I forget what their code name was. That Japanese lieutenant was stripped of all his belongings, but he still had his precious body left. Of course, the military got the diary off of him, and the GA translated it and then it was sent to us when we had our first reunion in Nashville. Like I say, no one knew what the other part of my group was doing. I only knew what was happening in my foxhole; the other guys knew what happened in theirs. It took 20 or 30 years later for the full story to come out. Amazing!

Even though the Japanese were our enemy and they could have killed my buddies and me, I don't have animosity towards them now—but I did then. I am sorry. I did very much. A lot of the infantry guys, with the dead Japanese lying around, would kick them. The Japanese were very small in stature. I was surprised at how small they looked. Of course, they were on the ground, dead. They had dynamite strapped to them. They were going to blow up our camp. But anyway, some of our infantry guys went and kicked the dead bodies. I knew they were our enemies, but I could not do that. When the Army came in, they brought a bulldozer and dug a hole and pushed all of the bodies into the hole and buried them like that. We weren't there too long because they had to get us off. I should say that by 10:00, we were all off our base.

You know, speaking of the Japanese and Pearl Harbor, you hear stories of how cruel they were and how they treated our prisoners and the natives. Whether those stories are true or not, I do not know. What we think is that when those natives were running, one of the Japanese could have mistreated one of the women. Probably one of the natives killed the Japanese. I don't know. But the natives were deadly scared of them, so they were running. By the way, I had a brother who was lost in the service, too. He was a B-29 navigator.[1] He was lost, so I suppose I have a reason to hate the Japanese to this day—but no, I forgive them. Some people to this day hate

---

1. See Douglas MacArthur's condolence letter in Part III of this book.

the Japanese and the Germans, and maybe some of them hate Americans, too. It is probably true, but I was brought up to forgive your enemies. It is hard! But I feel that I have to do that because it is my upbringing. I believe in Jesus Christ, but it is still hard to forgive.

My Christian faith always was pretty strong. I thought of the priesthood during my high school days or shortly after that, but I had one thing that I really wanted to do—I wanted to be a golf pro. Of course, I suppose you could be a golf pro and a priest at the same time. *(Laughter)* But meanwhile, this girl sneaks into my life! *(Lots of laughter)* And eventually she would be my wife. As you know, you can be a devout Catholic and still not be a priest, but you can keep your faith anyway.

Like I say, I did think of the priesthood, and I was this close *(pinching fingers)*. But I was a pretty good golfer years ago. I worked for the typewriter shop in town, and my boss was a friend with the man who owned a hotel in town. He wanted to learn golf, and he knew I was a good golfer, so my boss asked me to teach him. I don't remember too much about the details, but the hotel owner did say the next year that he would sponsor me on a golf tour. I don't remember if it was just a tournament or what it was. But then, in 1941, December 7 came along, and that changed everybody's plans. Which is good. I mean, I have a family of 10—beautiful children, which God gave me, and I couldn't have...well, being on the golf tour, you couldn't be a family man. I was drafted then, shortly after Pearl Harbor.

I didn't go in right away after I was drafted. They had a process, so it was usually a few months before you actually went for basic training. I don't remember exactly when I was drafted. See, at that time, we all had to register. We all had numbers. When your number came up, you knew it was coming up. When your local draft board would get notified that they had to find so many men in Stearns County, they drew numbers, like a lottery. For example, they would call 46, 110 and two. If one of those was your number, you were bound to go. It was probably in August or September. I knew I was scheduled to go, and I asked for a deferment until after my baby was born because I knew our baby would be born in December, but they would not give me a deferment. I was very bitter about it and I knew I had to go, but I wanted to wait until my baby came—but no! They would send all recruits by bus—the whole group of us—to Fort Snelling, and then you would have a physical exam, your tests and everything. Then you would come back home for another two weeks and then go back to Fort Snelling. Once you were there, you knew you would go to basic training. I wasn't drafted when Pearl Harbor happened. I definitely did feel a strong sense of patriotism after December 7, but I didn't want to go until I had to, although I knew I was going to go eventually.

You know how I heard about the Pearl Harbor bombing? My wife, Gertrude, my mom and my dad went to the Twin Cities (Minneapolis and St. Paul) to visit some relatives. While we were all driving around in my car, Gertrude got a headache, so we stopped at a drugstore to get some aspirin. The druggist asked us if we had heard the news, and we told him no. So he told us the Japanese had bombed Pearl Harbor. Right then I told Gertrude goodbye because I knew I was going to be going soon, but I wanted that to be delayed until I was called.

You know, a lot of people in the U.S. didn't even know where Pearl Harbor was; but I liked history, so I knew where Pearl Harbor was. I am not saying that I knew where New Guinea was, but I knew Europe and stuff like that. I was always so lucky. I knew nothing about electronics—nothing! But in those days, when I was a kid growing up, we couldn't afford a radio. We were poor. So I made a crystal set. You would get a crystal and a set of earphones, and you would put an antenna out and put cat whiskers on certain spots—and you could pick up a radio signal. I knew how to take the wire and wrap it around a spool of thread—an empty spool with so many turns—then you would hook up the earphone, and then you could pick up a radio signal. Believe it or not! Guess what the first thing I got on it was? Babe Ruth, when he hit a home run. Wasn't that something? Now, I do not know what year that was, but I was already an adult. I don't think I was married then. No…I was home. Yeah. But anyway, when you are drafted, they give you all these tests. I had no idea what I was doing, but evidently I had enough knowledge for them to say that I was fit to go to electronics school. See how lucky I was?

When I got to Fort Snelling for the second time, they sent me to Miami Beach with six or seven other guys, all by ourselves. We had a pass and we went to Miami Beach and someone met us, and before long we were in the Air Force. We had basic training. Basic training was just marching up and down the street, counting 1-2-3-4-HUT! 1-2-3-4. All I remember is a sergeant telling us that we had two left feet. What that was teaching us was respect and how to listen and react. Then they sent me to Kansas

City to electronics school. I lived in a hotel. The Army took over the school in Kansas City. So I was going to electronics school and living in a hotel, but not as a civilian—everyone in our platoon lived in that hotel. Then we would march to the school and march back to the hotel after school.

We never had much training with guns or ammo. I guess we must have had some target practice later when I was up at Miami Beach. I can remember going to the firing range and there were targets, but I do not remember what I shot or anything like that. It wasn't new to me because I was a hunter. Did you know that 18 percent of the American fighter pilots killed 89 percent of the enemy? Do you know what these 18 percent were in civilian life? What their occupation was? Farmers! They knew how to hunt! When a duck came out, they knew how to hit it. You don't learn that when you are in the Army. You've got to know that, and that is why they were such good pilots. You cannot teach a guy who has never fired a gun how to shoot enemy planes.

I am sorry that I am sniffling so much here, but I've got hay fever—and it is the first time I have had hay fever in my 86 years. I have never had hay fever except for this year. I wonder what that's all about? *(Laughter)* Anyway, back to basic training! We were on the firing range for about an hour a day, and that was it.

Remember I said before that I wanted a deferment from going into the service right away because my wife was going to have a baby? Well, they refused that, and I had to leave just a couple months before the baby was due in December. It was very sad. I was away from home for almost four years. The saddest part...don't make me cry. When I was in the military television school in Kansas City, it was close to Christmas, and I knew my wife was due any day. I became very sad because I could not get a pass to come home. I wanted to come home for the baby. *(Crying)* The man in St. Cloud who owned the funeral parlor was also the head of the Red Cross. He met my wife on the street and asked her when the baby was due, and she told him. He asked her when I was coming home, and she told him I wasn't. So he fixed it up with the Red Cross to have me come home for an emergency. I remember—I don't know if it was a wire or what—I got the call to come home, that my wife was desperate. One of my instructors said to me that if I wasn't back by New Year's Eve, then I was going to be court martialed. Back then everything was court martialed!

So they put me on a train, and I got home by Christmas Eve. I can't remember too much, but on December 29 I took my wife to the hospital in the morning, and then the baby was born. The nurse came out and told me I had a baby girl, and she put a mask on me and brought the baby to me, and I held my daughter for 15 minutes. Then I gave her back to the nurse, kissed my wife goodbye—and that was the last I saw of my little daughter for nearly four years. *(Crying)* The next time I saw her is when they met me at the train depot when I was discharged. I saw this little girl running up to me. She was probably three and a half years old. I can remember her jumping into my arms because her mother had instructed her to do so. That is all I can remember.

Remember when I said before that I was lucky? The guy who was my master sergeant in Kansas City became the VA representative for the district between Fargo and Chicago. He would stop in and see me. When I got out of the service, I went to work for Robertson Radio Service—there was no television at that time. I was doing radio repair. He said television was coming out and there were good television schools and he knew the best one was in St. Paul—Northwest Electronics School, or something like that. He told me that I should go there, but I didn't apply. He would stop by every week to see how I was doing. He'd ask me if I had turned in my application yet, but I had no intention of doing so. I didn't think television was going to take off in St. Cloud because we had very poor television reception in St. Cloud—we were too far away from the Twin Cities at the time. There were a couple of dealers who had televisions in the window, with all "snow" in the pictures. Well, he stopped by three or four times, and he filled out the application for me himself and sent it in. He pressured me to go to television school. And I am glad I went. Certainly!

I was real fortunate because I had a sister who lived down in the Cities, so I stayed with her. When I went to television school, that was a year or two—and you had to start from scratch, see? I said that I wasn't going to start from scratch because I had already had all of that training in the service, but they told me that I had to. I told them I couldn't afford to because I had three or four kids. They told me that they would give me a test. I passed that test with flying colors. So I just got into the television course because I was lucky, and I got out of television school in six months' time. Yes. I was very, very fortunate because the GI Bill paid for much of the schooling. It really wasn't too much money, actually, but it sure helped. My wife and I lived upstairs at her father's house here.

Anyway, I passed the TV course with flying colors, and I got into television repair and came back and worked for Mr. Robertson for a few months. Then I had an opportunity to go out on my own, and I did. I was scared to tell Mr. Robertson I was leaving because he had hired me right after I got out of the service, but he took it well. He told me congratulations. That is how I got started in the business. Well, several years after the war, when I was back in St. Cloud, I opened an electronics repair store. It eventually was called Zylla TV Repair. That was me. I retired from that when I was 62. I am 86 now. That would have been about 1980. I have fixed a lot of televisions. You see, with that I was lucky. I learned that trade in the service—not television, but electronics.

It was a hell of a long time in New Guinea. A hell of a long time. The only thing that kept us sane was knowing that our outfit was going to be sent back for leave, but we had to wait for the other outfits to go first. They told everybody that. If they told us we were going to stay there until the end of the war, we would have gone nuts. We kept thinking that our turn was coming for a leave, and that is what kept us going.

We were not prepared for WWII. There wasn't supposed to be any more war. I think it was President Roosevelt who said we weren't going to be involved in any more wars and that we had nothing to worry about. When it hit, we knew it was a matter of survival. They had attacked *us*.

Glen E. Dawson, Sr.
and wife Marilyn (on their wedding day)
1945

Born: 1923

Military history: Enlisted; entered service 1942

Branch of service: U.S. Navy

Length of service: Three years, eight months

Highest rank: Pharmacist's Mate 2nd Class

Note: Mr. Dawson died on March 22, 1995. This commentary is excerpted from his journals. Grateful acknowledgment is extended to Glen Dawson, Jr., for making his father's journal available for this book.

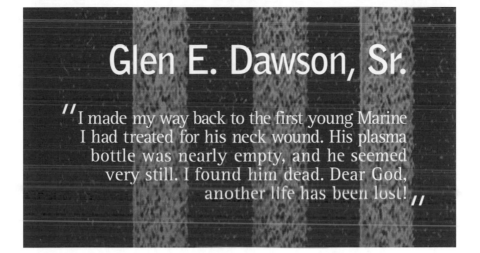

Glen E. Dawson, Sr.

"I made my way back to the first young Marine I had treated for his neck wound. His plasma bottle was nearly empty, and he seemed very still. I found him dead. Dear God, another life has been lost!"

Anyone who wasn't raised in the Ozark Mountains in south central Missouri probably would think that it wouldn't be a great place to be brought up in, but that wasn't so in my case. I was born, raised, and educated there. I never got out of the state of Missouri until a few months before WWII, when I took a job with the Dow Chemical Company in Pittsburg, California. Then I joined the Navy in 1942, when I was 19 years old.

After having mulled it over and over in my mind as to what to do after Pearl Harbor was attacked, deciding to join the military was a rather quick decision. Dow was considered to be a military dependent, which meant that everyone working for the company was exempt from military service. This was a cloak of shelter where a lot of young men my age took refuge. The town of Antioch, California, where I lived at that time, was three miles from Pittsburg, a beautiful little town set on the banks of the Sacramento River. We were all a pretty close bunch at Dow. At least the young people my age were. Western boots and dirty jeans were "in" for most of the guys, as were pleated skirts and sweaters for our gals. Being from the Ozarks, I preferred to hold on to the traditional western boots and clean jeans accepted by most.

A military camp was built between Antioch and Pittsburg. Camp Stoneman was an embarkation base for Army personnel leaving the west coast for the South Pacific. The camp was very hastily built and was very hastily filled after Pearl Harbor. Our big thing in Antioch was the Saturday night dance at the American Legion Club—the biggest building in town, outside of the cannery. Believe it or not, name bands played at those dances, so it was popular and everyone went. I was dating a young lady named Celia, and she and I were among the couples who attended one dance. In those days, if you took a date to a dance, it was an unwritten law that she was your date for the whole evening. To make a long story short, on this particular Saturday night, a young soldier from Camp Stoneman showed up alone. Celia knew the guy and had dated him or had met him at the local USO, a very popular group during WWII. Anyway, this guy Fred, as we shall call him, decided to take over all the dances and anything else that had to do with Celia's evening. I should have ignored all of this and walked away from it, but having been brought up in Missouri, where no man shows fear from any other man or from very few women, I decided to challenge the young soldier to leave my date to me and get lost. He refused, and I beat the hell out of him. Now, being sympathetic to servicemen was very popular in those days, and anyone in my age group who wasn't a serviceman was looked down on: "How come you're not in the service?" If a civilian challenged a serviceman, as I had just done with Fred, the civilian was always thought to be wrong.

Anyway, the next day I went to San Francisco and joined the Navy. Celia never forgave me for joining the Navy. Dow Chemical Company scoffed at my leaving, and more than a few of my friends said that I was a damned fool for leaving a safe and comfortable set up like Dow. I suppose that I could have stayed in Antioch and turned out chemicals for Dow. Who knows? I might have even married Celia—a lovely lady to remember, but difficult to forget.

But now, let me skip ahead to the time that I met, fell in love, and married my beautiful Marilyn Rose—certainly the happiest day of my life. It was springtime in 1945, and I was stationed on a base in Hawaii. It wasn't too surprising to us to hear that a regiment of women Marines was being transferred overseas. The Territory of Hawaii (TH) was then considered overseas duty. Our first reports of women Marines being transferred to TH seemed a little far fetched, but arrival notices suddenly alerted us to the fact that they would indeed be there in a few days. So what do we do? Ignore the whole thing, or invite all of those beauties to a welcome-to-Hawaii party and dance? We chose the latter.

Our plans for the party took shape, and everything worked out pretty well. We secured a Red Cross headquarters building and hired a band and scrounged around for food and drinks. Our ships arrived on time, our escorts were on time, our military police escort was much better than expected, and the serving of dinner came off perfectly. The only catch was a torrential downpour, which Hawaii is famous for. The girls arrived in covered transports but had to be escorted into the building over plywood and planks to keep them from getting mired in Hawaiian clay. My job wasn't too important. I was the pharmacist's mate assigned to ensure that no one left with a broken leg or was unattended. When the girls showed up, the band played. Everyone stood at attention until they had all arrived, and then the crowd was quiet. Our company welcomed all of the women Marines and their officers to Hawaii, and finally the party was declared open.

I had just recently returned from a tour of duty in the South Pacific and also a 15-day tour in the States, where I watched my mother slowly die. My leave did not permit me to go to Missouri to attend her funeral. Not being too much in a party mood, I reserved myself to a corner table and watched. One of my friends attending the party, a guy named Jim, was a medic from Oklahoma. He was dancing with a girl who was obviously struggling with his considerable lack of ability to dance. As they moved toward me, I could see her problem. When she looked me straight in the eyes and shrugged her shoulder and even motioned with her left hand to help her out, I arose to the occasion. I cut in and said thanks to Jim. At that very moment, when I took that girl in my arms to dance, I had a feeling that this was the woman that I would do my damndest to have for myself.

The party ended with all the girls getting aboard transport vehicles to be taken back to their quarters, which were on a different compound than ours and separated by gates and wire fences. Such was the military routine about relationships between men and women in those days. The name of the girl I met that night was Marilyn Rose Welch, PFC. She was in the Women's Marine Corps. Her name was known not only to me but also was familiar to several other military men because she was beautiful and very popular. I finally convinced her that I should be the only one that she should socialize with and that she should forget about a few hundred other guys waiting to dance with her. I admit it wasn't easy with eight-to-one in her favor; yet despite those odds, she still picked me. I pondered a lot of questions and wondered if I should even ask her them. What were our chances of being married under the circumstances and knowing my status? Being shipped out any day was inevitable. We proceeded to challenge the civilian courts and the military to issue us a license to be married. Opposition suddenly came from every corner. I still believe if it hadn't been for a sympathetic commandant who I knew personally and who had a little more pull at headquarters, our marriage would never have come off. At least not in the military.

We had a great wedding day on April 11, 1945. We were married in a local church in Honolulu with our close friends in attendance and had a gala champagne reception afterwards followed by a booze party that just about did us in. At least me, anyway—I had been aboard hospital duty for 72 hours previous to our wedding day. Thank heaven for the following days of our short honeymoon and for my beautiful Marilyn Rose. As I have said, our honeymoon was short and my wife's commanding officers intended to keep us separated. So they made plans to get me transferred immediately—and that they did. I had never had a regular leave since joining the military, so in order to get rid of me and not slight the other people in my outfit, they sent us all home for a 30-day leave. After that leave, we had orders to return to San Francisco for reassignment.

But I should go back now to begin to tell of my experiences—or, should I say, a tale of one man's war. December 1941: I was sitting with some friends at their home in Antioch, California, listening to our favorite San Francisco radio station, eating spaghetti and meatballs, and drinking a glass of red wine. All of a sudden there was a break in the regular program. They announced the attack on Pearl Harbor. Frankly and truthfully, I, in my ignorance, had never heard of Pearl Harbor: Hawaii and Oahu, yes—but not Pearl Harbor. As the program progressed, we all suddenly set aside our wine, left our spaghetti on our plates, and looked at each other aghast, not knowing what to say. One of the younger women there suggested dessert, but without any response. Then she walked over to me and said in a low voice, "Maybe you and Charlie should leave." I nodded a yes and motioned to my friend Charlie. His response was immediate, and we left. I waved a kiss to them all and received the usual "We love you" from them in return. I had never left their home before without that feeling and have never forgotten it. Imagine: a hillbilly from Missouri being accepted into a prominent family and receiving affection.

Our famous Great Bear Division at Dow Chemical was noted for saline separations and all Allied products, including ferric chloride, hexonth, CO_2, and hexachlorophene—all of which were military related. Mobilization was also starting, and we were asked to be cautious as to who was loyal and not loyal and were told not to take chances on people.

I remember one Italian man who had never taken out U.S. citizenship papers but who had worked for Dow Chemical Company for 20 years. He was suddenly considered an alien and exempted from his job. I went to his home to pay my respects and say how I felt about his situation. I told him how sorry I felt and how unfair I thought our government was being to him. I tried to cry at being so insulted by our government, but I just sat there and felt ashamed. This was a part of my reason for joining the Navy.

I went to the recruitment center and applied without telling my supervisor at Dow Chemical. I was immediately accepted by the Navy and even offered NCO (noncommissioned officer) rating because of my previous experiences in the late 1930s with the CCC (Civilian Conservation Corps), where I worked in the civilian medical service. Well, at any rate, I was accepted as a medic. I went back to tell my boss and plant supervisor that I had joined the Navy. Explosion isn't the word for their reaction. The plant manager nearly strangled me and gave me a lecture like you have never heard about how the company had worked so hard to defer its workers from military service. I told him that despite all that, I had already decided, and I had to go. After a handshake we parted as friends, and I punched out for my last time and left Dow Chemical Company.

After six weeks of naval training—which was thrown at us like a whirlwind typhoon—we were sent on our different ways. I was sent to Bal Boa Naval Hospital, which didn't mean much. Two days later I was on a plane to Panama to pick up some Navy personnel who had contracted polio. After my trip back from Panama, I suddenly found myself—gear and all—aboard the aircraft carrier *John Cabot*, headed for the South Pacific. Seventy-two hours out of San Diego we were in Pearl Harbor, refueling for a trip to Guadalcanal and Toulagi. We were on a converted cruiser with a limited flight deck but as fast as anything afloat. We outran and outmaneuvered all that the Japs had to stop us with, and we landed all of the planes we had on Henderson Field. After picking up casualties, we headed for New Hefurdies and new patients. Then my work really began.

I didn't know much about surgery, but I soon learned. I quickly grasped how to scrub, gown, and glove myself and, under the direction of some wonderful surgeons, how to hand them their instruments, assist in closing wounds, and bandage surgical operations. So by the time I returned to San Diego, I considered myself somewhat of a naval medical corpsman.

For the next six months, my experiences included helping to set up a hospital at Corona, California. This was formerly the Lake Narconian Country Club, an exclusive spa for the elite of Los Angeles and Hollywood. But it was bought by the Navy and transformed into a hospital with a TB sanitarium next to it. A million words couldn't describe all the things that went on in setting up that hospital or all the things involved in making it a place to live or the people who were involved in making it work—both military and civilian.

I left the Navy ranks to join the Marine Corps in 1942, still as a Navy medical corpsman but attached to Marine ranks and fighting battalions. I went first to a training center at Camp Pendleton, California, not for a long time but long enough to help make a movie called *Guadalcanal Diary*, in which I played the part of a Navy medic. It was quite an episode. I met a lot of movie stars, including Anthony Quinn in his very first role. His scene lasted about two minutes, but it showed Hollywood that he could play a part. So much for movies. I next found myself in a series of land-hopping events with the 5th Amphibious Corps, the "Alligator and Star" outfit that supported the first, second, third, fourth, and fifth provisional divisions in their South Pacific escapades from Eniwetok through Saipan and Okinawa. I didn't get in on all of those invasions, but I do remember getting my ass busted on a few of them.

Before I get ahead of myself: I was sent to a training session at the Ailea Naval Hospital on top of a mountain overlooking Pearl Harbor. My training was in surgery and surgical techniques designed for a corpsman on detached duty. That means service without a doctor. It would take a book to describe my training. Any surgeons and doctors who might read this: listen very carefully. I have done surgery that some of you will probably never do. I have assisted some of the world's most renowned surgeons in their specialized fields. The Navy had a medical corps that was the best in the world.

After all that training, I was destined for some exciting adventures that you probably wouldn't believe. Before we decided to hit the Philippines—

or "return to" the Philippines, as Douglas MacArthur had promised to do—there were a few things that had to be cleared up. One was a "jamming station" on the island of Luzon. A jamming station involved radio communications interference created by an electronics station built specifically to block our radio frequencies. Well, the Japs had a damned good one. So before we could take the Philippines, we had to knock that one out.

We didn't know exactly where it was located, but we had a general idea where it was. So a recon group was formed to find it and make a location for future demolition before we decided to take the Island. I was selected for part of that group. My training in medics and demolition made me a prime part of the group. However, after being set ashore and advancing toward our objective, I began to get the symptoms of malaria. Anyone who has ever had malaria knows that it sometimes comes on very quickly, which in my case it did. Now, the problem was what to do with a sick man on an important mission like this. After some brief brainstorming, we decided that I should stay at a designated area and take my chances with a malaria attack, and then a patrol would find me later on their way out and rescue me.

I was left on a trail, which proved to be a trail used by the natives. Well, before I knew what was happening, a whole group of Filipinos found me—two entire families, to be exact. You can imagine their surprise at seeing me sitting on their trail with an M-1 across my legs and a half delirious stare that didn't mean anything to them—but it meant that they would be in trouble with the Japs if they were caught with me. There were about eight of them altogether. They finally realized that I was no threat to them after I stumbled to my feet and motioned them on their way, with me trying to follow. I made it to their home area, which consisted of two or three huts, their chickens, dogs, and belongings. Sometime during the night I fell asleep, delirious with fever and chills—during which time my native friends went on their way. They left with all of their possessions that they could carry except for some food, which they left for me.

I waited 27 days. That's a very long time. But when one is quite ill, it seems even longer. I was camping in a creek bed, where there was water and cover. One day, I heard noises and some voices mumbling in the distance. I hid. The voices sounded like they were having a little bit of an argument about which way to go. But after a little while, as I was lying there in the weeds close to their feet, I realized that they were talking English. It was a party of Australian rangers sent in to blow up the jamming station! Not only that—it was the same outfit that I'd helped get out of a jungle in New Guinea. Very dramatic indeed.

Battle surgery is a field of medicine where every man is a surgeon. Perhaps he is not a noted graduate from one of our greater institutions, and probably he is not a graduate from any institution at all. Yet when the task is set before him, he is a surgeon using only his ingenuity and whatever conveniences that are at hand. For a scalpel, he uses a jackknife or perhaps a trench knife. For a tourniquet, he uses a belt. For anesthesia, he prays to his God; and for a post-operative dressing, he uses anything available.

Let me give you an example of what I am talking about. Let's say a man has been wounded and all but a few clinging ligaments of his lower leg have been shot away. The man is bleeding seriously, and the remaining portion of the leg should be amputated. Who is going to do this operation? The only available person in his immediate area is a former lumberjack or perhaps a doctor who, having lost all his medical and surgical supplies is helpless beyond his knowledge of knowing what should be done. So the battle surgeon has to rely on what is at hand. Taking his own belt from around his waist and a trench knife from the prostrate body of the wounded man, he begins his operation.

There was another case where one of our noted neurological associates was performing a tedious craniotomy. His operating room was a secluded spot about 200 yards behind the main line of fire. His operating table was a litter resting on some empty fuel containers, his instruments were a field surgical set consisting of the bare necessities, and his sole assistant and instrument nurse was a hospital corpsman. And yet, with all his encumbrances and lack of proper equipment—not to mention lack of sleep and proper nourishment—he accomplished the task set before him as best he could. Battle surgery consists not only of wounds and their behavior, but also of all kinds of surgery that confront our surgeons in everyday life. If there is no other way out, then it has to be done in the thick of battle. Perhaps if the surgeon is lucky enough to be working at a field hospital some distance behind the lines, he will have more conveniences and some form of sterile technique. But if he is working in the front lines, then the bare necessities and his own ingenuity are the only tools available to accomplish his great success.

It is difficult to describe the sounds and the tension and the fear as the ship you were on is approaching its destination for battle. We were supposed to attack an island at Bougainville. It was the dead of night, and we were trying to sleep. But we kept hearing a far-off bombing sound. The sound didn't seem right. It wasn't the usual sound of surf against the bulkhead. The sound seemed like far-off thunder. Falling to sleep again, just to be reawakened by the booming, I finally realized we had reached our destination. The sound was the firing of big guns from three heavy cruisers sitting off shore and shelling the island that we were supposed to attack at Bougainville. When you suddenly realize that the hour that you have been trained for has arrived and that the sounds of the attack have already begun, you wonder what will happen next.

At 0500, everyone who was still asleep was awakened, and we were all told to get our gear in order. We had already packed our assault packs with the items that we would need for at least three days: K-rations, ammo for our weapons, water and, for some of the Marines, some wound packs and sulfur powder. All other medical supplies were carried by Navy medics along with their personal gear and whatever weapon they chose to carry. Nobody was really ready, and everyone wondered if something was missing. At 0600, we were called for breakfast. Some forgot to take off their packs and ate their breakfast in full gear. Our breakfast was beans, cornbread, pork—beef for the Jews—black coffee, sweet rice, and bread.

Higgins boats were already being lowered from the troop ship for the assault. No one talked much. It just seemed to be a time for thinking and wondering what was ahead. At 0800, we were all ordered topside. Each one had already been assigned to his squad and placed in a position to be ready to go over the side on command. At 1300, we were still in order and waiting. A break was called and we were fed simple food again. If I remember right, it was rice with chicken à la king, hot buttered bread, powered milk or coffee, and cookies. Topside again, we waited.

Higgins boats were again circling the assault carrier ship. The landing net was already dropped over the side. We all looked at the situation as being maybe a beginning of the end. At 1400, our planes were coming in over us toward the island. Bombs were being dropped, and napalm was being sent in. Confusion is always a problem in an attack landing. This one was no different. Twelve Higgins boats filled with Marines and their support left our ship about 1500. "Follow the leader" seemed to be the norm, except we left for an invasion about two miles south of the original landing. We drew no small fire or shelling because the Japs had their hands full with the main assault. Digging in and securing a section of beach was a surprise to all of us. We were ordered to stay put and not to advance until further orders.

If you were wondering what I might be carrying on me as a field medic, here's a rundown: I always carried a weapon. This time it was a grease gun—a small, 45-caliber, fully automatic weapon that I could tape on an extra clip back to back. Also, one breast pack of medical supplies, six units of plasma, a lot of compress bandages, two hip units, sulfa drugs (powder), morphine curettes, bandages, and an extra supply of water. I actually had to carry more things than an assault Marine.

Anyway, when it was my turn to climb down the landing net, I knew that the war was on and that I might never see this same ship again.

After reaching the beach, we all dug in. I moved forward, always wondering what the high tide might be. I assembled the other medics in my charge and told them to spread out with their dig-ins. Night was coming, and we were still not under fire. I crawled around, checking the Marines to see if any one was hurt. In the Marine Corps, the saying is, "If you are not bleeding, you are not hurting." Securing our position for the night seemed to be easy. I again checked with our medics and told them to eat K-rations and use what water they needed for food only. Our CO was a Marine captain. I gave him our stats on the med team, and he said we should all do the best we could. He handed me a small radio, which I gave to one of my medics in case we needed help evacuating.

Day two was a different story. All hell broke loose. The Japs figured out that we were at their flank and began their assault on us. We were only three squads—no artillery—and only had small arms and a few mortars. We called for backup and were told that air or ground fire couldn't help us out. Our casualties grew, and our medical supplies dwindled. Plasma was running out, and water was a "sip if you have it"—a Marine Corps phrase. Suddenly, all of the shelling stopped. We all looked at each other and sort of said, "What the hell do we do now?"

I made my way to look around and found that most of our wounded had been taken care of and that we had only lost three men. You cry for one man, but you cry three times as loud if you have lost three. In respect to the war, I always wondered about men who perished on the battlefield. They were not me...but why? I live today, and I think of all the friends tho I lost in the war—including my brother. And I wonder why it couldn't have been just a dream instead of a reality—that maybe the world today could be a more peaceful union than it is.

Being a field medic is an experience that can't really be explained, but I will try. On that second day on the Island of Bougainville, I was at the front lines. Our forces were being beaten badly and taking a lot of casualties. The first casualty I came cross was a Marine lying pretty much face down on his side. I didn't know if he was alive or not. As I turned him over, blood spurted from a wound in his neck and hit me in the face and ran down over my lips. I quickly clamped off the ends of a severed artery with hemostats and tied them off with sutures to stop the bleeding. I inserted a plasma unit using his M-1 rifle as a prop. I gave him a curette of morphine and dressed his wounds with sulfa powder and compress bandages. I taped a red tag on his helmet, took a blanket from his pack, and laid it over him.

Another Marine was screaming with pain a few yards away. I crawled over to him. The kid was more scared than hurt. His upper arm had been shattered by a bullet. He hadn't lost too much blood, so I cleaned the wound as best I could and bandaged him up, gave him two shots of morphine to kill the pain, and gave him some water. I stuck his rifle bayonet in the ground and taped a blue tag on his helmet.

Another young Marine was screaming nearby. First off was an injection of morphine. His problem was a chest wound. That is a very difficult dilemma to manage out in the field. I clamped off the blood veins that were strangling him and left them in place, applied a big field pack, and tied a red tag to his leg. (I found out later that that kid did live, thanks to some blood work done at an aid station.)

I decided I should check back with some of the Marines I had already treated to see how they were getting along. I made my way back to that first young Marine I had treated for a neck wound. His plasma bottle was nearly empty, and he seemed very still. I found him dead. Dear God, another life was lost! Perhaps I should have said only a third of a life had been lost because he was only about 20 years old. Perhaps if we had known about CPR, we might have saved a lot more field casualties.

To be quite truthful, we weren't given the proper training or equipment to save lives in the early invasions in the South Pacific. Even our doctors admitted that. Other islands were taken with about the same tactics—always losing hundreds of Marines, stupidly. Our General Douglas MacArthur (1880–1964) was a killer, not a general. I saw more than one assault that was strictly his own idea that got hundreds of Marines killed, for no reason whatsoever. MacArthur was a real asshole as a general. Had we not had Admirals Chester Nimitz (1885–1966) and William Halsey (1882–1959), we would have lost the war in the South Pacific. I worked under Admiral Nimitz—a hell of a person. He was quiet and always alert to what was going on around him. William "Bull" Halsey was a different person. He was a confirmed alcoholic—but even with a full snoot of brandy, he could direct his fleet command with the best of them.

Another example of MacArthur's mismanagement or incompetence involved a good friend of mine named Ethan, who had just gotten married when he was taken into the service. This young lieutenant was killed in New Guinea in a senseless campaign cooked up by General MacArthur. It was one of MacArthur's many stupid mistakes. I say it here and now that I bear no allegiance to General Douglas MacArthur. He was as stupid a man as he was a general, and he was responsible for killing too many of my friends and too many Americans.

My good friend Ethan will be remembered fondly by all of us who knew him. There were two other guys—friends I grew up with—who were also killed in the same campaign as Ethan. A brother of one of those guys survived to tell us the true story of what happened in that campaign.

I often think back to those war years, and I remember also the innocence of my years growing up in the Ozarks. What a sharp contrast those two segments of my live have been!

Harry C. Bemlott
1942

Harry and Theresa Bemlott
(on their wedding day)
1945

Born: 1918

Present home: White Bear Lake, Minnesota

Military history: Drafted; entered service 1942

Branch of service: U.S. Army

Length of service: Three years, six months

Highest rank: Staff Sergeant

Date/place of interview: February 18, 2005
White Bear Lake, Minnesota

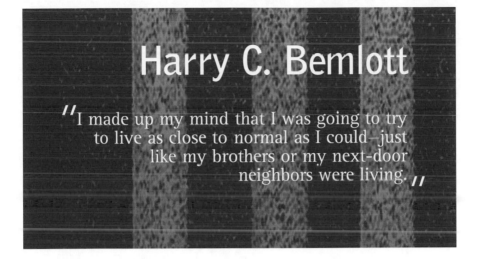

Harry C. Bemlott

"I made up my mind that I was going to try to live as close to normal as I could—just like my brothers or my next-door neighbors were living."

To begin at the beginning, I entered service on May 6, 1942. I was 24 years old. That was less than a year after Pearl Harbor. That happened in December the previous year. I remember where I was when I heard the news that Pearl Harbor had been attacked. I was driving my Ford from St. Paul up Highway 61 when I heard it on the car radio. I had a radio in my car in those days. I was driving north on 61, and I pulled into the filling station where I always bought my gas and to talk to the guy who ran the station there. I was sitting behind the wheel and he was standing next to my car—and then we heard the news on the car radio. We were visiting and started talking about the war with Japan and Pearl Harbor. Of course, I was only a hop, skip, and a jump from our farm when I left the gas station. You know, I had never heard of Pearl Harbor until that day. Anyway, I got a physical and was happy to pass it because I felt it was my patriotic duty to do that so I could serve my country.

First of all, we were stationed nine months in England after we got overseas. We landed in Liverpool, England, and then we were transferred to a town that is in southwestern England next to Salisbury. We were there for nine months, maneuvering. I was in an armored division, so we had tanks and tank destroyers—all that good stuff. We had some really big vehicles, you know. Before going abroad, though, I had my basic training at Fort Knox, Kentucky, for four months. I hadn't traveled very much before then.

The farthest I had ever been out of Minnesota, before I went into the war, was a trip to Wisconsin.

Once we got into military action I was in France, and it was on the second day I was in combat that I got wounded. That was right after the Normandy invasion on June 6, 1944. My wound was considered superficial because the bullet had not hit any vital organs, but they had to dig the shrapnel from my back at three in the morning in the hospital tent. The hospital tent was basically covered in sheets so they could make the lights brighter. I remember the next morning, when it was breakfast time, I couldn't even sit up to eat breakfast because my entire back was so sore. They had to dig that shrapnel out of my back. The pain was incredible. Yeah. It was. I had to lie on my side to eat my breakfast. I wasn't wounded otherwise, but I stayed there in France. I also went to a convalescent hospital in France. At the hospital they gave us different jobs to work on while healing up, and they had me relieving the person who was running the telephone—you know, the kind of phone with the crank? I relieved the regular guy there at noon; that was my job while my back was healing up over there.

I went back to combat in seven weeks. They would send you to a "repo-depo"—a replacement unit—unless you volunteered to go back to your regular outfit. They didn't deny you that choice. I thought I would go back to my old outfit to see all of the guys I knew, but after seven weeks, when I got back there, out of the 20 faces from seven weeks before, 19 of them were new, strange guys. I knew only one guy from before being wounded. There were a lot of replacements in those seven weeks. So I wouldn't have had to go back to my regular unit after all. I could have gone back anywhere. The only other people I knew were the drivers of the kitchen truck and the supply truck. The guys who weren't there anymore weren't necessarily casualties. They had just moved up into northern France during the time that I was in the hospital.

After I got back with my unit, we went through Luxemburg and into southern Belgium, and we walked up to the southern part of Holland. We swung into eastern Germany and northern Belgium before we got into Holland. It was on September 12, 1944, when we got into Germany. The going got a lot slower. We had spearheaded through Belgium and liberated numerous towns.

Just a side note here: A few years ago, my sister's grandson went to high school in Europe as an exchange student. He liked it so well that he went to college in Belgium. He met a Flemish girl and they got married, and he is still over there. He is working for a bank there now. Funny that 60 years earlier I had been in the same place!

Anyway, back to the past: Liberating towns along the way was a wonderful experience. The Belgian people were a lot nicer to us than the French people were when we liberated them. The Belgians would give us just about anything that they had. They gave us bottles of wine and chicken eggs. We would only be in each town for 15 minutes or so, and then we would have to move on. We liberated many, many towns over there.

Once we got into Germany, we were in the Siegfried line. Those fortifications had these dragon's teeth and "pillboxes" that were eight feet of concrete walls. Can you imagine? On a couple of occasions, after we would take them over, we would sleep in them. I remember sleeping in a pillbox for a couple of nights with the eight-foot walls. I felt pretty safe. This was September of 1944. We were 25 miles west of the Rhine River when I got hit the last time.

We were west of Cologne, Germany. I never got that far, but I did get to a little town along the way. That is when I was blinded and also hit in the leg. I also had shrapnel go right through my left leg here, right below the knee. *(Lifts his trousers to show wound)* I was in a cast for four and a half months in the hospital. After that they had to put a metal brace that would bend at the knee into the heel of my shoe. My left leg is shorter than the other. It atrophied, so it is not as big as the other leg. I have gotten along for 32 years working at my concession stand and being on my legs for about nine hours a day. My leg has never bothered me. Some might say that's because I'm a tough guy. Well, at least I was able to stay on my feet.

As for the blindness, that happened at the same time as the leg wound. A 120mm mortar shell dropped in front of me. I was in the 1st American Army commanded by General Courtney Hodges. We were in an area of slag, like an old zinc mine. We had our foxholes dug in this slag, and we had to board them up because they would cave in otherwise. We were there for about three weeks because Patton's 3rd Army was south of us. The 7th Army with General Patches was the first Army unit south of us in Germany. Then Patton's unit was south of the 7th Army. They had run out of ammunition so we had to stay where we were, otherwise we would be cut off if we kept moving out in front. The day before I was wounded on the 30th of October, I wrote three letters: to my mom, to my sister, and to my sweetheart, Theresa. All three of them had letters from me dated the 29th.

You know, the Germans would just start firing, just like they were punching a clock. At eight o'clock, they would start firing. If we did not fire at them, then they would start to fire at us. Ironically, the first time I was hit was on the 30th of June, and the second time I was hit was on the 30th of October.

Anyway, we were in this holding area waiting for Patton to get ammunition. By the way, a lot of the stories that we heard about Patton were built up. Everybody who had to deal with a tank in the war claimed that they were under Patton. That was not true. There were about 20 armored divisions, and Patton had only about four of them under his command. The rest were under other units. You know that movie, *Patton*, with George C. Scott in it? I think I have listened to it a couple of times. It was way overblown. The part about Patton slapping that kid at the hospital was not overblown; that was true. The kid was there because he could not stand to be on the front, and he needed that slap to bring him back to his senses.

There were a lot of those frightened kids there. Some of them were only 19 or 20 years old. But in Hitler's army, near the end of the war, he was running out of soldiers, and he was drafting kids that were as young as 15 or 16 and some older men as well. While I was over there, I had taken a total of 18 German prisoners. Sometimes the men we captured would be 45 to 50 years old. Imagine how scared *they* were! Imagine how scared we *all* were! If they came out of that war and said that they were *not* scared, they were the biggest liars. We were all scared. It was a question of whether we could control it or not. Many of our soldiers could not control it, and we would have to send them back. They would tell me right out. See, I became a squad leader out there. I sent numerous guys back because I knew they were not going to do us any good. They couldn't stand it. A lot of them were left with warped minds after the war. It was a tough situation.

When I got hit the second time and was blinded, I was unconscious for 14 days. I was air ambulanced back to Bristol, England, to an American

Army hospital there, and that is where I regained consciousness. That is when I knew that my eyes were all bandaged up. I knew I could see light because I was in a bed on the east side of the room facing west, and in the afternoon the sun would bother me. I had to cover my eyes because all I could see through the bandages was that big glare of light from the sun. One eye was enucleated and the other eye was still there, but the retina was damaged. It never made a picture; it only made a glare of light. But it didn't stay. It diminished as time went on. I had light perception at first, but it didn't help me with travel or anything. When my perception of light finally faded, I guess the reality that I was blind set in. I imagine that I did go through a period of depression, but I never thought of it much as depression. I guess we never had names for such things back then.

I was there a couple more weeks, and then they sent me on an American hospital ship back to America. I was on that ship for a long time—18 days and 18 nights. We went down around Azores, where the water was smoother, and we landed in Charleston, South Carolina. At that time there were two Army eye centers in the United States—one was at Valley Forge in Pennsylvania, and the other was in California. If your home was east of the Mississippi River, you would automatically be sent to Valley Forge. If you lived west, you would go to California. When they filled out the rec-ommendation sheet while I was at Stark General in South Carolina, they asked me what state I was from. Minnesota was considered west of the Mississippi. When they filled out the form and they asked me what state I was born in, I said West Virginia. *(Laughter)* You see, I heard that Valley Forge had a really excellent eye specialist—an ophthalmologist. They told me on the way back that I had a chance of having sight in my right eye. I thought that I should go to the hospital where I would be able to see the best doctor. I went there and I saw him, and he was very good. I made my mind up that I was going to Pennsylvania, to Valley Forge, so that is why I told them that I was born in West Virginia. Actually, I had never been out of Minnesota—except for that one trip to Wisconsin—in my entire life, until I went into the Army. *(Laughter)* I don't think that that was a serious lie, so I was not too worried about it.

I was a vet patient at Valley Forge for four and a half months. My leg was in a cast up to my hip. I had to have my meals in bed, and I had to go to eye treatment in a wheelchair. I had to do that until they put my leg in a brace and I could walk around on my own. I didn't get any "road treatment," which is the term they used for learning how to walk with a white cane and all of that. I finally got to go to the school I had to attend up in Connecticut. It was a high school for wealthy kids. I guess the Kennedy boys, or most of them, had graduated from there. I think Jack Kennedy graduated from high school in 1935, because I graduated from high school in 1936. Jack Kennedy was a year older than I. This was a very exclusive private school. It was up in Avon, Connecticut.

Anyway, blind folks like me had to spend 18 weeks there to learn how to do different things, like learning Braille. There were a bunch of trades we could learn there, as well—even repairing cars! They had an area where you could learn how to repair cars. They also had a program where you could learn how to run a concession. You would work and serve your friends Cokes and candy and that sort of stuff. Believe it or not, I never even took that course when I was there—and I ended up running a concession stand for 32 years! *(Laughter)* Lots of people wonder how blind people could tell the denominations of the money people were giving them. If they told me it was over a dollar, I would ask someone I knew who worked around there to verify it. I wouldn't take the money unless I had it verified by someone else. Of course, when they gave me loose change, I could tell what it was in a second. So I got used to handling change and dollar bills. It is a pretty low form of human being who would slip a blind man a $1 bill and say it's a $20, but there are people who would do that. We were instructed not to accept anything over a dollar unless we had someone to verify it. Of course, there was always someone around there that I knew, even if it was a patient. I got to know some of those patients very well over the years at my concession stand at Fort Snelling.

Anyway, back to the past. I lay in bed in that hospital in Valley Forge for several months. I sure had a lot of stuff going through my mind. Theresa was my sweetheart when I went into the Army, and I was waiting to get back and get married when the war was over. We had talked about marriage before I went over, but I wanted to get the war out of the way first. I was 24 years old. Two days before my twenty-fourth birthday I was drafted. After I got down to the hospital at Valley Forge on New Year's Day of 1945, my mom decided to come down to visit me, and Theresa said that she wanted to go along as well. The two of them went from St. Paul to Pennsylvania by Greyhound Bus in January. I had only been there 12 days when they arrived. The day after they got there, the doctor came in and told me that I would never see again. He gave me that news the day after my mom and Theresa came. That was quite a shocker. Then I started to plan my life without sight. When I was lying in bed, I had the chance to think about it, obviously. I made up my mind that I was going to try to live as close to normal as I could—just like my brothers or my next-door neighbors were living. I had the feeling that I was pretty close to normal. After living in a couple of older houses, Theresa and I decided to build a new house. This house where we are sitting right now was built in 1955, and we moved in right after the holidays in 1956. I have been living here for 19 years now.

Theresa and I started dating in September of 1939. I guess people just tend to remember these things. In a way, it is pretty wonderful. Theresa hadn't turned 18 yet. She was still a kid. This was September, and she turned 18 in October and I was already 21. I think it is amazing that I was able to carry this image of her through our many, many years of marriage. That was pretty wonderful. I was so lucky that I got to see her before I was blinded. I thought that Theresa was a real looker. She was my honey. In April it will be 60 years since we were married. We got married on April 28, 1945, over in Valley Forge, in a little chapel by the hospital. Theresa asked a couple who lived by us to be our attendants. They were 49 and 50 years old at the time, and we thought they were pretty old! *(Laughter)* I didn't want to wait until I got home to Minnesota to get married because all I would have had there would be my relatives, gawking at me during the ceremony, and I did not want that. Theresa would have preferred to be married at home, but I knew what that would have been like, and I didn't want to have to go through it. I told her that I would rather get married in Valley Forge, so she agreed. She stuck by me.

Of course, this was after I tried to coax her to leave me and go home and find a sighted husband. But she wouldn't go. *(Pause)* I said that that was the original deal I had made with her: that we would get married only if I came home from the war normal. But she said that she loved me and *(starting to cry)* that she wasn't going to let me go. Turn off the tape recorder, will you please? I'll be okay in a little while.

(Break in interview)

So, is the tape recorder running again? Okay. It was a simple wedding. Yeah, it was just a simple wedding. Theresa got a job putting cookies in boxes at a cookie factory. She got to know a lot of the girls there, and they came to the wedding. Some of the patients from the hospital who knew me came to the wedding, too.

We went to Philadelphia with our attendants and had dinner together, just the four of us. We had made reservations at a hotel, a prominent one, and after dinner our attendants went home and left Theresa and me at the hotel. This was a Saturday night and I had to be back to the hospital on Monday morning, so that was a short honeymoon. Yes. Not even a full weekend. And so that was our wedding. We were married almost 60 years. That's really a long time, isn't it? We knew each other longer than that— for 66 years—until her death last month. She was my chauffeur, my eyes, my everything. *(Pause)*

We had five wonderful children. Our oldest son, Mike, died in a construction accident during the summer after his freshman year in college, when he was 20 years old. *(Long pause)*

When I came home from the service, Theresa did not know how to drive, and I, of course, could not drive. I had signed my car over to my father because they told us that if we had anything of value before we went into the war, then we should get rid of it. I let my father keep the car, and he had it for another 10 years. In 1950, Theresa still hadn't learned how to drive, so I bought an old Chevy—and then she had lots of teachers! Of course, they were not willing to let her drive *their* vehicles—but when I bought one for her, then they came out of the woodwork to teach her to drive! *(Laughter)* She learned within a couple of months to drive very well. I traded that old Chevy off for a two-year-old Chevy. About a year after that, I received a certificate from the government for a new car for blinded veterans. The certificate was for $1,600 to help purchase a new car in 1952. I wrote numerous letters to President Truman, who was against this idea. He pocket vetoed it. He felt that someone else would get more use out of a car than a blinded veteran would. The Senate, however, made it a law, with a two-third's majority vote over Truman's veto, and that's how we were able to get it. I got a new Pontiac. I had heard that the Pontiac was the nicest-looking vehicle on the road, so that is what we bought.

You know, as I look back on all of this now, I remember having been told that since my father was a farmer and he was 60-some years old and I was the only one left at home to help, I could have gotten out of serving in the military. I felt good that I had passed the physical exam, but before that I did not really want to go to war. It was because I passed the exam and felt good about it—that is why I went into the war. A lot of guys my age weren't able to pass that test.

As I said earlier, after Pearl Harbor was attacked, I thought about getting involved in the war. At that time, I had been working for two years at a meat packing plant with a fellow named Art Blom from Minneapolis. This was right after Pearl Harbor was bombed. We were kicking around the idea of joining up and had our minds made up that we were going to join, but he got drafted. We had our minds made up that we were going to join the Air Force, but he got drafted in March of 1942. I didn't do anything, and then two months later I got drafted in May. That is how that happened. My friend Art Blom was in the 90th Division, and he got killed in the war. He got drafted in March, and that was the last I heard of him. He was a nice guy. Another guy who I had gone to school with was hauling gas on the front lines, and a shell hit his truck and he was blown to kingdom come. He was the same age as I was; we went to grade school together. He was also in the 90th. That division saw a lot of action. That is how that went. So anyway, I was pretty close to enlistment, but in the end I got drafted instead. I got the "Greetings" from good old Uncle Sam!

After I got out, I was treated very well by the government. As long as I was hospitalized out at the VA, they would buy me a shaver and a radio. They supplied me with lots of things like that, in addition to my compensation. About a week after Theresa died, I got a letter from the VA notifying me that they were cutting my compensation. I had been paid some for having a spouse, but the VA cut that payment right after her funeral. I thought that was sort of poor timing on their part, but Theresa's portion of the compensation wasn't a lot. I thought it was going to be more than that. Actually, I didn't even think about it until I got the letter.

Not that I'm bragging or anything, but you might be interested in knowing what special honors the Army awarded me. I received the Purple Heart, the Oak Leaf Cluster, the Bronze Star, a Combat Infantry Badge, and a Rifleman Sharpshooter Badge. I am very, very proud of all these recognitions.

You know, on May 8, just a few months from now, I'm going to have my eighty-seventh birthday. I remember when I was a kid, I thought that 87 was ancient. It *is* ancient! *(Laughter)*

William V. Schleppegrell
1943

Born: 1923

Present home: Hibbing, Minnesota

Military history: Enlisted; entered service 1942

Branch of service: U.S. Air Force

Length of service: Three years (including six months in a German POW camp)

Highest rank: 2nd Lieutenant

Note: This interview was transcribed from a videotaped interview of Mr. Schleppegrell's prisoner-of-war experience. The video was produced by Fig Leaf Productions (William V. Schleppegrell, Jr., producer). Grateful acknowledgment is extended to William Schleppegrel, Sr., and William Schleppegrell, Jr., for permission to use the transcription here.

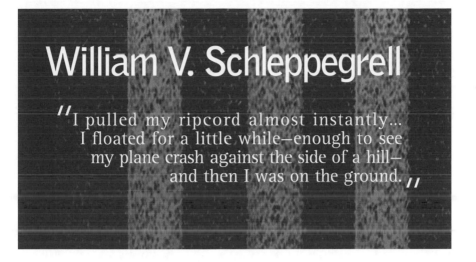

William V. Schleppegrell

"I pulled my ripcord almost instantly...
I floated for a little while—enough to see
my plane crash against the side of a hill—
and then I was on the ground."

J anuary 1945—*Germany holds over 28,000 prisoners of war. Of these, more than 8,000 are Air Corps officers. This is the story of one of them.*

I am an ex-prisoner of war. I was a prisoner of war in Germany in Stalag[1] One, which was located up on the Baltic Sea in Barth, Germany. I was there from the middle of January of 1945 until the end of the war—and a little after until the end of May. We lived in barracks. I was in a room with 23 other men. The whole camp of Stalag One was for airmen—people shot down and taken prisoner who were flying bombers, men who were navigators and bombardiers, engineers and fighter pilots. I was a fighter pilot. I flew a P-47 Thunderbolt. In camp, we were confined to a very small room. There were eight tiered bunks, three bunks high, and I was in the top bunk. We had straw mattresses that were fairly soft when we first lay down on them, but after a few days and weeks, they became hard as boards. Since we were being fed very meagerly, we found that our bodies were becoming bruised—black and blue—just from the boards on the bed. It is just like the *Princess and the Pea*.

---

1. "Stalag" is the name the Germans used for their prisoner-of-war camps. It is a shortened form of the German word *Stammlager*—"base camp"—from *Stamm*, meaning base, and *Lager*, meaning camp.

We had three "meals" a day. In the morning we had coffee and a slice of bread with either—well, usually, just margarine on it. At noon or around noon, we would usually have a cup of soup or stew and another piece of bread and maybe some jam. That was it. I think I had the jam or the marmalade in the morning and the margarine at noon. Then at night, again, we would have another slice of bread and coffee. We were supposed to get Red Cross parcels from Sweden and from Switzerland—each person was to have one parcel each week while we were prisoners of war. Well, by the time I got to Germany in 1945, the transportation system was so upset that Red Cross parcels no longer were arriving. When they were arriving and stored, very often they were bombed out. So we had to share a parcel every few weeks with other members of our group. The contents of these parcels was rather interesting. We would get a little tin of margarine, a piece of chocolate, a package of cigarettes, a can of Spam, and a package of dried toast. I really cannot remember anything else we got. We would begin our trading. Since I didn't smoke and I loved chocolate, I traded my cigarettes for chocolate—and a lot of other people did, too. We were allowed to go outside during the day for our physical education. We would do some calisthenics outside—usually someone would lead us in calisthenics. In fact, at this time of the war, the Russians were approaching from the east, and we had high hopes that we would be liberated by the Russians. In our calisthenics, instead of counting 1-2-3-4, we would say things like, "Come on, Joe!" because it was Joseph Stalin who was the leader of the Russians at the time. We weren't allowed to do this for very long before the Germans caught on to what we were doing. We were forbidden to use that expression.

We called the guards "goons" until they discovered what the goons were. Young people nowadays maybe don't know what the goons were, but in the *Popeye* comic strip they had a series of weird-looking characters that were called goons, so that was really why we were calling the German guards goons.

The bread that we got was a loaf of bread or a couple of loaves of bread that had to be shared by the 24 of us. The loaf was cut into thin slices. The soup varied, and sometimes we had pieces of meat in it that we found out later was horsemeat. The vegetables were almost always rutabagas and potatoes—and sometimes carrots. Every once in a while, we would get the news that we were having real meat at the midday meal, and it would turn out to be a great big bone from a horse. The meat would be carved from that, and we would have a piece of meat—which really didn't taste bad, by the way.

We gradually all lost weight. I, myself, weighed around 150 to 155 pounds, I think, when I was in the service and when we were in active training. By the time I got out of prison camp and had the chance to weigh myself when we got to Camp Lucky Strike in France, I was down to about 115 pounds. So I had lost quite a bit of weight. I had frozen my feet before we got to camp, and so I spent a lot of the time in camp with my feet facing the sun coming in the window because my feet had turned black, and they were peeling. That seemed to help, because the skin peeled off and I got new skin. My feet still remain sensitive today, and I still have a numb feeling on the soles of my feet. We were not able to get hot water for showers and soon became infested with body lice. From time to time, they would have us strip and shoot us with powder for the lice, then sterilize our clothes or burn them. We had to stay out of our rooms while they sprayed for lice, but this was not much help as the lice soon returned.

The morale that we had was rather positive because at night we would get an updated radio report. Somewhere in the camp there was a secret radio, and someone had a typewriter and would type out the latest news. We did get news from the Germans, but we also knew that that news was colored—they would say that the Allies were in Hamburg and the British were in Hamburg and approaching or pushing up from Hamburg. We knew that the British would probably be in Hamburg for a considerable amount of time and were getting closer to us. The same thing with the Russians coming from the east: They would say that they were approaching Frankfurt from the border, and we knew from the American reports that the Russians were already in Frankfurt and were approaching Berlin. We did have that news of communication.

Our morale was good that way. We spent the time playing cards because most of us were officers and were not allowed to do physical work, according to the Geneva Convention. Personally, I would rather have been occupied doing some work than just be sitting. We did have a small library, but they were books from Great Britain—old books from the past. I did manage to wade my way through *David Copperfield* and several other British novels that I never thought I would read, but there was nothing really up to date or interesting. They had newspapers and magazines; and, as I said, we played cards a lot—bridge and cribbage, mostly—and we talked about our war stories. I learned things there that were rather depressing. I guess I had an uplifted spirit about American heroes and pilots; but then when you get into a room with 23 other men and they begin telling you some of the things they were a party to and did, you begin to realize that a number of atrocities were committed on *both* sides of the fighting powers. I began to question a lot of things about why we were fighting and how we were fighting and what the outcome was going to be.

On April 30, 1945, the Germans left Stalag One. On May 1, the Russians entered the camp and liberated over 3,000 men who were held there.

Before I got to the camp, I was flying out of the airfield in Nancy, France. We had moved there from another location farther south and east in France—Dijon, France. It was during the Battle of the Bulge. This was one of the last attempts by Hitler to push through the Allied lines. He almost succeeded, by the way—but all the force of our armies and Air Force were directed towards stymieing the German push in the Battle of the Bulge. We were doing a lot of dive-bombing at targets like railroad yards, bridges, airfields, railroad centers—that type of thing. I happened to be on my seventeenth mission. We were dive-bombing some areas near Saarbrücken, and I happened to be the last person in the flight that day. There were 16 of us, and I was the sixteenth in line to go down on those targets. We would start down at a certain altitude and go into a steep dive and focus on the target. As I pulled up after releasing my bombs—we carried two 500-pound bombs, one under each wing—I released my bombs on the target and pulled up and began climbing. And all of a sudden I felt this tremendous shock in the plane, and I knew anti-aircraft had hit my plane.

Fortunately, I was flying a P-47 Thunderbolt, which was a really heavily armor-plated plane. I think otherwise—had I been flying a P-51, which was another plane that was used more on pursuits—I think that my plane would have disintegrated, and that would have been the end. I felt this tremendous hit in my plane, but I was still flying. I was still going up. There was no explosion. I knew my gas tank had not been hit, or I hoped it hadn't. I pulled back up and rejoined my flight—there were four of us in each flight. It was at that time that I began to notice that I had a little faltering in my engine, I had checked my instruments, and I found that they were all normal. I did tell the flight leader that I had been hit and that I felt I was having some engine trouble. He directed me to fly back toward my base and directed one of the flight members to accompany me. So the two of us took a direction southwest toward our base. As we were flying back, I noticed that I was losing altitude. My engine was losing power and my oil pressure began to drop, and I realized that my oil had been struck by part of the anti-aircraft fire. I knew that this wasn't going to take long. A plane just doesn't fly without oil—and actually, a plane not being propelled forward falls at a pretty rapid rate.

As we flew closer and closer to the front line, I began to have hopes that I wouldn't have to bail out over enemy territory— that I would be able to reach the front lines and be able to bail out over friendly territory. But it was not to be. I was getting down to about the lowest altitude at which it was safe to bail out. My engine was gasping and my power was failing, and it finally failed. I told the other pilot that I was going to have to bail out, but he was having problems understanding me due to the static on his radio. I had to repeat it and wasn't sure if he heard me or not, but I ripped off my helmet and ripped open the canopy of my plane. I bumped myself getting out because I had lunged over the side. I pulled my ripcord almost instantly because I was so close to the ground. My parachute opened. I floated for a little while—enough to see my plane crash against the side of a hill—and then I was on the ground.[2]

I got out of my parachute. It was a cold day. I had ripped my pant leg getting out of the plane, so I had to rip the pant leg off and was bare-kneed to the middle of my thigh. I hurt my leg when I landed, but not too bad. I knew I hadn't broken it, and I got out of my parachute. Our instructions had been that if you ever had to bail out, you should bury your chute—that is, find a hiding place for it. There wasn't a hiding place for mine. I was in an open field. Of course, I was scared, and I wasn't dressed for winter at all because our planes were so hot, so warm, that most of the pilots did not wear winter outfits at all. We wore summer outfits and wanted to be comfortable. We never thought we would be shot down, of course. Fortunately, I looked around and noticed it was a wooded area. Now, a

---

2. See Part III of this book for copies of some of William Schleppergrell's letters about the downing of his plane and his prisoner-of-war experiences.

wooded area in Germany is not the same as northern Minnesota. This was a forest that had been cultivated and recultivated and cut down, and I could hear saws working in the distance and knew that there were people around. I thought, where do I head for?

The best way to head was southwest because that was towards the front lines. Actually, I could hear guns in the distance, so I knew I was not that far from the front line. I had no idea what to do. I saw a road, a country road, and I thought, well, I will go down this road—at least in that general direction. I had evidently cut my forehead or my eyebrow on the plane when I jumped out because all of a sudden I realized that I had some blood on my face. As I headed down the road I thought, well, I am just going to act as though I belong here—which was very foolish, now that I think about it. Around the corner, ahead of me, came a bicycle. It was quite a distance away, and it was an old man riding a bicycle. I thought, now, do I run? There wasn't a place to hide. Should I run into the forest here? Or do I just pretend that I am going somewhere? I thought, well, I am just going to keep walking. I kept walking and the bicycle kept getting nearer and nearer; and all of a sudden, I think, he must have seen my torn clothes and the blood on my face because his eyes got really big, and I could tell he knew I didn't "just belong there." He passed by me very fast and got behind me. I didn't even look back. He started yelling. When I looked back, he had gotten off his bike and was yelling at the top of his voice, but I just kept walking faster, away from him. Down the same bend in the road came a Jeep—a German Jeep—and two soldiers came out of it, and they picked me up.

I am rambling on...but that is the way I got picked up. From that point on, I had a couple of weeks—a couple of weeks which were the worst time of my experience. I was in solitary confinement. I was put in coal cellars all by myself. I was put in civilian jails all by myself. When I was finally put together with other groups, it was on a train; and then we had to march when we would get to town, and we would have to march through the town. For instance, I remember in one town which was pretty bombed out—where we had to get off the train and walk through the center of town, which was really just a heap of rubble—civilians were standing on the sidelines, throwing stones and rocks at us and yelling. People would come brandishing big sticks and try to get at us. Our guards kept telling us to keep moving ahead. We finally got through, but not before some of us had rocks and sticks hit us. I remember another time when we were traveling on a train. It was close to evening, and the train stopped suddenly and everybody had to get off the train and go into a bomb shelter, which was out in the middle of nowhere. We were put in with civilians. They were very angry, of course, because we were being dive-bombed. We did not know what was going to happen. We did not understand the language. It was a very frightening experience, going to our destination, walking and riding on trains.

From there we were processed and sent to Stalag One. I was interrogated. They brought me into this bombed-out basement and into a room where an officer was sitting behind a desk. In very good English, he asked me to sit down. He asked me my name, and I told him—Schleppegrell. He said, "Your first name?" I said, "William." He told me it was a German name, and I said, "No. It's Danish. My grandparents came from Denmark." Since then, I have learned that it really *is* German, but at that time I had thought, "Ha-ha-ha! I am not a German!" When he asked me my rank, I said, "Second lieutenant." He asked for my serial number, and I said, "715009." He asked, "What plane were you flying on?" I told him that I couldn't tell him any more. I told him I could only tell him my name, rank, and serial number. He kind of laughed and said, "We are not asking any questions that are going to be incriminating for anyone. We need to know some of these things. What type of plane were you flying?" I told him, "No, you don't! All you need to know is my name, rank, and serial number." He said, "We are having problems with spies. We are having people who are claiming to be pilots or claiming to be soldiers who are really spies who have been coming over the front lines. We have to make sure you are who you say you are." He rang a little bell, and another guy came in. He said that guy, "We'll bring him back later. Take him somewhere." This was all said in German.

So the other guy led me to a door, and he opened it up and told me to go in. He closed the door behind me, and I was in the coal room. It was just coal—and it was cold. There were three windows that were colored over so you couldn't see outside, but you could see if it was still light. I think they were blue. They were up high—just small windows. There was nothing to do there but pace because it was so cold in there. I had to keep walking. I walked and walked and walked until I finally realized that the Germans were interrogating other soldiers in a room right next door, and

I could actually hear what was going on over there. I could hear them asking someone what their name was and if they were American. They would say, "John Jones." "And your rank?" They would answer, "Corporal." "And your serial number?" They would rattle off their serial number. Then they would ask what outfit they were with, and they would say, "362nd Infantry Division." They would ask where they were when they were captured, and they would say, "I was by this little village." They would go on and on, answering all of the questions.

I became very angry when I heard them give the Germans all of that information. Not that that happened all of the time—but we were told just to say our name, rank, and serial number. That was all. It made me angry to think that some would let the other information out. What we were told was that if we were to give out more information, bits and pieces of information, the Germans could find out what altitude we were flying our planes, when we began our dive-bombing runs, where our bases were located, and what was going on there. A lot of the things discussed would be detrimental to our Army. I knew the Geneva Convention said, "Name, rank, and serial number" only. That was it, although at times I began to question it and how it was going to affect me.

I stayed in that room for a long time. I could tell that it was night. I had been shot down at about 10:00 in the morning or 9:00, maybe. I hadn't had anything to eat yet—just some breakfast that morning. I was cold and scared. I tried sitting down to rest, but my butt got cold sitting on the coal. I walked and walked, and the next day came. I could see daylight through the three little colored windows.

Sometime during the day the door opened, and they took me back to the same room I had been in before. The same man acted like he had never seen me before. He asked me what my name was. I told him, "Schleppegrell." This time he didn't say anything about it being a German name, but he asked me my rank and serial number, and I told him. Then he asked the same questions again about what group I was with, and I told him that I wasn't going to tell him any more. So then they put me back into the coal bin. I was there for the whole day, because the next time the door opened it was night again.

I was really hungry by this time. They brought me out and put me into a car with another serviceman who spoke English, so we were able to speak to one another. It was one of the scariest rides I had ever had because we didn't know where we were going or where they were taking us. It was a small car, perhaps a Volkswagen. They took us over these roads, and there were no lights on. You could see flashes of anti-aircraft fire all around. We kept going and going, and finally we got to a tar road. Then we were put with another group of prisoners in a house that wasn't bombed out. It was a house with a kitchen. They had soup on the stove, and there was bread. We were given soup and bread to eat. I can remember that we could have as much soup as we wanted. Then we were told to go into the other room and find a spot to lie down. There were a lot of us, but the house did not have any furniture in it. There were just some ticks (mats) on the floor. So I found a place next to the wall, and I lay down there. I must have gone to sleep right away. I awoke to them prodding me and saying, "Schleppegrell!" They brought me out again and took me by myself and put me into a jail that was in town. From that jail cell I could look out and see dive-bombers—P-47s, actually— flying and dive-bombing in the area. I thought how ironic it would be if they would dive-bomb the town.

I was there overnight and then put with a group of other prisoners and had to march. That began the story of the marches: the rides on the trains, staying overnight in barns, and things like that. The only other interrogation I ever underwent was when we got to the concentration point where prisoners were sent to different prison camps throughout Germany. I was interrogated there again, and I answered in the same way as before. A German major asked the questions this time. It was a plush office, and he asked me if all I would tell him was name, rank, and serial number. I told him yes, that was all I could give. He told me that after a few days I would change my mind. He had the guard take me and put me into a cell. It was a small, narrow room with just a cot and a blanket—one GI blanket. There was a radiator that came on once in the morning and once in the evening. If I sat on the radiator, I could feel my butt get warm. Otherwise, it was cold in there. I spent most of my time just lying on the bed, wrapped up in the blanket. I could hear a clock chiming outside, so I could tell what time of day or night it was. I lost track after a while. I noticed on the wall that there were marks that people—prisoners who had been there before—had left on the walls. There were about 21 marks, which meant 21 days.

After about three days, I began to have thoughts about whether I was ever going to get out of there. I didn't know if they had forgotten about me or what. I had nothing to do. The guard would come with a piece of bread in the morning, a bowl of broth at noon, and another piece of bread at night—and coffee. I thought, "Gee—I'd do anything to get out of here!" I pounded on the door once, and after a few days I pointed to my head and said, "Headache!" I thought they would take me to the infirmary and I could get out of there. Also, when I needed to go to the bathroom, they would take me out of the cell and down the hall to the bathroom, and a guard would stand there while I did my business. I thought if I could get to the infirmary, he might leave me alone. Well, he left; and then he came back with a couple of aspirins for me, and that was the end of that.

I figured I was in that cold, little cell eight days. On the eighth night I was awakened when they came and brought me out. They took me into the same room as they had before. The major was there, and he had on his desk in front of him three folders—403, 404 and 405 Squadrons. He looked at me and said, "I want to tell you a few things about your squadron. You're in the 405th squadron." He picked up the folder and opened it up and said, "Your commanding officer is Major Leonard." Right away I thought, "Well, at least your spy work isn't up to date." Leonard wasn't a major any longer; he was a lieutenant colonel. He had been transferred to another unit at Christmastime. Then the major told me that I was with the Ninth Air Force, 405th Squadron. Then he said, "Oh! Pardon me! He isn't Major Leonard. He is Lieutenant Leonard. He just got his promotion!" I thought boy, they really are up to date on their knowledge of what is going on. He asked me if I was surprised, and I told him I was. He said, "You are going to be even more surprised when you find out who else is here!" He called for his assistant and gave him something, and then the assistant brought in another fellow from my squadron who had been shot down and taken prisoner. That guy had told them everything! I said to him, "Why did you give them more than your name, rank, and serial number?" He said, "Oh, they knew all that stuff anyway!" Fortunately, we did not wind up in the same room at the prison camp. I did not have very good feelings toward him.

How did I get in the Army? Well, I was a student at the University of Minnesota. I was in pre-med and was doing poorly in school. I just wasn't very motivated. I was from a small town—Littlefork—and went down to the "big" city to go to the university. I was kind of a small fish in a big pond. I wasn't living on campus; I was living with my aunt.

When Sunday, December 7, 1941, came, my aunt and I were sitting around the radio, listening to some program. They interrupted the program to say that the Japanese had bombed Pearl Harbor. We were good and ready from that point on until war was declared. Everyone was talking about war. They were saying how students would be exempted. I was in my second year of school by that time and was still doing poorly, but I was also thinking romantically of doing something for my country. It was all about patriotism and the flag. We knew we had a just cause. We knew they needed men over there. The Axis needed to be defeated.

I somehow got the idea to go into the Army Air Corps. They were looking for people who had two years of college, which I did. On December 7, 1942—a year after war was declared—I went down to the courthouse in Minneapolis and enlisted in the Army Air Corps. That is how I got in. In February of the following year, 1943, I was called up and sent to basic training in Missouri. That was my first experience in the Army. Then I went on into preflight school in Lansing, Michigan. I went to primary school at Cimarron Field in Oklahoma City. I went for basic in Victoria, Texas, advanced, graduated, and got my wings in March of 1944. I took gunnery practice down in the Madagarda Islands in the Gulf of Mexico. I then went out east to Richmond Air Base for training there. After that, I went to Long Island at Suffolk Field. I went to Bradley Field in Connecticut, where I got into single-engine P-47 training. Back in those days, we got to decide if we wanted to go into single-engine or multiple-engine planes. I picked single-engine planes. I flew P-47s and P-40s in training. Then we were shipped overseas. We landed in England, and I had a little bit more training there. We were then flown to Paris and went by truck to Dijon, France, where we got our planes and began our mission. That is really my history.

How has this war experience affected my life? I know it has affected my life in many ways. I think one of the very negative things that happened was that I didn't learn how to eat properly. When I got out of prison camp, I just went all out for food—for sweets, for fat stuff, for anything! I had no sense of eating properly. Consequently, I put on a lot of weight, and ever since I have had a weight problem. Before that I had been active in sports and didn't have a problem with weight; but after being deprived of food and then getting back on food, I found it to be a really difficult thing. The last couple of years, thanks to being a member of TOPS, I have been able to get control of myself and TAKE OFF POUNDS SENSIBLY.

I still have dreams. I know I have post-traumatic stress. I think I deal with it okay. At least I have tried to. It has helped me a lot to be able to talk about my experience. I felt at fault with the U.S. Government because it took them 40-some years to call me back to debrief me. I think it would have helped if I had come back to the United States and been able to talk this out with some counselor who knew all about the trauma and the stress of being a prisoner of war. I think that would have solved some of my problems a lot earlier.

A lot of positive things have come out of it, too. I became a German teacher. I felt that these were people I had to know more about. I had to know more about the language. I had to know more about the culture. How could a group of people perform the horrible things that they performed in their country? Was everyone like that? Was everyone a Nazi? Those were questions that I had; and because I became involved in the way that I did, I think it helped me determine what my future course in life was going to be. I did go into education and become a German teacher. Since then, I have tried to show my students and my friends by example. But also, in the classroom, I have used my story, somewhat, to try to show that there are people who are bad and others who are good in all countries. We have a beautiful country. I wouldn't want to be a member of any other country but this. I am an American citizen, and I am proud to an American.

I also realize that a German citizen is proud to be a German and proud of their language and heritage. I feel that is the importance of learning a foreign language and learning about a foreign country. You begin to see that America is not the only country in the world. There are other countries and other people who also have feelings. They get up in the morning and go to bed at night. They get married and divorced. They do things that we all do. I think I have learned that, and I tried to instill that in my students. I believe that having been in solitary confinement and having been able to do so much thinking, I realize how lucky I really am to be where I am today.

I have a beautiful family, a beautiful wife. I really owe them for what I am today because I feel that I would have been a completely different person had I not met Norma, my wife, and had the family that we have. I wish I could instill in my children and my grandchildren the feeling of "questioning" things, of learning as much as you can. Another lesson: Don't act before you think. Think of what implications your actions are going to have, and think of the people you really love and who love you. Before you go off on some screwy angle and then say afterwards, "Oh, I wish I would have known better. I wish I would have thought before I did that." That is part of how I think my war experience has affected my life.

I find it hard to interact with people in large groups. I do not know why that should be since I was in solitary so much. You would think that I would be more comfortable in large groups, but I am not. I am not an out-going person. At the Newman Club at the university after the war, they jokingly called me "Loudmouth" because I was just the opposite of being a loudmouth. I have learned to become more talkative, I guess. I am married to a talkative person, and she keeps me going that way. My kids all love me, and they are good to me. We are good to them. My grandchildren are coming along, and I love all of them and they love me, too. Now I have great-grandchildren! I am hoping to spend my life with my wife in good health, which I have had so far. I have been very lucky that way. I have lived to be an old man. And you know what? I don't even *feel* old!

Leland "Lee" James
1944

Born: 1926

Present home: Edina, Minnesota

Military history: Enlisted; entered service 1944

Branch of service: U.S. Navy; later, active duty in Korean Conflict

Length of service: WWII – about two years
Korea – about one year

Highest rank: Petty Officer 3rd Class

Date/place of interview: February 11, 2005
Edina, Minnesota

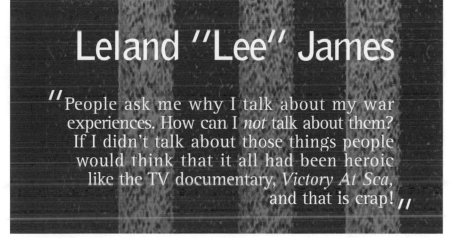

Leland "Lee" James

"People ask me why I talk about my war experiences. How can I not talk about them? If I didn't talk about those things people would think that it all had been heroic like the TV documentary, Victory At Sea, and that is crap!"

Where was I and what was I doing when Pearl Harbor was attacked on that Sunday early in December of 1941? Well, I was only 15 years old in 1941, and a buddy of mine and I were out at the Field Museum in Chicago, where I lived at the time, trying to pick up girls. Well, we didn't hear anything about Pearl Harbor until Sunday afternoon. We weren't having much luck attracting girls, and suddenly the guard came in and asked us if we had heard about Pearl Harbor. We said we hadn't, and he told us that the Japs had attacked Pearl Harbor. We said, "Oh. Thanks." My buddy and I then had a moment to talk to each other, and we asked each other what we should we do. We just decided to pick up where we left off and continue what we were doing. In other words, the attack meant nothing to us. We didn't even know where Pearl Harbor was.

I had a better idea about the Japanese than most people did, however. coming from a mostly Chinese family, which I did—my stepfather was Chinese. We had been at war with the Japanese since 1936. My family had Chinese restaurants in Minneapolis and Chicago. The reason why I lived in Chicago was because my stepfather was down there, and that is where I lived and went to school. In a way, I was raised partially Chinese. My mentor was the Consul General for the Republic of China, Dr. Chang Lok Chen. He was down in Chicago at that time. Dr. Chen always kept me abreast of the war with China. When my buddy went home that Sunday afternoon, I went back to the restaurant, and Pearl Harbor was all the buzz. We were all wondering what was going to happen. Dr. Chen came in for his evening meal, and I heard quite a bit more. He had gotten some information by that time. Personally, it never affected me. I was only 15.

Since many people don't know the difference between who is Chinese, Japanese, Korean, etc., you'd think people would have treated us Chinese with hate after Pearl Harbor, but they didn't. Most people came into the restaurant to commiserate, thank us, and say that we were all in this together, and so on and so on. They had read all about the Japanese attack in the paper, but nothing really got close to them. Now, all of a sudden, things *were* close to them. As far back as 1936 on, my family always had a dislike for the Japanese and a strong hatred because of Nanking. We were very familiar with the "Rape of Nanking."[1] Dr. Chen had a lot of diplomatic information and descriptions about what had happened at Nanking. It was appalling. There was not much love in our family for the Japanese empire or for any Japanese. The Nanking incident happened in 1938. See, I had a different view of this Pearl Harbor area because I was 15, but I really didn't know how to assimilate this stuff—so in my case, add another layer of, "I don't like the Japs." Besides, at age 15, I was more interested in chasing girls! *(Laughter)* That is right. That was a high priority.

Anyway, I graduated from high school in 1943, and my life did change after that. I was in the Junior ROTC, the Reserve Officers Training Corps, at Lane Technical High School in Chicago. This changed things entirely for me because they got pretty tough with us in the ROTC. I ended up being a line captain with my own company in the Lane Regiment when I graduated down there. The Lane Regiment had about 1,300 cadets in 1943. When I graduated from high school in June of 1943, I had just turned 17 four months before. Don't ask me how I got out of school so young.

I was immediately urged to be accepted as a sergeant in the Organized Army Reserves if I was old enough, but I *wasn't* old enough. They told me that I could also be a second lieutenant in the Illinois National Guard if I would join up. Don't ask me why I joined the Navy; I don't know why

---

1. See the footnote in Kenneth Porwoll's interview for details on the "Rape of Nanking."

I did. *(Laughter)* I think the reason why I did sign up for the Navy was because it seemed as if people got shot at in the Army, and that didn't happen as much in the Navy. I had thought about getting into the Navy, the Air Force and the like, but my eyes had never been good, so I thought I wouldn't qualify. Finally, in February 1944, I was going to be 18 in two weeks, so I went down to join the Navy. They told me that I would have to take an eye exam. That scared me. My eyes had stopped me from everything. One of the things that was kismet was that when they put me in line for the eye exam, they put me right next to the eye chart. This line of guys wasn't moving very fast, so I memorized the eye chart forward and backward. I memorized what was on line four, what was on line three—and I can still remember: E-F-P-T-O-Z-P-O-A-N-H-E-F. I can't do them backward, though. By the way, they don't use that chart anymore. They use different things. This was my only chance at the time. I went up there and told myself that I could not think about anything but the letters that I had just memorized. I passed the eye exam! I will never forget that, and I will never forget how I felt. I felt great!

By that time, the war had been going on for about three years. I got into it in the middle of it, but we had many other battles to fight yet and go through. The ship I was on, the *Makin Island*, went down to New Guinea, where we practiced troop landings. The Aussies and New Zealanders had been fighting there since 1942.

I am jumping way ahead here, so let me backtrack a bit. I was on an escort aircraft carrier, what they called a CVE or a baby-flattop. The number was CVE-93, and her name was *Makin Island*. As far as the Navy guys were concerned, the initials CVE stood for combustible, vulnerable, and expendable! *(Laughter)* But the Navy sure didn't call it that! The CVs were the big ones. The first carrier I got on was the old *"Sara" (Saratoga)* (CV-3). I was on her for only four hours when I got shipped to the baby CVE. What an eye-opener! It was a good thing that I got off the *"Sara"* because that huge ship was torpedo junction. The kamikazes loved her. The Japs loved her and gave her lots of "attention," if you know what I mean. Yeah, the old *"Sara"*. She was the one that they took down in Bikini Atoll, and I still feel bad about it. I look at the movies of the Bikini attack, and I see the old *"Sara"* getting deluged.

Maybe I should tell you a little bit about my early childhood. It was rather unusual. When I was about three weeks old, my mother gave me away to a family up in Lindstrom, Minnesota. I lived with them for quite a few years. Then later, I lived with an aunt and uncle in Chicago for quite a few years. I lived with my mother for only about three years. My mother was in the restaurant business with my stepfather, and she didn't have any time for me. I got shoved around from pillar to post, and during that time I basically lived everywhere and learned to live with everybody.

Anyhow, after I joined the Navy, I went to Great Lakes and into boot camp and learned about the Navy and about being in the Navy. After all these years, I can still remember vignettes—little things, like getting food in the chow line, shooting a 20mm machine gun, learning how to march, and the like. They soon found out that I had been a captain in the ROTC in school, so they made me the guidon bearer, and they kept step with me. Believe it or not, I have a picture of my graduation class. Would you like to see it? *(Shows the photo)*

After boot camp, they sent me down for Naval Air Tactical Training in Norman, Oklahoma, to be an aviation machinist. That was fine with me. I was down there for the spring and summer of 1944. I went through the usual stuff. I came back home for a little bit, and then I went to the Landing Forces Training Camp at Shoemaker, California, which was a major training camp for the Navy and Marines in 1944. I still have my bayonet downstairs. Would you believe it? I've still got that bayonet! Suddenly, they took me out of there, and I was shipped to San Francisco and put on good old Goat Island there. A few hours later I was on a "goal poster"—Navy slang for cargo ships with their own big, on-board cranes for loading cargo. They didn't tell us where we were heading. All you had was your sea bag, and they only told you on what ship you were to go. One of the things that I remember about the landing forces camp at Shoemaker was that if you volunteered to be in the chow line, that meant you would have to work as a dishwasher. But the added bonus was that you had extra liberty. I wasn't worried about it. I was willing to wash dishes for something better, like more liberty, which is how I got to go to San Francisco. It was the city of dreams. I had many great adventures there, but *not* Navy related. *(Laughter)* And you don't want to hear all of those details! *(More laughter)*

Anyhow, we got on the old "goal poster" and eventually got down to Pearl Harbor. I had been sleeping outside of the regular bunk area. Down inside one of those ships, there were 2,000 enlisted men on one side and 500 officers on the other side. You'd go down and find out where you were going to sleep, and the bunks were crowded. I am not going to describe the smell! I wrapped up everything I had and found one of the ship's crew and asked him where the best place would be to sleep on deck where I wouldn't get rained on too much, and he told me that I could sleep outside. I told him that was fine, and he told me to go to the bridge area and go below to the scupper. He told me to put my sea bag right in front of the scupper and told me that I wouldn't get wet. The rain would go into the scupper. A scupper is a dent in the deck where the water comes down and just runs off—a gutter. So that is where I slept through rain, storm, and shine. And no smell! The Navy gives you very good stuff for sleeping outside; maybe the whole Navy never got it, but I did. Another thing was that if you were in the middle of the ship and it rocks from side to side, you don't rock. When you are in the center of the ship, the bow goes up and down, but you don't. The ship wiggles from side to side; but since you are close to the center, you don't wiggle. In other words, with the six degrees of freedom, you are just about in the center of it. I didn't get seasick. I got very queasy, but not seasick.

When we finally got into Pearl—this is still 1944—it was night. You want to know some weird stories, right? Well, we got into Pearl at night. We needed to eat and hadn't had any food, so they put us onto a school bus, and we went to some Army camps that were outside of Pearl Harbor. The name of the island was Ford Island. It was where all the battleships were sunk. We didn't see anything except for these massive shadows of the ships and people working on them. After three hours of hunting for food, we wound up back at Pearl Harbor at the island there, and they didn't have a place for us to sleep. They told us that they had a hangar for us. There weren't any beds, so they gave us cots. We had our sea bags; *we never let go of our sea bags*! That was our home. They put us into this huge hangar and we put up the cots, which were all nicely lined up. They didn't tell us that they tested and ran planes outside of that hangar for 24/7. It was noisy, but we were pretty tired. The next morning, they put us into the regular outgoing unit barracks. I wasn't there long. We couldn't see the ships in the harbor, but I knew about two ships: the *West Virginia* and the *California*. I remember those ships because they were great! They were bombardment ships which, along with the carriers, supported the landings. They were the bombardment ships that supported the troops down there. I wasn't in the outgoing unit for very long.

By the way, in the outgoing unit the bunks were stacked three high. First thing, you'd get yourself a bottom bunk on the floor where all four legs are in coffee cans and the coffee cans are full of bug killer or kerosene to keep bedbugs from the other bunks. The bedbugs were known to travel from bunk to bunk. You soon learned what a bedbug looked like and all of that. I got myself on the top bunk.

So, as I've already mentioned, after a short time in the outgoing unit, my name was called, and I was put on the *Saratoga*, which was the CV-3. I thought, wow! It was very big to me. I was assigned a bunk, and I had no more than gotten my sea bag settled in and found where I was going to live when they called out my name and pulled me over to a baby carrier, the *Makin Island* (CVE-93). So very quickly I had gotten off of this big old honker, the *Saratoga*. I could certainly make a comparison between the *Saratoga* and the little *Makin Island*, which was not so little, but comparatively. That began my sea duty, my real sea duty.

One of the things about the *Makin Island* that was very, very lucky was that it was going to be the flagship for Rear Admiral Calvin T. Durgin, Commander of the Escort Carrier Force. The Escort Carrier Force that he commanded was composed of 37 escort carriers—a formidable force. It was a new job for escort carriers that were going to be attack support. We were going along with every invasion—not just the same carriers all of the time—but there were about 16 of us that were pretty strong. Our airplanes and crews were all trained to support the troops. The little carriers carried about 12 to 14 fighters: FM-2 Wildcats and about 10 TBM Avengers, which were torpedo bombers. We operated about four at a time together, which was pretty good. We found out that we could do about 19 miles an hour at top speed. Destroyers hated us. Nothing that could go 25 or 30 miles per hour liked us because they could go circles around us.

Some of the guys I worked with on that ship and on other carriers did die in action. Yeah. We were all one big mess of classes. Some of us got out at the same time and met each other because it was new to serve on escort carriers, and in a Navy way we all sort of gravitated towards one another. Just recently, in a class for senior people called "End of Life," they asked me to talk about death in combat. So I told them: When you are 18, you can't hit your fanny with both hands—I don't care what you say. But anyhow, we knew nothing about death. We hadn't lost anybody yet.

The importance of death built on us slowly in the war. We got bombed, but we still had no deaths. The smart guys would hear the bombs and look up. The bombs just dropped around us. We would think it was just like sitting in a movie. Yeah, sure! You have to remember, we were 18. This was our first invasion, and we really didn't have any idea about what was happening. The Japanese would be flying around in their bombers, and you would have *Makin Island* sailors lined up on the flight deck saying, "Look at the Jap! Look at the Jap!" Well, the rear gunner in the Jap bomber would see all of the sailors lined up on the deck and shoot away at them like mad. You would see the little flashes, and the gunner would range in on us. All of this would happen in a fraction of a second. The slugs started hitting the sponsons[2] on each side of the ship. The *Makin Island* had three sponsons down there that were fairly close to the water line, so as the slugs came, they started hitting. Suddenly, it occurred to us that we were getting shot at. Guys on the bridge starting yelling at us to get off the flight deck! Get off of the flight deck! This was our first taste of combat. It was comedic, funny, and stupid. And we were so young! After that, we found out what happened to the guys downstairs. Actually, not much happened to them after the time the slugs got to them. That was our first taste of death.

The second taste of death where we really got the idea was when we were going through the straits of Linguayen Gulf and Surigao Straits for the invasion of the Philippines. This was where the Japs hung out behind the islands, and they came over the hills and dove right on us. Did you know that in some places in the straits there was only a three-mile wide neck, and all of the ships had to go through there? The Japs could pick us off very easily, and they did. They sank escort carriers. Our ship just about got hit. We didn't, but just about.

By the time Iwo Jima came around, we really knew what death was. The night of February 21—the night I mark every year—was the night that our sister carrier, the *Bismarck Sea* (CVE-95), was sunk. On that night, the *"Sara"* was also about five miles ahead of us. She was on fire like a torch because she had taken at least four or five hits from the kamikazes. After that and this I cannot prove—the Japanese came down and strafed the guys from the *Bismarck Sea*. They came down and strafed them in the

2. A "sponson" is a projection (as a gun platform) from the side of a ship or a tank.

water. "Strafed" means sort of gliding. The Japanese would fly down about 100 feet over the water and shoot all the guys who were in the water. If they missed some of the guys in the water, they would open up the doors of the plane and throw grenades out. There were about 235 guys dead from the *Bismarck Sea*. The Navy gave us these little battery-operated lamps so that you could be picked up at night in case you fell off the ship or something. The *Bismarck Sea* was off our starboard side and we had slowed down—God only knows why. We didn't want to catch up to the *"Sara"* because she was nothing but a target. I mean, you could see her for miles. The only other thing I remember about that night was another carrier with us, the *Lunga Point* (CVE-94), being hit several times. A friend of mine from that ship whom I met at a beer bust later said he'd never seen a mess like that until he had to clean up about 20 feet of Jap guts off the flight deck. So then, that was the reality of death.

Along came Okinawa, and that was also our biggest scare. The Sakashima Gunto was a bunch of islands southwest of Okinawa. The Japanese had several landing strips and camps down there. What was assigned to keep them down there? The whole British Navy that was left over—which was pretty good. Their carriers had steel flight decks, and they were pretty good at keeping watch over the area. It turns out that British ships are very short legged and are best suited for coastal waters. That is, the ships can't stay out for days and days like American ships can. They were not like American carriers. I can't remember how many carriers they had there—it was either two or four. When they needed fuel they left, and we took their place. We did not want to get caught, naturally, and we could not fight back like the British Navy. We were only out there two nights, but we went only four or five miles an hour so we would not leave a wake. We could hear the Japanese searching for us out there. Now, that is fear! That is fear! If anybody would have shown a light of any kind, that would have been it. I remember that as being one of the scariest times during the war. You couldn't turn the ship because when you did turn, you would leave a wake. I remember that so clearly.

Now, those British ships were the good old British battleships. They were not American made. They were the big carriers. When the kamikazes would try to smash into them, they wouldn't do anything to those ships! If a bomb would go off, you would only have a little dent. Our decks were made of oak. The worst things that we had were splinters. When our planes landed, we always wanted them to land nicely. If any of them nosed down and landed wrong, the props would chew into the planking of the deck. If you were idiot enough to have your head in the wrong place to watch a plane land, God would say that it was your time to get a splinter right between the eyes. You never had a lot of people standing around. *We* had to because we were the catapulting crew and the arresting gear crew. We had to be up there, standing around. When planes would have accidents during landing, the props would tip down and chew into the oak planking—and we were out there, exposed.

One time we had to catapult some New Zealand Corsair fighters. That was fine with us. We knew that our ships were too small for airplanes to take off by themselves, unless the wind was blowing with hurricane force—so we had to use the catapult and learn how to propel the plane with that. Basically, the catapult shoots the plane off from the deck. There is a bridle that you hook the plane on to, and the bridle is hooked on to a small shuttle, which is the working part of the catapult. Within 70 feet, you have the airplane going over 70 miles per hour. That is how we got the planes in the air. When they came in for a landing, they had to be stopped with regular landing wires. Our ships were small! I think that our flight deck was only 460 to 480 feet long. That was all. So that's why we had to catapult the planes.

There were so many brave men who died in that war. The statistics are amazing. I was just a grunt. You would never see John Wayne playing Lee James. *(Laughter)* There were millions of us involved, and so many died heroically.

Anyway, that is how the escort carriers worked. We could land, take off, and pretty much work as a group. The sister carriers of the *Makin Island* (CVE-93) were the *Lunga Point* (CVE-94), the *Salamaua* (CVE-96), and the *Bismarck Sea* (CVE-95). One time, the *Salamaua* got hit right by her fuel tanks and next to the catapult, but it did not blow. A friend of mine got wounded, but he didn't know it until a few days later when he went to take a shower. One of the guys told him that he had blood on his back. The guy looked closer at his back and found several pieces of shrapnel. At least he got an honest Purple Heart out of that one.

You know, you get to meet a wide range of people in the military. In my boot camp school, half of us were from Chicago, and the other half were from Kentucky and Tennessee. One of the first things that some of these guys learned—and I am sorry for sounding nasty—but they had to learn to take showers and change their socks and all sorts of other things about personal cleanliness which some of these boys didn't seem to know about.

It is kind of funny, when you think about it: When Pearl Harbor was attacked in 1941, I was just an innocent 15-year-old kid trying to pick up girls at the Field Museum. But just a few short years later I was involved in the war, and I met many diverse people and got to see many distant places in the world.

By the way: Lots of people wonder if President Truman's decision to drop the atomic bombs on Japan in August 1945 was the right thing to do. Oh, my God, yes! It certainly *was* the right thing to do. There were plans being made by the U.S. government for the invasion of Japan, and Japan also had plans for its defense against such an invasion. The main U.S. plan was called Operation Olympic.[3] Then the Japanese suspected these invasions were being planned, so they used the code name *Ketsu-Go* for their own plan to repulse the landings.

We sailors found out by scuttlebutt in July of 1945 that we were going to be part of Operation Olympic because Rear Admiral Calvin T. Durgin was going to go in there with 14 or 15 small carriers to support the landing. As to why the awful Honshu attacks never took place, I think I can thank General Leslie R. Groves for that more than Truman. Groves was appointed to head the Manhattan Project.[4] But the Japanese were very stubborn in their plans to battle any invasion by U.S. troops. Even when the world leaders at the Potsdam Conference ordered Japan to surrender or face destruction, they refused.[5]

Anyway, after the war was finally over and Japan surrendered, I was sent home on leave and stayed at my mother's place in Chicago. This was in December of 1945. My mother was very good to me. I was living in downtown Chicago at the time because that is where I had my 30-day survivor leave, or whatever they called it. Often at night I would wake up screaming, and that would wake my mother up. She would pour Scotch in me to calm me down. I would have the same damned dream every night. I mean the *same* dream. I can still describe it to you. In my nightmare, the

---

3, 4 and 5. See the endnotes at the conclusion of this interview.

Japanese plane is coming in and coming in, closer and closer. You could see parts of the wing shot off and puffs of smoke. Just as the plane is about to come in, I would suddenly wake up. I had that dream for about a week or two, and then it went away. I have never had it since, but the memory of it has stuck in my brain. We were attacked at Okinawa almost 100 times by kamikazes, but we were among the survivors…with only these vivid memories and nightmares.

The only other time I broke down was when I was over at a girlfriend's house. I was just sitting there, alone, looking at the Christmas tree. This was also in December of 1945. I looked at the tree and remembered Christmas Eve in 1944 and how we had just been told that we were going to go into the invasion of the Philippines and what it was going to be like. I started to cry and couldn't stop. My girlfriend came in and comforted me and got a shot of booze to quiet me down.

On the night that the *"Sara"* and the *Bismarck Sea* were attacked, we had to take some of the planes off of the *"Sara"* because she had a few holes in her flight deck. We were not made for those landings, but we took them in. We lost one F-6 pilot, but we were able to get six of them aboard, and one Corsair. The fighters and TBMs could not take off by themselves on our tiny deck. My catapult crew's job was to hook the planes to the catapult. I crawled under the little fighter planes and hooked the bridle underneath a Wildcat. The prop was approximately eight to 12 inches from my head, and the pilot was gunning it up like mad because it was his only chance to find out how his engine was working. My glasses were tightly bound around my head. If I didn't pay attention to what I was doing, then the plane would just roll up the middle of my body.

You know, there were so-called Black Shoe Admirals in the Navy. They could be on aircraft carriers, airplanes, or battleships. Black Shoe Admirals were from the old school. Even though we were in the middle of a war, they expected you to have everything clean and polished. Our officers were not like that; they were up there with the sailors all of the time. When the catapult had a major malfunction and the cable pulled out of the absolute stop, you had 16 tons of everything—plus hydraulic pressure—going berserk in the catapult room. I was down there once when we were trying to get the buffers to come out by hitting them with a big hammer. There I was with my hammer, smacking the thing. It was about time that old catapult had an overhaul. Suddenly it blew on us, and the towing cable pulled out. The cable whipped. It was 49-strand, one-inch steel cable. I can't remember how many miles of cable strands there were, but part of it caught me on the left inside arm—and that was all. It took some skin off and caused a lot of bleeding, but that was all. The guy who started the stop and pulled the trigger down there had gotten it really bad. My arm was not too good, and the other two guys weren't much better. But we started fixing the catapult anyway because we knew it had to be done.

Anyhow, the catapult officer saw what we were doing. Then the commander came down and the captain came down and then the executive officer came down. All those guys did was watch! But then Admiral Durgin came in. Durgin rolled up his sleeves and said that we weren't able to move until the catapult was fixed and secured. He worked as hard as we did. He was always working with his men. Wherever his carriers were, there he was. We never hollered against him because we respected him so much. By the way, our navigator on the ship happened to be Richard T. Reynolds, head of Reynolds Tobacco Company—and that is why we never ran out of cigarettes. *(Laughter)*

After the war was over, I stayed with the Reserves, which was a mistake. When the Korean conflict started in 1950, I was called to active duty. That was President Harry Truman's idea! After that was over, I went back to the University of Minnesota and finished my Bachelor of Business Administration degree in 1952.

People often ask me why I talk about my war experiences. How can I not? If I *didn't* talk about those things, people would think that it all had been like the TV documentary film, *Victory at Sea*—and that is just crap.

---

3. The overall code name for Operation Olympic and Operation Coronet was Operation Downfall. Those plans were preceded by some very severe battles which cost both sides casualties numbering in the hundreds of thousands.

In America's continuing attempt to be victorious over Japan, the plan was to conquer and control several islands to the south of Japan that were strategic Japanese bases of defense. After many weeks of bombing the tiny island of Iwo Jima, U.S. forces landed there on February 19, 1945. The bloody battle continued for over a month, and the U.S. forces claimed victory on March 26. But casualties were heavy: Nearly 7,000 U.S. soldiers were killed, and 18,000 were wounded. Of the 21,000 Japanese soldiers stationed on the island, all were killed except for 212 taken by the Americans as prisoners of war.

The next major American offensive was the invasion of Okinawa in late March 1945. America was ultimately victorious, and the battle ended on June 23. Again, casualties were heavy: About 7,000 U.S. soldiers were killed in action. The Japanese military losses numbered about 110,000, in addition to 40,000 civilian deaths.

After securing Okinawa, the next U.S. plan was to make the relatively short 400-mile distance to the southern tip of Kyushu to destroy the Japanese forces there and, primarily, to seize the Japanese air fields and bases for use by the U.S. forces as a main base of operations. This plan was called Operation Olympic and was scheduled to occur on November 1, 1945.

The second phase, known as Operation Coronet, was to be the total U.S. invasion of Honshu, which was scheduled for March 1946.

The Americans expected retaliation from the kamikazes and the formidable Japanese air force in Operation Coronet. The plan of defense by the Japanese military had the code name *Ketsu-Go*, and it called for nearly 5,000 planes to attack the estimated 1,000 U.S. transports. The Japanese also assigned 300 kamikaze planes to attack U.S. carriers.

Of course, none of these plans regarding Honshu was ever carried out due to the atomic bomb blasts on Hiroshima and Nagasaki, Japan, in early August 1945, after which Japan surrendered. When one sees the massive number of casualties on both sides in the Iwo Jima and Okinawa battles, one can easily speculate as to the many hundreds of thousands of lives which might have been lost if Operation Olympic, Operation Coronet, and *Ketsu-Go* had taken place. The number of lives lost in the two atomic-bomb blasts, while terrible and considerable, was a fraction of how many lives *might* have been lost if the war with Japan had played out through traditional air and naval battles.

---

4. In 1942, President Roosevelt established the Manhattan Engineer District, known as the Manhattan Project, with the sole directive of creating as quickly as possible an atomic bomb, regardless of the expense. General Leslie R. Groves was appointed as the head. Groves then appointed J. Robert Oppenheimer to head the Los Alamos laboratory where the bomb was constructed. Some of the greatest scientific minds in America were involved in the Manhattan Project.

When the bomb was completed, Groves wrote the following order to the head of Air Force Operations in the Pacific: "Deliver (the) first special bomb as soon as weather will permit visual bombing after about 3 August, 1945."

Groves did credit President Truman with the decision to use the atomic bomb against Japan, but he qualified this by saying, "As far as I was concerned, (Truman's) decision was one of noninterference—basically, a decision not to upset the existing plans."

Groves was the primary mover in getting the atomic bomb built in such a short time. He also was the person who decided where it would be used, and when it would be used. (Source: Leslie R. Grove's book *Now It Can Be Told*. Internet entry.)

---

5. Truman, Churchill, and Stalin met in a suburb of Berlin for the Potsdam Conference from July17 to August 2, 1945. The leaders discussed many post-war issues, but one of their statements was directed at Japan: "We call upon the government of Japan to proclaim now the unconditional surrender of all Japanese armed forces, and to provide proper and adequate assurances of their good faith in such action. The alternative for Japan is prompt and utter destruction."

When Japan refused, the U.S. dropped an atomic bomb on Hiroshima, Japan, on August 6, 1945. A second atomic bomb was dropped on Nagasaki, Japan, on August 9, 1945. Japan surrendered on August 10, and President Truman proclaimed V-J (Victory Over Japan) Day on August 14.

Oscar A. Backlund
1945

(front row, second from right)
1944

Born: 1926

Present home: Bloomington, Minnesota

Military history: Drafted; entered service 1944

Branch of service: U.S. Army

Length of service: Nearly two years

Highest rank: Private 1st Class

Date/place of interview: June 2, 2005
Bloomington, Minnesota

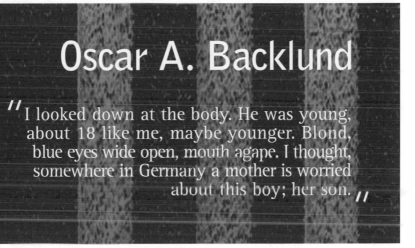

Oscar A. Backlund

"I looked down at the body. He was young, about 18 like me, maybe younger. Blond, blue eyes wide open, mouth agape. I thought, somewhere in Germany a mother is worried about this boy; her son."

I was drafted fairly late in the war, and I was 15 years old when Pearl Harbor was attacked. I remember exactly where I was and what I was doing on December 7. I was reading a *Batman* comic book, sitting in a booth at Tibb's Pharmacy at the corner of 38th Street and Bloomington Avenue. They had the radio on behind the soda fountain—they had soda fountains back then—and I heard about the bombing of Pearl Harbor. I wondered where that was, and somebody told me. They said that it was in Hawaii. That is how I found out about it.

I did not graduate from high school. I had another year to go, but I got drafted because I was 18. I was a year behind in school due to illness when I was younger. I was drafted in the fall of 1944, and after I got out of the service in 1946, I took the GED test and got my high school diploma. I went on to school at the University of Minnesota, but first I went to television school. That is a different story entirely.

Skipping ahead: At the end of the war, on the way home, we docked in the New York Harbor, where we had our leave. We had a whole troop ship full of people. We went into a bar in lower Manhattan, and at the end of the counter, above the bar, there was a box on the wall with a picture in it. There was a Laurel and Hardy film playing on that box. We wondered what that was. The bartender told us that it was television. We barely knew what television was or that it had progressed so far. I said to myself right then and there that television was the business that I was going to get into. It took a while. When I came home, there wasn't any television here in the Midwest, so I waited. A television school finally opened, and I went there. I graduated from the television school and tried to get a job with the local stations. By that time there were two stations on the air locally, but there weren't any jobs available, so I went to the University of Minnesota. I was there for two years when I got a phone call from one of my former teachers who was working at one of the TV stations. He asked me if I wanted a job in television, and I told him that I did. So I quit the U of M and went into television. That was 1951. I stayed there until 1993, when I retired. The station was WTCN at that time; then they switched over while I was there, and it became WCCO.

I was there for two years. Then I left WCCO, and a few of us went down to Peoria to put the NBC station there on the air. It was the first station in central Illinois. Then I got a call that Channel 11 was going to go on the air in Minneapolis, and they wanted me to help them put that station on the air. I stayed in Minneapolis for 40 years. One of my very good friends was Dave Moore.[1] Dave actually started in TV in October of 1950. I started in March of 1951. Because we were the new kids on the block, we had to work weekends. We got to know each other very well. Dave was more of a theatre man by training than a television person. He loved theatre in general. He did plays out at the Old Log Theatre in Excelsior, Minnesota. That theatre is celebrating its sixty-fifth year of operation this year. Amazing! I appeared in a show there in 1952.

Well, now, back to my war experience. After I was drafted, I went out to Fort Snelling and got on the train and took it down to Kansas to Fort Leavenworth. We stayed there overnight. They just gave us general information about the Army. I went from there to Camp Wolters in Texas, where I had basic training for 13 weeks. I came home for a week, and then I was shipped overseas out of Boston. Our ship went down the coast of America, and we went across the ocean to the Azores, where we met the convoy. There were ships from all over, and they all became a convoy that went along the coast of France. It stopped in South Hampton and stayed there until night. Then we went across the English Channel. The destroyers were dropping depth charges because they had heard there were subs

---

1. Dave Moore was a prominent television news anchor for many decades in the Twin Cities of Minneapolis and St. Paul, Minnesota.

around. That kept us awake. We were trying to sleep while we were going across the Channel. We landed in Le Havre, France, early in the morning after sunrise. We had breakfast in a warehouse on a pier. They then put us in boxcars, and we went down towards Paris and saw the top of the Eiffel Tower. Then we went across into Belgium. We spent one night somewhere, but we never knew where we were. We could still hear occasional gunshots, even though this part of Europe was pretty well clear by that time.

I was assigned guard duty for a POW camp where German prisoners were held. We were right on the Dutch border, on the west side of the Rhine River. I would have to get my German map to show you the exact location. I was a replacement for the 106th Division, which was reorganizing because they were practically wiped out in the Battle of the Bulge. This was in March of 1945. We stayed in München Gladbach for a while. Then a few of us were driven up to the northern part of the Rhine to be guards at the prison compound for German prisoners of war. We arrived at the camp late at night. A sergeant asked me where I was from. When I said "Minnesota," he said, "You should feel right at home here. This is the 3rd Minnesota Regiment." Actually, I think I was the only Minnesotan in the outfit. I was told to get a couple hours of sleep and that I would be called for guard duty before long. That is where I really started. My ultimate military assignment was to be a guard at that POW camp. What I saw there made me grow up in a hurry.

The trip up was a really interesting experience. We were just a bunch of green kids. Occasionally, we wondered about all the bundles of clothes we saw in the ditch. Then we realized that they weren't just bundles of clothes; they were bodies that hadn't been picked up yet. This was a long time after the armies had gone through. This was the beginning of the end for Germany. We had a feeling that the war was almost over. Roosevelt had died and, after a while, Hitler committed suicide, so we all wondered what was going to happen next. We didn't hear about Mussolini's death until later.

There were a few thousand prisoners at that camp, at least. We took a crew of eight German POWs across the Rhine River into northern Wesel, which was bombed because it was the rail head of Germany. We went in there to raid whatever wood that we needed. I got to know the German crew because I worked with them every day. One day there was a woman who went to a pump and pumped a big pail full of water, but she was having trouble carrying it. I told this one German officer who was standing around to go give her a hand. He said he wouldn't do it. I told him he had better do it and so he did, but he grumbled all of the way. When we got back to camp, I told the truck driver to tell whoever was sending these people out that we didn't want officers anymore. The next morning I got on the truck, and the other Germans wondered where the German officer was. I told them he was gone. They were all happy to hear that because he was just too much. They didn't like him at all because he was so arrogant. He was like the German officers in the movies. He didn't seem to realize that the war was over for him, that he was a prisoner, and that his rank was of no value anymore.

In the camp there were three buildings, as I recall. One was a hospital that wasn't used much because we sent the guys into town when they needed the hospital. There was an administrative building and a cook shack. Other than that, the prisoners slept in holes in the ground. That is why we had prisoners die. There is a book out called *Other Losses*.[2] It is a story about the American or Allied camps and how the Americans mistreated German POWs. The book was put out just to show that it wasn't lilacs and roses on either side.

On my first day, just before dawn, I was out on sentry duty at the main gate of the compound. As the sun came up, I got my first view of the prison camp. It was a huge open field surrounded by a high fence topped with barbed wire. The prisoners living in holes in the ground were covered with whatever they could find to protect themselves from the elements. This was a very cold spring. Just after sunrise, they started carrying out the bodies of the prisoners who had died during the night. They placed four of the bodies on their backs in the grass a little ways from me. They placed the fifth one next to me.

I looked down at the body. He was young—probably 18, like me; maybe younger. Blond, blue eyes wide open, mouth agape. I thought: Somewhere in Germany, a mother is worried about her boy—just as I knew my mother back in Minneapolis was worried about me. He looked just like the blond, blue-eyed kid who lived down the block from us back home. As I

---

2. See *Other Losses* by James Bacque. Second revised edition, 2004. Little Brown and Company, Ltd., Bolton Ontario, Canada.

looked down at him, a large fly landed on his face. It walked up his cheek and across his open eye. It made me blink. I still blink now every time I think of it. Where the fly came from on that chilly morning, I will never know. I waved my arm, and the fly flew away. A little while later, two German civilians arrived with a horse and wagon. They put the bodies in the wagon and carted them off to the local cemetery in the town of Rhineburg.

It has been 60 years, and that young man's body has long since turned to dust. But I can still see that young, dead face. He was my enemy. He wore a different uniform and spoke a different language. But I don't believe he was that much different from me or that other blond, blue-eyed kid who lived down the block from us in Minneapolis.

Some of the soldiers in our camp were taking it out on the Germans. I remember that we had one German prisoner who was a big mouth. He liked to make fun of the "crazy" Americans. One day one of our sergeants who had been through hell in the war took the guy with him, and they went for a walk in the woods. The sergeant came back alone. I never saw the German guy again. I assume he had been "disposed of" in the woods. This sergeant had all kinds of friends who had been killed by the Germans, and he just couldn't take that taunting from the big-mouth Germany anymore. I also had relatives who had been killed by the Germans. I had a cousin who was a tail-gunner on a B-24. He went down over the North Sea. We never thought that we would hear about him or find him or his plane again; but in 1946 there was a big storm on the North Sea, and the wreckage of that B-24 washed up on the shore with all of the bodies still in it. They are buried together, all of the guys on that plane, down in Missouri at the National Cemetery in St. Louis.

We had lots of awful things going on at the camp. There were guys who were so hungry that they would jump into the latrine and eat the feces. In that book, *Other Losses*, they say that Eisenhower put out the order to let the prisoners starve, but who knows if he did that or not? That is what is in the book, and the author apparently did careful research. That book also has drawings of the camp that I was in, which was just called the Rhineburg.

Near the end of the war, Hitler had drafted very young guys, teenagers and younger, for his army. If you talk to the veterans who had to fight them, they would say that the young Germans were the worst because they wouldn't give up. You had to kill them. Have you ever seen the film *Europa, Europa*? Well, one of the characters pretends not to be circumcised so he could pass as being non-Jewish. There was a very interesting program on public television the other night. It was about a German Jew who was not circumcised because his family was not religious. They were all treated like regular Germans. He lived through the war and had relatives who had been killed in the camps, but he survived. After the war, he went to Chicago and made films. This PBS program was a documentary that he made his first trip back to Germany, which was just this year. He went into a classroom of young Germans and told them he was still alive because he had not been circumcised. He asked the boys in the class if they were circumcised, and only two of them raised their hands. I think they were shocked because they were talking about personal stuff. There were only two in the whole class, and they weren't Jewish.

Speaking of Hitler's treatment of Jews: We had heard that there were concentration camps where people were not killed, but where they were being held like political prisoners. Nothing had leaked out at that time about the death camps, the ovens, and all the rest. By the time I got into the service, the Allied forces had already started to move in and had liberated some of the camps. The death camps were in the eastern part of Germany. There were a couple of American armies; they opened up some of the camps, and the Russians went into the others. Films were also made of the liberation of the camps. After the war, I was one of the GIs who forced the citizens of one German town that we were in to go into the movie theatre to watch films of the camps. Of course, they didn't believe what they saw. They thought it was fiction.

Talk about the strong smell near some of the cities! That first summer, we didn't want to go into the big cities because from a mile away you could smell the stench coming from the ruins. There was a strong smell of decaying bodies coming from under the rubble of bombed-out buildings. That smell did not come from the death camps; it came from the rotting bodies of civilian casualties.

Here's another one of my stories. It was early in May of 1945, and I was an 18-year-old GI guarding German POWs. One night while I was off duty, I was sleeping on the second floor of a house across the road from the POW compound. I was awakened by singing and shouting coming from the camp. I looked up at the ceiling of our room, and I saw reflec tions of flames. I jumped out of my sleeping bag and ran to the window. The compound was covered with small campfires, and I could hear the singing of German songs echoing through the night. There was one beautiful voice in particular, a fantastic tenor that could be heard above all the others. I saw a buddy of mine standing by the gate to our house, and I asked him what was going on. He said the prisoners were celebrating because the war was over.

I got dressed and went down to the compound and asked a lieutenant on guard duty about it. He said, "We have no official word that the war is over." I went back to my sleeping bag and fell asleep listening to the beautiful singing.

We did not get the official word of the Armistice until a day or two later: V-E Day, May 8, 1945. But I will never forget that tenor voice coming from the camp. He must have had training in opera. In my memory, he could have out-sung Caruso and Pavarotti.

Christmastime away from home when you're only 19 years old can be pretty difficult. Actually, I was in the war for only one Christmas, but I was in basic training for the other. It was Christmas Eve, 1945. The war had been over since May, and we GIs in Germany were waiting to be sent home. A few of us drove our Jeep into the small city of Esslingen for Christmas Eve. As we entered the town square, a large number of Germans was standing around the fountain in front of the old town hall, singing Christmas carols. We didn't understand the German lyrics, but the tunes were familiar. We got out of our Jeep and started singing the carols along with them—only we sang them in English. As we were singing, the snow started falling, and the floodlights were turned on. The lights illuminated the front of the colorful town hall and also the castle on the hill. It was beautiful! I had been away from home and family for two Christmases. I had tears in my eyes as we sang "Silent Night, Holy Night" and the Germans sang *Stille Nacht, Heilige Nacht.*

There we were, singing Christmas carols together, when just a few months before we had been enemies. The Germans invited us across the square to their church for the Christmas Eve service. We didn't understand the sermon, but we loved the music and their friendship. Their kindness to a few lonely GIs away from home at Christmas was truly wonderful. It was a

Christmas Eve I will never forget. Christmas can be very lonely when you are away from home—especially when you are young. When you get older, it is just another holiday.

Here is another interesting story. A few weeks after the end of the war, I was walking through one of the many devastated German cities. I can't remember which city it was because we were being moved down the Rhine River every few days. It was either Coblenz or Cologne. Anyway, I was approached by a woman holding two little children, a boy and a girl. The woman spoke perfect English, and she asked me for food for her children. I shouldn't even have been talking to her because of the fraternization ban which was in effect for a few months after the war: no talking to German civilians unless it had to do with the military occupation. I asked her why she spoke such good English, and she said she taught English in German schools. I looked at her two children, and they did not look very healthy. I asked the woman where they lived, and she pointed to a building across the road. Half of the building was a pile of rubble. I told her I would see what I could do about getting them some food.

I talked to a buddy of mine who was an assistant to the mess sergeant, and he came up with a box of Army rations. We threw in a few Hershey bars for the children. When I showed up with the food at the small apartment she was sharing with her elderly mother, it was like I had presented them with an early Christmas gift. They kept saying, "Danke! Danke!"

"I don't know how I can repay you," the woman said. "I have no money." I said, "We don't like to see children starve." Then she went to a small cabinet and opened a drawer. She brought out a little medal. She said, "This was given to me by the Nazis for being a good German mother. By giving birth to two children, I have contributed to Hitler's goal of having a 'master race.'" She turned the medal over and showed me where Hitler's name was inscribed. "I don't want this medal anymore," she said. "Look what Hitler did to my beautiful city." I thanked her for the medal and walked out of the building. I never asked her what her name was, and I never saw her again. The next day we moved on down the Rhine. That medal is one of my prized souvenirs of WWII.

I did make friends with some of the German prisoners I looked after. Once, when we were in some town, digging around in a shop for wood, we came across a wheel of blue cheese. Back then I didn't eat blue cheese, but the Germans were wild about it. They used my bayonet and cut the mold off and served up the blue cheese. They gave me a chunk. I looked at that cheese, with all of the blue veins running through it, and they insisted that I try it. I tried it and liked it! To this day I love blue cheese. I was familiar with smelly cheese because my father was from Sweden and loved exotic aged cheeses, but my family hated them. But that German blue cheese was milder than the cheese my father liked.

A few years ago, I went back to Germany and took a river cruise up to Amsterdam. We went through the Danube to the Rhine. I saw areas where I had been 60 years ago. It had all changed. It is so much more beautiful now than it was back then. I think that most of the people I met during my first time there are dead now. I traveled with a 90-year-old friend of mine. My wife and I had been planning to take that trip for a long time, but then she became very ill. After she died, my friend said he'd go with me—and so we went.

PART II

They Were Also Involved

Roy H. Saigo
(with brother Takeshi, on left)
1943

Born: 1940

Present home: St. Cloud, Minnesota

Present position: President, St. Cloud State University

Date/place of interview: October 15, 2003
St. Cloud, Minnesota

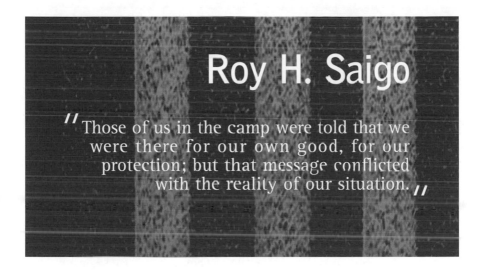

Roy H. Saigo

*"*Those of us in the camp were told that we
were there for our own good, for our
protection; but that message conflicted
with the reality of our situation. *"*

Note: On February 19, 1942, within a few weeks of the Pearl Harbor attack, President Franklin D. Roosevelt issued Executive Order #9066, which ordered that 110,000 Japanese Americans living in the U.S. coastal areas were to be placed in camps many hundreds of miles inland. Roy Saigo was affected profoundly by that Executive Order. Most people now agree that this action stands as one of the most shameful and embarrassing events in American history.

M
y family was given only a few days' notice to pack all of our belongings and be prepared to be taken away to one of the many internment camps which were established throughout the United States.[1] My family consisted of my mother, Fumiko, my father, Toshiaki, my sister Chiyo (age nine), and my brother Takeshi (age 11). I was 18 months old at the time.

We were only allowed to take whatever we could carry, so we gave things

---

1. The official word most commonly used to describe these camps was "internment" rather than "concentration." Presumably this was because the latter word held negative connotations associated with the atrocities in Hitler's death camps. The world was gradually becoming aware of the horrors of Hitler's concentration camps by 1942. But no matter what label was used for the American camps for the Japanese people, there was no doubt that they were indeed prison camps.

away, and we left things stored with neighbors. Most of our worldly possessions and all of our livelihood were left behind

We were taken from our farm in Vacaville, California, and transported to a dusty and hot camp in Gila River, Arizona.[2] We lived in that camp for over three years. We lived in multifamily barracks built by internees, who also constructed furniture from lumber scraps. We shared communal dining areas and bathroom facilities. There was very little privacy. My younger brother Joe was born in the camp.[3] Giving birth in such a shared living environment rather than in her own home or in a hospital was very difficult for my mother.

My parents were very worried about what might happen to us. They didn't know if we might be gassed or shot. They felt great insecurities, but they didn't talk too much about those insecurities with us. The reason for their silence is based in part in the Japanese culture, which taught that people should not complain. One Japanese word, *ganbatte*, means "hold on, keep at it." Related to that concept is *gon-ko*, which refers to stubbornness. A particularly useful Japanese phrase is *Shikata ga nai*, which suggests that people should have a certain degree of resignation about things over which they have no control—an attitude of "that's the way it is; forget it and move on." I think my mother was the embodiment of these concepts. She was only five feet tall and weighed about 100 pounds. She was resigned to accept the things she could not change. She was not one to complain, but she was not one to show weakness, either. Believe me, she was tough!

Those of us in the camp were told that we were there for our own good, for our protection, but that message conflicted with the reality of our situation. The camp was surrounded by barbed wire, and they would shoot you if you tried to leave. The kids in the camp, especially the younger ones, had fun playing games and going to school with all the other kids, so for them it may not have been so bad. The older children and the adults,

2. Vacaville, California, is located between San Francisco and Sacramento, and Gila River is southeast of Phoenix. The camps at Gila River opened on July 20, 1942, and were closed on November 20, 1945. At its busiest, the camp housed over 13,000 people who came mainly from the Sacramento, Fresno, and Los Angeles areas.

3. Joe Saigo is now a doctor living in Washington state. He is Roy Saigo's only immediate family member still living.

however, realized that they had been taken from their homes and were being held as captives.

When we were finally released from the camp and returned to California, we had lost the land we had and our home. Most of the Japanese people lost these things, so everybody had to start over. We had to live in a high school gymnasium for a time while my father found farm work near Sacramento. My parents did not talk much about their experience in the camp. They accepted their circumstances, but my father was very bitter.

Getting out of the camp and being back in California was not always pleasant. We were constantly reminded, sometimes quite violently, that we were not liked. We were indeed hated, and we were different from the other Americans. I can give you one example of this: When we went back to school once we were back in California, the Japanese freshmen were made to crawl on their hands and knees under the legs of the older white students standing over them. The older students would take turns beating the crawling Japanese students with belts as they passed under them. My brother Takeshi was about 14 years old then, and I remember very clearly how painful it was for him, both physically and emotionally. I vividly recall seeing my mom swabbing his backside with ointments to stop the bleeding.

Knowing that I was different and being constantly reminded that I was hated and being subjected to cruel treatment because of my "difference" have only strengthened my resolve to fight racism and injustice wherever I encounter it. I detest bullies, and in my position as president of St. Cloud State University, I feel that I am in a leadership position to counteract prejudice, whether it is based on ignorance, insensitivity or outright racism. I firmly believe that my own experiences, and the memories of my parents' quiet spiritual strength in the face of adversity, have prepared me to do this.

After the September 11 World Trade Center disaster, there was much talk of retaliation against Arab and Muslim Americans. This attitude occurred to some extent on the St. Cloud State University campus as well as elsewhere in the country. My own memories of the internment camp rushed into my mind. The parallels were very obvious to me. I called a meeting of all international students on campus to assure them that they were safe here and to express to them that I understood all too well what they were experiencing. I promised them that I would do everything in my power to protect them. I could not let history repeat itself. The principles upon which a university is built could not permit any kind of retaliation aimed at innocent people just because they are of a different race or religion or heritage than the mainstream student body, or just because they happened to be of the same race or religion or heritage as the people who attacked the World Trade Center. Ignorance can cause fear, and that is why I value education as the antidote to that fear.

Author's Note: While the bulk of these comments came from my interview with Dr. Saigo, I found additional background information on him in a fine article written by *St. Cloud Times* staff writer Michelle Tan: "SCSU President Draws on Life in Internment Camp to Help Others" (October 15, 2001).

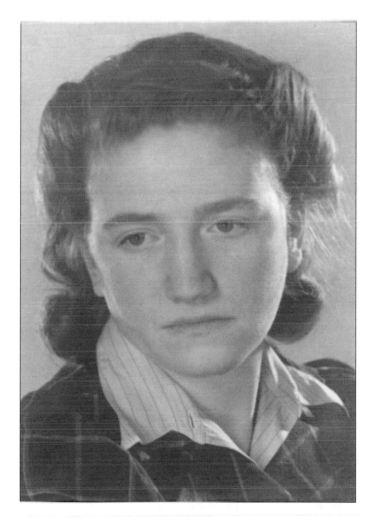

Margot DeWilde
1942

Born: 1921 in Berlin, Germany

Present home: Plymouth, Minnesota

Date/place of interview: February 28, 2005
Plymouth, Minnesota

Also present: Margot's husband, Rudy DeWilde

Note: Rudy DeWilde died on April 7, 2005.

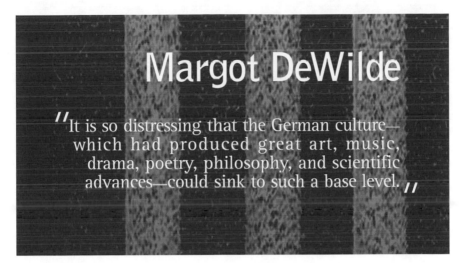

Margot DeWilde

"It is so distressing that the German culture—which had produced great art, music, drama, poetry, philosophy, and scientific advances—could sink to such a base level."

I believe that nothing is an island of itself. Everything is a source and continuing toward the future. I cannot believe in only one thing, and that is why I can't make this a short interview. Germany, after WWI, itself was in a very poor financial state. When my father married my mother, she was one of seven children who survived to adulthood. My grandfather had a department store in Mainz, Germany, and part of the dowry that you were given at that time when you were married was that the husbands would be involved in the department store—which, of course, in 1920 went kaput. People had to look for other occupations. Most people in Germany were forced to find other work. There was a lot of unemployment and poverty. Inflation also came about during that time. Germany was in a bad condition—plus losing WWI, on top of it.

A person came along with big ideas. His name was Adolf Hitler, and he had an enormous way of hypnotizing people. He came up with the idea that you had to find a scapegoat: the Jews to start with, and eventually other people as well. He was trying to make their lives so bitter and lousy that they had to go someplace else. There is one thing that I blame America for: The U.S. did not enlarge its immigration quota because they did not see that coming. There were many people who did not think that it was that bad in Germany, but whoever did leave had to leave all their possessions behind. That was the system. That is how Hitler built up his army and Socialist society. I had some aunts and uncles who decided to stay in Germany. They did not think that it would be so bad. One aunt could go sometimes to Holland for vacation; she got permission and money to go there. But for most people, Hitler's idea was to make their lives so miserable that they got out of Germany, if they could, but they had to leave all their belongings behind. None of them survived.

In general, it worked fine. The immigration part started, and many people went to Holland because it was a very hospitable country. The emperor of Germany escaped to Holland after WWI, and many famous people ended up in Holland. It was no big problem because they *all* had to start over. It was a community, but it still wasn't a community within itself. The people who were a little bit more educated started living in the same neighborhood. Regardless of having been robbed of everything, sometimes they had some background for money. This was not the case for our family when we left Berlin in June of 1932. My father's brother was living in Amsterdam, and he helped us quite a bit from the beginning. Later my mother learned a trade. Her sister was married to a Swiss man who was still living in Berlin. They told her to come to Berlin in 1934 and take a course in making intimate apparel for heavy-set people. It was not like it is here, where you can get a bra in size 55. You had to have it made to measure. She built up a very nice business.

I went to school in Holland and to art school later, but I had to leave school in order to take care of the household. My father was so-called "helping" my mother, but it was a symbolic thing. Whatever he touched, it did not work. He was like Willy Loman in the play *Death of a Salesman*. He was a very intelligent person and could write tremendously well and make poems for everything—but business-wise, it never went right. We moved several times in the same neighborhood because when you moved to Holland, you received several months of free rent. That helped, of course; but we always moved within a four-block area all of the time. Through other Jewish groups and sport clubs, I met other people.

One day I was with my aunt at a resort town, 20 miles away from Amsterdam. By coincidence, I was sitting at the front of the terrace in a Jewish restaurant, either writing something or reading...I don't know. Two young men came walking by, and one of them was from a group of people I knew. He introduced me to the other young man, and they came back later to ask me if I wanted to go for a walk. That young man's name was Lo. We got better acquainted, and I learned that he was a student at the agricultural university because he wanted to go to Israel and have a farm there. So I decided that if I wanted to have a serious relationship with Lo, I would have to start delving into that direction a little bit more; and later I went to a *kibbutz* to learn the traditions of kosher housekeeping. A *kibbutz* is a communal farm or settlement. All of this was happening in 1938 and 1939.

It was a peculiar situation. I called Lo's home during weekends when he was in town and we talked quite a bit, but I wasn't introduced to his parents. Whenever he and I went someplace for a concert or an opera, it happened that his parents were sitting close by us. At a certain point his father said that it was too crazy, and he said that he was going with his wife for a walk and told Lo to come from the other side of the street to introduce me to them. At that time, Lo still had a lady friend in Switzerland who he had to finish it off with because they had grown apart. Lo finally introduced me to his parents in 1939, it must have been. Shortly afterwards, Holland was mobilized, and Lo went into the army. But being a religious person in the Jewish faith, he could not eat the army food, and the army was not prepared for kosher food yet. I once went with his parents in a chauffeur-driven car to deliver a few days' load of food where he was stationed.

On May 10, 1940, the war broke out in Holland. My friend at that time was in the army. He was close to the part of Holland with the canal by Amsterdam. We heard the radio signals, and it was an alarm for parachutists. Parachutists were landing, and they were wearing camouflage clothing. They were dressed as nurses and other outlandish things as well as in Dutch soldiers' uniforms—the Germans had stolen a load of uniforms from a train in September. They started bombing the port city, and that went on for a day or two. The defense of Holland was made by inundating the land with water. You see, Holland was kept dry by the dikes. The dikes were mechanical devices used to close off the water. Like locks—like what is used to close off the Mississippi River in Minneapolis. They would use the locks to flood the streets and roadsides away. They believed that if they did this, then the Germans would not be able to find their way. But the Germans flew over the city, in the sky. It didn't work.

After the bombing of Rotterdam for two or three days, Holland surrendered to the Germans. A lot of people committed suicide because they were hopeless. In general, the Germans behaved quite decently. Nothing was done in the first landing. They marched into Amsterdam with troops and war materials and everything, but nothing happened. They took over and ruined things a little bit, but not much. People eventually simmered down, like in Germany. After a while, the Dutch people did not think that it would be so bad for the Germans to occupy Holland.

Well, anyway…I got engaged to Lo in 1941. His father was still alive. The Germans slowly brought in some rules and regulations in the shape of a Jewish committee, and we had to do what they told us to do. In Holland, people had always been registered with their name, surname, and religion since the days of Napoleon. It was not done by force, but done voluntarily. Most of the people were registered as Jewish. So now the Germans started having this Jewish committee. First of all, they installed identification papers for the whole country. I still have mine. Everybody had to do this. The Jews got ones with a "J" on it—a red "J". All the others had what was like a driver's license with their name, address, and fingerprint on it. Of course, at that time, we started to have underground work, and we would make false papers. The non-Jewish people would go and tell the government that they had lost their papers and were issued new ones, and then they gave their new papers to the underground groups. What we did in the underground was to soak off the pictures and put a new picture on top and connect the points of the mark that was on there. That way you could become another person—a whole new identify. I also have the papers from my parents, who were in hiding.

There came a time when everybody had to bring in their radios. Also, the Germans started to order the Jews to bring in their bicycles. Jews were not permitted to have any jewelry, either. We had shopping hours at certain times and at certain stores, when others couldn't shop. Every sort of entertainment, including movie houses, was forbidden to us. The schools had to disperse their Jewish students, and those students had to go to Jewish schools. My fiancé at that time was still at an out-of-town university, and they were not as strict there. When you got married, the ceremony had to take place at a special town hall only for Jews. When we got married, my husband and I were married in the student center at the university where he studied. We were married by the mayor of the city. It was completely different from getting married in the big cities.

When I got married, I got a different name, of course. So I went to the city hall to change my papers. The guy who gave me my papers gave me the papers without the "J" on them. This made it seem like I wasn't Jewish but my husband was. At that time, mixed marriages between Jews and non-Jews were frowned upon, and I was worried that I would bring my husband into danger. So I told that gentleman at city hall to add the "J" on my ID papers. It was stupid of me. People do not always think about what could happen later. If you focus on one certain thing, then you forget everything else. The only thing I could have done is to say that I had lost my papers and go back after a few days and get new ones with a "J" on them. But I didn't do that.

My in-laws had applied for immigration to the United States. They were fairly well-to-do financially. They had money in the United States and in Switzerland. It was not forbidden for them to have an income. They got the papers for all of us on the day Pearl Harbor was bombed. That took away all of our chances of going to the United States because the U.S. was not a neutral country anymore. I had two brothers-in-law who were kind of smart. My father-in-law by that time had died. He died in my arms, and I stayed with my mother-in-law. On the day of our marriage, I was sitting with Lo, my husband, and my mother-in-law called out to ask me if I was going to bed. It showed how little it meant to be married because it was only meant for legal reasons—like if I was to come along on my way to go someplace else. My brothers-in-law got to know a Swiss guy who had a connection with the German higher-ups. They said that they would develop a plan to get us out of Holland. In return, they would get a payment of a decent sum of money. It took a while, but during that time we were protected. We didn't have to be afraid of being picked up during a raid because in 1942 the Germans had started calling up young men to go to labor camps. It turned out that they were needed to build the concentration camps. None of the young men was ever heard from again.

Of course, there were always rumors about the camps in those years. My father had been playing cards with a friend who was not Jewish but who had a Jewish wife, and this friend had a brother in the Army. From him, my father learned about what was going on. We knew, for instance, that people would be taken to shower rooms in the camps, which were not shower rooms at all, but gas chambers. This was the only information that we really had about what was happening. My brother in law worked with those Germans. The wife of my oldest brother-in-law (who also was not

Jewish) had a baby that was two weeks old. In mid-March, we got notice that we should get prepared to go to Switzerland. But the wife of that Jewish brother-in-law could not go along because a German officer said that it was too tiresome for his wife after just being pregnant and that it was not good for the baby to go on that trip. On the day we left, we had to leave everything in the house as it was. In that case, it was the non-Jewish wife who stayed and got many valuables out of the house. We got the news to be at the train station at such-and-such a time. I do not remember how we got there. I don't remember a lot of things about those days.

Once we were at the station, we were escorted to a part of the train with a compartment reserved for us. With us was another family that included a diamond tradesman, who had money, and his wife and two kids. When we got to our first German stop, we were informed by our escort that we had to get off the train and get our visas and our passports. Switzerland was a neutral country. We got off the train in Cologne and were immediately arrested—all of us. They accused us of trying to smuggle things, and they interrogated us for three days while we were in the Gestapo prison—which was the worst that you could imagine. But they had to let us go. That time they put us into a regular train with several Jews from Cologne, and we were sent to Berlin to a collection camp for German Jews.

I had an uncle who was a lawyer working in the Jewish committee in Berlin. When I got to Berlin, I started asking questions. I remembered my mother's girlfriend, with whom she had been friends since she was five years old. She had a brother who was a headmaster at a Jewish school. It turned out that he was the leader at this collection camp. I went to his office and introduced myself, and he almost fell off his chair. He asked me what I was doing there, so I had to tell him the story. As it turned out, he couldn't do anything for us because just a few weeks before he had had to send his own mother to a camp. The only one he had saved so far was his sister, my mother's friend. She visited us a few times and brought us something to eat. We were housed in classrooms with straw on the floor. I was about 20 years old at the time.

One day a Dutch truck driver came to deliver goods, and he asked right away if there were any Dutch persons. We talked to him, and he told us to write letters to whomever we wanted to write letters to and he would deliver the letters for us. He also gave us his address just in case we could manage to get out of there. My letter—which was sent to an in-between address for my father because I did not know where he was—did reach him.[1] In turn, he sent a letter to me from where he was in Berlin with some money and food. I talked to whomever I could talk to, and I found out that there was a doctor there named Lustig—which was my maiden name— but he did not want anything to do with me. He thought that I was just another one who wanted favors. We did not try to escape from that place because the Germans had promoted the story that we were going to a new country where we would be able to build a new life for ourselves. That was the story that was told to us, despite the fact that it was not true.

One day I had a sore throat, and I went to the nurse in the camp. The first thing that she asked me was if I was pregnant. I said I didn't know, so she gave me quinine in case I was pregnant, and that would abort it. I was complaining about my sore throat. There was a young doctor there, Dr. Erlich—which meant "Dr. Honest"—and he lived up to his name. He looked at my throat and said that I had scarlet fever. He sent me to the hospital for six weeks of quarantine. My husband stayed in the camp in the school, and my two brothers-in-law and my mother-in-law were sent on a transport before I got out of the hospital. While I was in the hospital, there was a Russian girl in the room with me who also had scarlet fever. Her mother came and visited often because the Russians were still under friendly terms with Germany. Jewish or not, she was Russian. This lady managed to send the letters which I wrote to my father. I had to write the letters in code, using secretive ways to tell him what had happened to us. That was an attempt to inform my father the best way that I could, but I didn't want the Germans to know what I was writing. My father sent some money, but there was no way that I could spend it. The only thing that I could do was hide it in my clothing. I was in the hospital for six weeks, and then I was released.

We were eventually loaded onto a cattle train with only one door, so no one could get out. We also had a part on the train that we had to use as a toilet, but people were so close together that it did not do any good. Many people died on the way there. When we got to our end station, it turned out to be Auschwitz.[2] We were unloaded amid screams and cusses and were sorted out into groups. Men went to one side, women to another side,

1. See some of Margot's letters and postcards in Part III of this book.

2. See the endnote at the conclusion of this interview.

old people to another, and women with children to another. Everybody was separated. In our group the women got orders from a man who turned out to be Dr. Joseph Mengele, who was a nice-looking guy.[3] He told the young married women to step forward. From those he sorted out—I don't remember how many there were—he selected several of us younger women. We didn't know what happened to the rest. We were loaded up onto a truck and taken through the gate to a collection of barracks and were all put into one barrack. There were people in this barrack who had already been sent there before. Some of those people turned out to be from Belgium.

The Germans did not do any of the work; they forced the Jewish prisoners to do everything. Everything was manned by prisoners. Even the gas chambers were manned by prisoners. When we got there, all of our hair was shaved off, all our clothes were taken from us, and we had to dress in prison attire. When I got to Auschwitz, before I got into the barracks, I knew that I would survive. I *knew* it! I was probably a little cocky because I could understand German. The people who didn't understand it were revolting against an order because they couldn't even understand it, and they got punished and mistreated oftentimes. When I was still in Holland with my false papers, I went to every place that I was not supposed to go to. Sometimes I even went up to a German soldier and asked directions on how I could get to different places. I think that is what helped me in the camp. I understood German, and I was not afraid. I believe that I have always had a guardian angel in my life. I knew I would come out alive.

After being in that camp in the barrack, we got some knowledge of what was going on. There were so-called medical experiments going on with all of those people. Mengele was in charge; he was the one who had selected us. It was not only his experiments; there were other people involved, too. We did not know for certain what kind of experiments were going on; it was all hearsay. There was a dental station in the barrack, too. There were women who sorted out dentures and put them on boards and sent them to Germany. Also, the gold was removed from the teeth of dead prisoners and collected there. Another group of experiments was done on 10 Greek girls. The Germans opened them up for a cesarean section and removed all of their female organs and then taped the girls together again. What

3. See the endnote at the conclusion of this interview.

else was done? There was a sickbay for German prostitutes who got sick. They had to be taken care of by a nurse from our station.

At that time, there was a new transfer coming with some people on board who had scarlet fever. We had a Polish (Jewish) doctor, who also was the head of the barrack. The entire block was supervised by the German SS, Hitler's secret police. The doctor decided to keep the scarlet fever matter quiet because if the Germans would have known, they would have emptied the whole barrack and gassed everyone because *they* wanted to be the killer and not something caused by nature. The block's supervising doctor asked if people who had had scarlet fever wanted to volunteer at the sickbay. I had had scarlet fever, so I volunteered to work in the sickbay.

The sickbay was overseen by two Polish women who would steal and get from others everything that they wanted. After I volunteered to work there, I became the cleaning lady of the barrack and later got promoted to nurse. It didn't bring me very much advantage, except that I could go and get some more soup because I had to bring the soup in for the patients. The person who dished out the soup was also a Polish woman who held herself in very high esteem because she had a powerful job. If she liked you, then she scooped down to the bottom of the soup kettle and brought up some solid food. If she didn't like you, she would just skim the broth from off the top. I had been known to be able to bring back with me four bowls of watery soup.

We often would get news about what was happening in other parts of the camp. They delivered food to our barrack and also to the men's hospital barrack. I got the news that my husband, Lo, had arrived at the men's barrack. Our windows were blocked, but with cooperation from someone else I managed to peep through a crack when the other party brought my husband to their windows. I could see how bad he looked after spending nine months at the labor camp. They took him to a sickbay only to kill him later. Because I had made friends with some of the higher-up people who were in my barrack and who were friends of the man at the men's sick barrack, I managed to keep Lo off the gassing list. They kept him off the list three or four times—but he finally died in the barrack from tuberculosis. At least I saved him from being taken to the gas chamber. Lo had come to the camp at the end of 1943, and he died in March or April of 1944. I sent him my solid food and a piece of bread every three or four days. I did that through the food carrier who would take my food from my barrack and bring it to Lo. But the bread and a small amount of food every three days were not enough.

As for the food, we got some brown substance in the morning that was warm, and at noon we had to stand in line again to get the soup or whatever. There were a few times when there was good food in the camp. One of those times was when I was sick. One time, I remember, we had some soup with little segments of bones in it, and I thought they were bones from human fingers, but they turned out to be tails from pigs. That was the only time that we really had something that was identifiable.

Meanwhile, most of us women had to submit to some medical tests. The prisoner "nurses" would take a big ear syringe with some substance in it, and they would put it in our vaginal area and then take an X-ray. After some weeks, they would take an X-ray again to see if whatever they had used had been successful. That turned out to be the test that they did on the young, married women. We later learned that this was for mass sterilization. I had to submit to the test, too. I really did not know what they were doing to us. Some of the women had pains, and others of us didn't. It was probably good that we did not know what the substance was that they injected in our vaginal area, but it turned out that they wanted to find an easy way to sterilize women so they could live and do whatever they wanted. There was to be no next generation. Hitler's goal was to keep his surrendering countries Aryan. Anyone who was not Aryan—gypsies, Jehovah's Witnesses, Catholics, other people who thought differently— would be eliminated for the next generation because of Hitler's sterilization policy.

On other blocks in the barrack, they did a lot of tests on twins, also. Dr. Mengele was particularly fascinated by twins. They treated one twin one way and the other twin another way. It was something so cruel that it was hard to imagine. It happened because the Nazis considered those people to be worthless, less than human, and inferior.

Despite all of these terrible things that I am telling you, I have never hated the Germans. Actually, I pitied them. It is so distressing that the German culture—which had produced great art, music, drama, poetry, philosophy, and scientific advances—could sink to such a low level.

From the Belgian transport, there was one woman who had been selected to be a nurse. She was the head of another sickroom. It turned out that she and I had been in a dance group together when we were young in Holland. She was very sweet to me, and right away she gave me sheets for the straw mattress on my bunk. It did not turn out to be such a good thing, though, because once the lights went out, all of the bedbugs would come down and be attracted to that white sheet. At night, the only thing that I could do was scratch and shake my sheet over the railing to get the bugs out.

As I said, the Germans would take everything away from you when you got off the trains at the camp. Incidentally, the reason that they shaved people's heads was so that no one could not keep anything hidden in their hair. They had a big warehouse with all of the things that they took from the prisoners when they first arrived. Even great piles of human hair were there. The warehouse was called "Canada."

I soon learned that if you had the right connections, you could get *any-thing*. There were some prisoners who sometimes managed to smuggle things out and pass them on to someone else. One day, I was with a group of people from the barrack who had to go to the medical warehouse to get a few medications needed for the experiments. When we got to the warehouse, there was an old officer in charge of the pharmacy unit. He asked us if we had had any coffee yet, and we told him "no" because we did not even know what coffee tasted like anymore. He came back with a big mug of some brown stuff that turned out to be crème de cacao. Since all of us didn't have much in our stomachs and we were not used to alcohol, we were high for the rest of the day. He told us to go ahead and take the meds we needed, but he did not want to see what we took. We were able to take a lot of things with us that were not on the list. So you see, if you had the right connections, you could get a lot of things. *(Laughter)*

Anyway, in September 1944, we were taken from the camp in Auschwitz to another barrack outside of the Auschwitz camp. It was a new barrack. I don't even remember if they continued the medical tests. I always volunteered for the work groups. They had us collect acorns for a foot wash for the soldiers to soak in. I don't remember what else we did in the work groups. One time we were taken down a little road. We had a basket, and we were supposed to pick up certain rocks from the road and take them to the other side of the road. The next day we had to go back to that same place, but this time we had to move the rocks back again to the other side of the road where they originally were. It was very degrading. It was done just to humiliate us. There was not point to it.

When we were in the new camp, I volunteered to be in a sewing group. We repaired the clothing for the prisoners. That was in September of 1944. I was sitting against the slanting-roof part of the building, and I asked the girl next to me to move over a little bit. I was uncomfortable there. Seconds after I moved over a big rock came through the roof. That was the only time that the Russians had dropped a bomb on a building close by. That was a close call. After a while, the Germans returned and herded us back to where we were supposed to be.

There are some very gray areas in my thinking about that time because the days went by, one after the other, without incident. I do remember that in January of 1945, we got called to stand outside to be counted. The climate was like Minnesota in the middle of winter. It was cold, with lots of snow, and we had no sufficient clothing or decent shoes. They started distributing loaves of bread. Of course, prisoners in that situation will crawl over bodies to get something good to eat. Some of them got more than one loaf, but others did not get anything. I never could fight, so I did not get a loaf of bread. Two girls from the Dutch group came up to me and noticed that I did not have any bread, and they told me to stay with them. They remembered how I had taken care of them when they were in the sickroom, and they told me that because of that, they would take care of me. So that is when we became "The Three Musketeers."

That same night, we were taken on a death march with hundreds of people. If you couldn't walk, you lay down in the snow and had a graceful death—if the dogs didn't get to you or if the guards didn't shoot you first. The march took three days and two nights. I remember only one time leaning against the building, so we must have walked day and night. I don't remember anything in between. If someone couldn't walk, you did your best to help them. It was a matter of camaraderie. We "Three Musketeers" helped each other.

We finally reached the end of the trip. It was probably 60 miles from the other camp. At the train depot, we were loaded onto open cattle cars. There were no facilities to use. Nothing! The only thing we had was our food bowl. At a certain point on the train nature would call, so we would have to use one of the food bowls to answer nature's call. One time, when the bowl was filled with waste, we took it up and threw it over the wall of the train car. There was a German soldier walking below, and he was splashed with what was in the bowl. He got mad, and he cussed and yelled. We had fun for that brief second because he could not get inside the cattle car and do anything. Besides, he didn't know who had dumped the bowl. That was a humorous highlight in our misery.

We got to Ravensbrück after a long train ride. The trip that was normally six hours took two and a half days. Many people died on that trip. It was very chaotic. We had bread to eat, and that was about all. When we got to Ravensbrück—which was a political camp near Berlin—after one or two days, there was a call asking who wanted to go to another camp. We "Three Musketeers" volunteered. We were loaded on trucks and driven to another camp that was close to the demarcation line of the Russian and British troops. There we were put in a civilian labor camp where the Germans put people who had disobeyed the law. All the prisoners had to work. It was like a work camp. All of a sudden there were so many more prisoners, but not enough room for all of them. We slept on the floor on hay, and we were all squeezed together like sardines. If you wanted to turn, you had to give some sort of a signal so the whole row would turn. If you did not do that, then you lost your spot. If you needed to go to the outhouse, then you had to sit up against a wall after returning. I had frozen my feet there, too. One time I had to stand up, and I noticed that I had a big lump under my foot. I tried to scrape it off, but I couldn't. It was a big blister. I got a pin from someone and broke the blister and pushed the fluid out, and I got a paper bandage for my foot.

In that camp, we "Three Musketeers" were selected to work at various jobs. One of my friends worked in the food preparation kitchen, peeling potatoes and vegetables. She had a way of getting food. I was selected to work in a factory that made cardboard boxes for ammunition. The owners were terrific. They had escaped from Leipzig and had built a little factory, and they employed us. Once they heard who we were, they immediately bought soup for us. We had a few beautiful days. That was until someone heard about it and took us from there. During that time, I was able to get extra food from my friend who worked in the kitchen, and I hid it in my clothes and took it to the camp. We were not checked when we returned. We had some extra food and had to pay the guards in charge of the fire to fry it for us. It was only for a short duration that we were employed that way.

At that last camp, we could also hear things going on in the area. We could hear trucks going by and sirens going off. We heard shooting at times, but we didn't know what was going on. At certain times it got busier. We decided that one of us should stay awake at night in case someone liberated us. One Polish woman who spoke a little bit of Russian volunteered to stay up; and since I could speak English, I also volunteered to stay up. Of course, nothing happened.

One morning we were awakened by the German guards, and I saw an American soldier in his blue suit with white stripes walking with an American flag. I thought to myself: Keep your mouth shut; you are hallucinating! Nothing happened. But after a while, some other prisoners came to the barracks and told us to get out because we were free. We went out, and we were not the only ones on the road. There were hundreds and thousands of Germans trying to get away from the Russians because they had done bad things to the Russians, as well. Nobody was feared more than the Russians. This must have been about April of 1945.

As we were walking on the road, we shared some food that people were cooking over an open fire. At night, all we had to do was look for a roof to go over our heads for the night. We were not the type of people who would throw Germans out of their homes, like they had done to us. The first night we slept on top of a haystack in a chicken coop. We had nothing to eat. In the morning, one of us volunteered to look for something to eat and came back with a little suckling pig. I asked her what she thought we would do with it because we weren't able to butcher it or boil it. She told us that she would go back and return it to the lady she had taken it from because that lady looked so mad at her when she first took it. We still did not have anything to eat. We decided to catch a chicken, but no one would kill it. We kept the chicken until it laid an egg, and then we let the chicken go again. We put the egg in our bowl and added some water to it and mixed it with our fingers and drank it. All three of us got sick, which delayed us half a day. We threw up. After we could not throw up anymore because we had nothing left in our stomachs, we started walking with the masses again.

The Russians caught us. They were on a different road than the Germans, and they had closed off an area of the road. We could prove to them that we were prisoners. There were a few of them who could speak other languages. When one of the officers who interrogated us heard that we were from Holland, he took—of all things!—a Dutch dictionary out of his pocket. He said he was very interested in Holland and hoped to get there some day because Czar Peter many years earlier had been there to learn the shipbuilding trade. He put us up in a house that the Germans had lived in but had deserted. We had a bed and a roof over our heads. We got a loaf of bread, but there was no running water. We had to go with a bucket to a lake close by to get some water. Somehow we heard that there was a post of the Red Cross post nearby. It turned out to be on the other side of a burning heather field. We decided to try to cross the field; we got through it somehow. It turned out to be the French Red Cross, but they said they would take care of us even though we weren't French.

After being treated so well by the Russians, we were put into tents in an open field by the French. I don't know how we got meals, but we were transported by trucks from one collection spot to another. We were escorted by Canadian soldiers. We finally got to Holland and were put into a school, deloused, and given a medical checkup. We were told that we could not go back to another part of Holland where we wanted to go because it had just been liberated in May of 1945 and they were still having trouble supplying the people who were already there. They didn't want any additional people coming into the country.

One day I saw a priest coming into the school, and I started talking to him. I asked him if he knew a certain manufacturer of textile goods and if that person was still living there. He told me that he would check on that. The manufacturer was a business connection of my father-in-law's who was a powerful textile wholesaler from Holland. The priest came back and said that the manufacturer was there and had asked me to come right away. I told him that I could not go alone because there were three of us—"The Three Musketeers," remember? *(Laughter)* Finally, I did receive word that all three of us could go.

When we went to visit this family, it was beautiful day in May. The lady of the house had decided to have a tea party outside. She told us to ask the three men who had escorted us all of the time to come with us, too. After those three Canadian soldiers joined us, another solider arrived as well. The hostess asked if one of us had *two* gentlemen, and we told her no! *(Laughter)* Then this young man walked up to her and turned around and looked at me—and it was my *brother*! He had volunteered in the Canadian army as an interpreter, so he had been given a pass to go from one part of

Holland to another. It was from my brother that I learned that my mother and my father had survived. He brought me a $10 bill and some clothing that my mother had saved for me. I felt like a queen because I had money, even though there was no place to spend it. That was a good feeling.

After some time, we got the news that the trains were running again—so off we went to Amsterdam. One of the three of us decided to go to a cousin of hers who was in a mixed marriage; she went to that address. I went to the address of the house where my father had been hiding, but I had to walk. I remember that I had a very nice coat that I kept from the prisoners' clothing supply. At the time, I had to put a big white cross on the back of it because I was a prisoner. A lady came up to me as I was walking and asked me if I knew that I had a big white cross on my back. Apparently, I had forgotten that I didn't need that anymore: The war was over! I walked about 20 to 35 minutes to where my father was. Our reunion was a big to-do.

There really weren't many families still intact like ours turned out to be. My friend Anne—this was about half a year later—she received a letter from a visitor who was looking for a photo of his wife. Well, it turned out that this "visitor" was in fact her husband! Not only did he receive the photo, but he received his wife as well. What a happy reunion *that* was! She, her husband and I stayed in touch for many years. Anne died in 1965.

Laura, the third of the "Musketeers," used to live in New York. Then she moved to Florida, where she got married. Anne and I saw her once in the airport. I am always the one who calls people because I need the contact. The last time I called Laura, the telephone had been disconnected and there was no forwarding address, so I lost touch with her.

There are lots of photos of prisoners in the concentration camps who were wearing striped uniforms, but we had regular clothes. The clothes had a big number on them and a red triangle with the point down. You were no longer a person; you were a number. They marked that number on your left arm. Right after they gave me my number and wrote it on my arm, I took dirt and tried to rub it out, but they caught me later and had it redone. I did a good job, but you can still see the little number underneath there. *(Pulls up her left sleeve to reveal the number etched on her arm)* My number is right here: 47574. It is still visible after all of these years. You will notice that a triangle is tattooed right through the number. That was the designation for the camp that you were in. The red triangle pointing down was for the Jewish. The purple triangle was Jehovah's Witnesses, and another triangle was for the gypsies. I think the homosexuals had a pink triangle.

A year after I was liberated from the camp, I met a guy in Holland who had been in a Japanese camp. He was in the Merchant Marines. His ship got bombed, and they ended up on an island in Indonesia, where the Japanese took them prisoner. He and I got together at a party. We felt that we could build a better future with the experiences that we both had had and that we could build a better world. After 17 years of being married to him, however, I decided that it was not the right way. I filed for a divorce and went into hiding because he would have pursued me and forced me to stay with him. After the divorce was final, I decided to go to the States to visit my brother in Minneapolis. I went on a long trip through the States—first to visit all my different acquaintances—and then I stayed with some friends in Santa Anna. While I was in California, I got a call from my sister-in-law that she was almost due with her baby. I returned to Minneapolis, but the baby didn't come. Rather than just waiting around, I decided that I needed to get out of there. So I took a bus downtown. I missed a connecting bus, and so did another lady who was trying to catch it as well. We started to talk about things, and she told me that she knew some people from Holland and would call them for me. One of those people called to tell me that there was a Dutch club meeting and that they would come and pick me up and take me to dinner with them. That's where I met Rudy, one of the brothers who had been dating the woman I met who had missed the bus, and we started talking. During that time, Rudy and I met a hundred times, and I promised him that I would come back to Minnesota. You see, my visa had expired, and I had to go back to Holland. I applied for my immigration visa, and I came back to Minneapolis in February 1961. Soon after, Rudy and I were married on March 4, 1961. We have been married over 40 years. *(Rudy smiles from across the room.)*

2. Auschwitz-Birkenau was Nazi Germany's largest concentration and extermination camp. By direct order of Adolf Hitler, Heinrich Himmler established the camp in April 1940. It was located near the provincial Polish town of Oshwiecim in Galacia. As part of Hitler's "Final Solution" (the elimination of as many Jews as possible), Hitler personally ordered the mass extermination of the Jews. As Nazi propagandist Joseph Goebbels wrote, "With regard to the Jewish question, the *Fuhrer* decided to make a clean sweep." It is estimated that between 1940 and 1945 about three million people died at Auschwitz. Those people met their death through gassing, starvation, disease, shooting, and burning. (Source: *Gate to Hell: Auschwitz*. Internet entry by Louis Bulow.)

3. Josef Mengele (1911–79) was called "The Angel of Death" because of his ruthless and bizarre medical experiments in the Auschwitz camp. As a youth and a young man, Mengele was intelligent, handsome, refined, and popular. He studied philosophy in Munich and earned his medical degree at Frankfurt University. His doctoral thesis dealt with racial differences in the structure of the lower jaw.

Mengele joined the Nazi party in 1937. In 1942, he was wounded at the Russian front and thus could no longer serve in the military, so he volunteered to work in the hospital in the Auschwitz camp, where he remained for 21 months until the war's end. His laboratory was located on Block 10 of Auschwitz I.

Mengele's horrible medical experiments made him a greatly feared legend at Auschwitz. For example, when he learned that a small number of inmates in a women's cell block was infected with lice, he gassed all 750 women in the cell block. On another occasion, when a mother hysterically begged not to be separated from her 13-year-old daughter, Mengele drew his revolver and shot them both, all while prisoners stood and watched. In a children's cell block, he drew a black line on the wall about five feet from the floor. Shorter children whose heads did not reach the line were sent to the gas chamber for extermination.

Mengele was fascinated by twins. Once, about 15 sets of young twins were brought to his laboratory, where they were carefully laid out on his dissection table and drugged. When they were asleep, chloroform was injected into their hearts, thus causing their immediate death. Mengele proceeded to dissect each set of twins, and he carefully arranged and catalogued each piece of their bodies.

It is estimated that Mengele conducted medical experiments on over 3,000 twins: chemical injections into the eyes to change color, surgeries performed without anesthesia, transfusions of blood from one twin to another, injections of deadly germs, sex-change operations, incestuous impregnations. One surviving twin gave an account of the horrific medical procedures performed on his twin brother, and he concluded his comments with these words: "It is not possible to state how I felt when my twin brother died. They had killed my mother, my father, my two older brothers—and finally my twin."

After the war, Josef Mengele escaped Germany and managed to hide under various aliases to avoid detection. He spent the last 35 years of his life in South America under an assumed name. One afternoon, while living in Brazil, he went swimming in the ocean, where he suffered a massive stroke. By the time he was dragged to the shore, he was dead. That was in 1979. It was not until 1992, however, that Mengele's body was positively identified through DNA tests. (Sources: *Mengele: The Complete Story* by Gerald L. Posner and John Ware; *The Nazi Doctors* by Robert Jay Lifton; and *Gate to Hell: Auschwitz*, Internet entry by Louis Bulow.)

Samuel Young

Born: 1928

Present homes: Honolulu, Hawaii, and St. Joseph, Minnesota

Military service: Drafted; entered service 1951, Korean Conflict

Branch of service: U.S. Army

Length of service: Two years

Highest rank: Corporal

Date/place of interview: August 5, 2003
St. Joseph, Minnesota

Note: Samuel Young was a teenager living in Honolulu when the Pearl Harbor attack occurred on December 7, 1941. He was not able to provide a photograph of himself from that time.

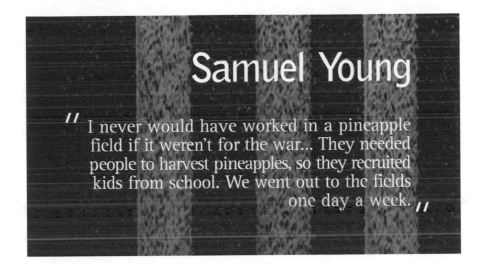

I was living in Honolulu on December 7, 1941, when the Japanese
attacked Pearl Harbor. I was 13 years old at that time. I think the attack
happened about 7:55 in the morning. I was in bed sleeping, I guess. It
was a Sunday, and nothing was going on. We just heard booming and
things like that off in the distance. We heard booming, but we just thought
it was practice because the military at Pearl had been practicing shooting a
great deal prior to December 7. So it was nothing unusual, at least for us—
until we heard the reports on the radio. To this day, I do not know why we
turned on the radio at that hour of the day, and on a Sunday.

I am pretty sure the Japanese planes flew over my neighborhood. I *know*
they did because after we heard on the radio the Japanese had attacked
Pearl Harbor, the radio announcer kept saying, "This is the Real McCoy."
I walked over to my sister's place. She only lived a block or so away—and
that is what I mean when I say the attack really made no impression on me.
I just thought I would go over to my sister's place for a visit. She was married and had kids. I know the Japanese planes flew over because as I was
walking over to my sister's house, I heard shooting and I looked up and saw
a Japanese plane. The reason I knew it was a Japanese plane is because I
did see the red ball, which was the Japanese insignia, and that is all. It did
not make an impression on me. Maybe it was because I was only 13.

The planes were flying low. It wasn't the way airplanes fly nowadays. The reason I looked up was because I heard firing, and I didn't know why they were firing or at whom. All I knew is that it was coming from an airplane. Our house was quite a ways from Pearl. Today it's a half-hour drive, but back then the roads were not nearly as good as they are today. But I could see smoke billowing out from the direction of the harbor. I don't recall if there were several waves of attacks. I mean, I didn't think too deeply about it at the time it was happening. But the next day, when Roosevelt referred to it as "a day that will live in infamy," it took on more significance for me. In retrospect, I don't know how much of those later comments influenced me. I knew there was more than one wave of planes attacking, but I knew nothing of it as it was happening, and I did not care.

There did not seem to be any panic among my neighbors. As I told you, I strolled over to my sister's place. I don't remember getting there, but I am sure I did; also, I don't remember what I did when I got there. But there was no mad rush to take cover, to assume we were under attack. We did not have the kind of panic that you see in the movies. Well, I am sure there could have been *some* panic elsewhere on the island. There probably was excitement and things like that; but where we were, it made no impression, at least to me. I did not know what war was, anyway.

I never did see that recent film, *Pearl Harbor*. There was no reason to see it. It had bad reviews anyway. *(Laughter)* And besides, they didn't invite me to the premiere! So I thought, forget it! *(Laughter)*

The next day would have been a school day, but I don't know whether I went to school or not. Probably not. I don't know, and I don't remember if my friends and I talked much about what happened. I don't remember if we talked about it or not. I know that certain things happened. My older brothers were working at Pearl Harbor, so they were called immediately. They left the house pretty quickly. What followed after? I do not know about time and passage of time from then until whatever happened. I don't even remember when we went back to school.

They did have things like the "blackouts"—you had to have blackouts. To "black out" a room meant more than just closing the drapes. It was just like actually papering over the windows so absolutely no light could be seen from outside. It was just black. At night you'd hear the wardens who would come by the house and yell, "Light showing!" That kind of thing. Again, the whole thing is so distant—it made no impression on me until later on.

I didn't pay that much attention. I know that my brothers were working in Pearl Harbor at different shifts. Life changed for my family; the pattern changed. For instance, before the attack, our family always ate together as a group. We would wait for someone to come home so that everybody would be eating at the same time. Obviously, after the war started, that routine had to change because of different work shifts. We did not eat at the same time. My father would always have some food for my brothers when they got home.

My brothers were much older than I. My youngest brother, the one closest to me, was at least six years older—about 19. They were adults and out of school. I suppose there was a fear among adults that it could happen again, that there might be another attack, but I never heard much talk of that in my immediate surroundings. I have no idea what the reaction was. The main thing was that the pattern of life changed for us.

I never did go out to Pearl Harbor once we were allowed out there. Part of the reason I didn't go, I think, was that it never occurred to me to want to go. I don't think my parents probably would have let us go because shortly after the attack, we were under martial law immediately. There were troops all around us. So I wouldn't ever venture out there. Besides, we didn't have a car. I think some of the buildings at Hickam Field still have bullet holes on them.

Before December 7, people were all coming to Hawaii, mostly by ship. Of course, the tourist trade was not to the degree it is now. After the bombing, I don't think there was anything else but shipping of goods and materials with those ships. There were only a couple major ship arrivals per week. I am not positive, though. Then, after the attack, all of those ships were, I think, taken over by the military and used for transport for supplies and troops.

I guess life for me did change, but I mean it was the pattern of daily life that changed. For instance, every Sunday we used to go over to the outdoor market, but I don't even remember if we still did that after the attack.

You probably wonder if, when I reflect on that December day, I think that I was part of an important historical event. Well, no, I don't. I didn't think in those terms. It happened; it just happened. And that's all.

I do remember when Roosevelt came over to Hawaii. He did that a number of times, I guess. I remember once when he came over—and I do not know how the word got around, but they always knew when he would be passing by a certain area. I guess you could tell because there usually were military police standing at a street corner, waiting. I remember once when we were waiting for him to go by, he went by and everyone cheered and he waved. I actually saw him! Yeah. If I remember correctly, he was in a convertible, and he had to be sitting on an elevated seat because he was way up and it was high. He probably didn't feel any danger, I am sure.

That is the thing: Of that day, there are snatches of things I remember. Otherwise, there was nothing that really had an impact on me. I don't think even the war itself had any impact on me until after I went to high school. I know it did in whatever grade I was in, but things like working in a pineapple field—I would never have worked in a pineapple field if it weren't for the war. You see, they needed people to harvest pineapples, so they recruited kids from school. We all went out to the fields one day a week.

Of course, Hawaii wasn't a state yet. In 1941, it was just a territory of the United States. We kind of resented the military's presence, in a way. The idea was typical for the people living in the States to think that people living in Hawaii were not Americans. We were brought up as Americans and nothing else. We were a territory but were still part of the United States. I think that is one of the things about people who refer to the States as if they are American and "you people out there" are not. "You people" were the Hawaiians. But it was common, and naturally so. We forgive you. *(Laughter)*

I think one of the things they did discover way back then is that the people in Hawaii—and I know I am generalizing here—the people in Hawaii knew more about America and its history than a lot of people living in the States. I mean, in school we had to *study* all of those things about America. That is how they indoctrinated us.

One of the things that happened after the war a matter of language. In Hawaii, many people speak what is called pidgin English. Those people were told to speak "American" and not pidgin English. Well, it has taken years to get over that. In many ways, Hawaii was thought to be backward and provincial—yet most Hawaiians were then and are now more aware of international and national things, I think, than the people in many places on the mainland. I know the major reason why Hawaiians knew more about the U.S. mainland was because we got so much news from the mainland. We knew more, in that sense.

PART III

Correspondence and Related Documents

DRAFT No. 1   December 7, 1941.

PROPOSED MESSAGE TO THE CONGRESS

Yesterday, December 7, 1941, a date which will live in ~~world history~~ *infamy*

the United States of America was ~~suddenly~~ *suddenly* and deliberately attacked

by naval and air forces of the Empire of Japan ~~without warning~~.

The United States was at the moment at peace with that nation and was

~~continuing the~~ *still in* conversation with its Government and its Emperor looking

toward the maintenance of peace in the Pacific. Indeed, one hour after

Japanese air squadrons had commenced bombing in ~~the American island of Oahu~~ *Oahu*

the Japanese Ambassador to the United States and his colleague delivered

to the Secretary of State a formal reply to a ~~former~~ *recent American* message. ~~from the~~

~~Secretary.~~ *While* This reply ~~contained a statement~~ *stated* *it seemed useless to*
that diplomatic negotiations

~~must be considered at an end, but~~ *it* contained no threat ~~and no~~ *or* hint of ~~war or~~

armed attack.

It will be recorded that the distance ~~of Hawaii, and especially~~ of

Hawaii from Japan makes it obvious that the attack ~~was~~ *was* deliberately

or even weeks
planned many days ago. During the intervening time the Japanese Govern-

ment has deliberately sought to deceive the United States by false

statements and expressions of hope for continued peace.

At about 5:00 p.m. on Sunday, December 7, 1941, President Roosevelt called his secretary, Grace Tully, to his study. He dictated the speech that he would deliver to Congress the following day. After Ms. Tully typed the speech, Mr. Roosevelt modified some of the wording in the script.

FDR signs the Declaration of War against Japan.

While hospitalized in Nebraska for a recurrence of malaria, Jack Rinsema wrote this letter to his brother. "Puddin'" is Jack's nickname for his wife Jean. Jack's brother George (nicknamed "Jud") was in the 38th Battalion of the U.S. Army. Judd participated in the invasion forces on D-Day. He was in charge of a tank destroyer and took party in much heavy fighting.

Tomorrow will be your birthday Jud but due to my illness it was forgotten until now. This will ~~United States Army~~ be late Jud but you know that we'll be wishing you a very enjoyable one under the circumstances —

Saturday

FORT CROOK, NEBRASKA 15th January - '44

Dear ~~Brother~~ George —

Well, Jud, I ~~guess~~ you as well as I and everyone else never expected me to write you from an Army hospital in Omaha Nebraska, but such is the truth. Strange things do happen occasionally. The effects of tropical habitation. I'll begin from the beginning of this deal.

We, (Jean & I) left Chicago Union Depot at 12:30 Noon Monday. The folks took us there and the kids were also with. About 3 hrs. later I told Puddin' I wasn't feeling well and expected an attack of Malaria. Severe chills took hold of me for three hours followed by a very high temperature which lasted about 2½ hrs. — Malaria is a very strange thing. It comes with attacks just the way I described this one but they begin with very weak ones about two days apart at first and becoming more severe each time. I had two of these during the previous week but said nothing because they were so slight. I thought I could make California before they would get too severe. — Well, I reported this to the M.P. on the train & he advised me to get off at Omaha to consult the Army Nurse stationed at the Depot. She in turn advised me to leave the train and go to this hospital immediately. She also made arrangements for that and transportation for same. But Jean was still with me and insisted on staying with me until I felt better. Her plans were to branch off at Omaha toward home. She took a hotel room at Omaha and came out here the next day. This place is about 12 mi.s outside the City.

Well Jud in five more minutes Puddin' will be here again so I'll have to. continue then. Boy how I look forward to those visits. I usually watch for her through the window next to my Bed. I'll ~~so~~ write more after she leaves.

Puddin' ~~come to visit~~ me at ita 8:00 P.M.

Well Jud there you have a brief narrative of a year and a half's experience but it isn't at all complete. I'll wait until I see you again to do justice to it, so I'll say good bye now and hope to ~~see~~ you soon. I'm feeling much better now, so I'll probably leave here in a few days. So Long Jud and write ~~soon~~ With love your Bro. Jack.

Jack Rinsema designed this Christmas card while on a Navy ship. Originally intended only for Jack's family, some senior Navy officers saw it, liked it, and asked Jack's permission to have several thousand of the cards printed to be used as the official Navy Christmas card that year.

Dear Bill + Lucille

Just a small Christmas
remembrance in a way.
We somehow come along
stores on the way to buy
cause so we make them.
This is a copy of ours we
made after a pattern & designed
a few days ago.
Sure have hoping that a
Christmas will be a
lot of joy and happiness
for you. We hoping to
hear from you folks again
so will for Jane Jack
now...

Just been waitin'
"fo" for this chance,
To send a word of cheer

And so it comes
to wish you joy
A victorious and —

Love
Always,

Mary James

Grand River & Redmond
U.S.E. California
San Francisco

Ebba Trontheim p/a Stibbe
Amsterdam Z.
Palestrinastr. 9.

[...] Berlin 25.6.[..]

These letters were written by Margot DeWilde from Auschwitz-Birkenau.
Grateful acknowledgment for the English translations is extended to Dr. Roland
Specht-Jarvis, Professor of Foreign Languages and Dean of the College of Fine
Arts and Humanities at St. Cloud State University in St. Cloud, Minnesota.

contact mit Euch hatte. Eva hatte auch Scharlach u.
ist da sie Ausländerin ist, frei. Sie u. ihre Mutter u. Schwester
waren reizend zu mir, sowie auch verschiedene Menschen,
die mir total unbekannt waren, unter Uns waren
das Leute die man kannte u. von denen man erwartete
dass sie etwas für einen tun würden. Hiermit meine ich
Leschl u. die sich leider, bis auf etwas Wurst zu schicken
nicht viel um uns bekümmert haben, er ist Lagerleiter
u. könnte viel für uns tun. Da wir 3 zusammen im
Krankenhaus waren u. ich anfangs nicht freigegeben war,
da ich auf erster Infectionsstation lag, waren wir solange
vom Transp. freigestellt, meldeten uns aber vorige Woche
freiwillig da der Transp. nach Theresienstadt gehen sollte
u. das somit von den 2 übeln das beste gewesen wäre.
Als wir schon vor dem Auto standen, holte uns der Com-
missar wieder zurück, da wir junge Leute sind u. im
Osten arbeiten können. So kamen wir wieder zu Haus
zurück, u. probierten noch alles was möglich war um doch
nach TH. zu kommen, da er aber nicht seine volle Unit
Arbeit gab, glückte bisher nicht. So werden wir also
Anfangs nächster Woche auf Transport nach dem Osten gehen, hoffen aber dass in der Zeit noch etwas
passieren wird. Behaltet auf jeden Fall contact mit
Eva, falls ich Euch nicht schreiben kann, gelt es viel-
leicht wohl zu ihnen zu schreiben. Das Geld sowie 3 Pak-
kete habe mit recht lieb Dank empfangen, leider konn-
te ich dies nicht mehr bis zum bewussten Mittwoch
bestätigen. Besonderheiten über den ganzen Fall werdet

Berlin, 25 June 1943

Dear One:

Finally I am in a position to report to you in this direct way. I had already once written a detailed letter and hoped that this one would have been picked up by an acquaintance, but that had not happened to date. She hopes, however, to welcome one of you.

That you are only hearing from me after such a long time is Aunt Iris' fault. She wanted to have the letter that I wrote on April 2 on its way immediately, but to no avail.

I was admitted to the hospital on April 11 with a diagnosis of scarlet fever, but if that is the case it was a mild form of it because I only suffered from symptoms of laryngitis and two days of having a fever. I spent a very exciting week there because another transport was scheduled to go at the beginning, and it was said that Lo must go with it. However, on the morning of the transport, he was postponed after a long and difficult endeavor to get him off due to a sudden illness of John and his mother, who were taken off the list after much ado. Thank God that he came into the hospital after three weeks with an angina pectoris, so that he can only be deported with the transport after next. Unfortunately, his mother-in-law was on the deportation transport.

Other than that, the time in the hospital was certainly the nicest time from this episode, especially when I was able to be in touch with you guys. Eva also came down with scarlet fever and got off the deportation list because she is a foreigner. She and her mother and sister were very kind to me, as were many different people whom I had not known at all but who turned out nicer than people whom we knew and of whom we could expect that they would do something for us. I am talking of Reschk, who did not take care of us in the least, with the exception of a tiny little bit of sausage that they sent. He is the director of a camp and could do a whole lot for us.

Since the three of us were together in the hospital and I was in the infectious disease station, we were kept off the deportation list for a while, but a week ago we volunteered because the transport was scheduled to go to Theresien concentration camp, and that would have been the better of two evils. When we were already lined up in front of the vehicle, the commandant sent us back because we are young people and able to work in the east. That is how we returned to Max and tried everything that was possible in order to make it to Theresien, but since we did not have his collaboration, nothing has fallen into place so far. So at the beginning of next week, we will be deported to the east, but we are hopeful that something will happen before that.

Be sure to stay in touch with Eva in case I cannot write to you; it may well be possible to write to them. The money, as well as three parcels, I have received, and I thank you from the bottom of my heart. Unfortuntely, I could not confirm the receipt until that certain Wednesday. The specifics about this entire case you will probably receive soon from Val and Getty.

Keep your heads up, as we'll do. So far everything has turned out better than we had thought, and I am hoping that it will continue to remain that way. In any case, we will try to stay in contact with you.

Now, my dear friends, we greet you and all our acquaintances from the bottom of our hearts and kiss you and hope that we will soon see you again.

Heads up.

Your Margot, who often thinks of you, Lo and John

Ebba Trautheim
A'dam. 2.
Palestrinastr. 9.

Berlin 25.6.43.

Meine Lieben

Endlich habe ich Gelegenheit Euch
mal auf direktem Wege etwas zukommen zu lassen.
Ich habe schon einmal einen ganz ausführlichen Brief
geschrieben u. hoffte, daß dieser bei Euch durch Deine
Bekannten abgeliefert [...] war bis jetzt noch nicht
geschehen ist. Sie hofft [...] bald einmal jemand
von Euch zu empfangen [...] ihr erst nach so lan-
ger Zeit von mir gehört habt, ist die Schuld von
Tante [...] den Brief, den ich am 2. [...]
schrieb, sofort weiter befördern lassen, daß [...]
nicht geschehen ist. Am 1. April kam ich ins Krankenhaus, angeblich hatte ich Scharlach, aber wenn dies
der Fall war, dann war es eine sehr leichte Form, da
ich nichts anderes als Halsschmerzen u. 2 Tage Fieber
hatte. Ich überlebte dort [...] eine sehr spannende Woche
[...] Transport ging und im Anfang hieß daß [...]
[...], es wurde am Morgen vom Transport du John
auch krank wurde, mit seiner Mutter, nach sehr langen
[...] u. großer Aufregung hergestellt. Gott sei
dank kam er nach 3 [...] mit einer Angina ins
Krankenhaus, so daß er über den nächsten Transport
weg kam. Leider kam [...] eine Schwiegermutter damit
weg [...] Sonst war die Zeit im Krankenhaus bestimmt
die schönste Zeit dieser Episode, überhaupt also ich

probieren ihr zu schreiben. Sie berichtet dann weiter.
Tante J u Max haben uns sehr enttäuscht. Freunde
haben für uns mehr als er, der, da er Lagerleiter ist, viel für uns hätte tun können.
Über die Pakete in das ... haben wir richtig gefreut
u danke ich ihnen dafür
Meine lieben, ich könnte noch Stunden schreiben,
aber da die Zeit gekommen ist werde ich es kurz
machen. Seid vorsichtig u behaltet den Kopf
hoch, wir werden es auch probieren, auch wenn es
noch so schwer ist. Macht euch keine Sorgen, denn
die Angst vor dem ... ist nicht wenn ist oft viel grö-
ßer als es in Wirklichkeit nötig ist. Wir haben bis jetzt
empfunden, dass bei allem es doch ganz anders, als
bis jetzt, doch noch besser gekommen ist als man
es sich vorstellte. Hoffen wir es weiterhin auch.
Nun, meine lieben seid ihr, sowie alle anderen
Bekannten recht innig gegrüßt u geküsst, u
hoffen auf ein baldiges Wiedersehen zuhause.
                    Eure Margot u. ...

257

Berlin, 25 June 1943

Dear LB:

Finally, I have the opportunity to write more completely.

Your package and money have arrived after all, if late, but just in time. You can learn what has happened to us from Val. In any case, it is nothing nice. Aunt T. had promised to write a comprehensive letter when we were admitted to the camp but probably did not do that. After that, I got acquainted with Lo in the hospital, where I had come down with what's called scarlet fever, but it was in no way so because I had few symptoms.

My clothing does not fit me anymore. Now, for the third time already, all of our luggage has been lost, so that hardly anything of what we were allowed to keep is available, and we only hope that we can stay together.

We suddenly have the opportunity to write to you because of a Dutch chauffeur who is here. Eva has a thorough report about everything with her and hopes that Ebba will also make it there. Be sure to stay in touch with her. In case we cannot write to you, we will try to write to her. She will then report on.

Aunt T. and Max have disappointed us a lot. Strangers have done more for us than he, who is a camp director who should have been able to do a lot for us. We have been most delighted about the packages and the money, and we thank you very much for them.

My dear ones, I could go on writing for hours, but time is limited, and I will keep it short.

Be cautious and carry your heads high, as we will try to do, even though it is so difficult. Don't worry about us because the fear of the unknown is often much greater than is necessary in reality. We have felt, to this point, that everything has turned out differently than anticipated, and so far it has still been better than we had feared. Let's hope it stays that way.

Now, my dear ones, as well as all our other acquaintances, we send you our warmest regards and kiss you and hope that we will soon see you again at home.

Your Margot and Lo

Absender: M. Mayera Lustig
Birkenau b. Neu Berun
O. Schlesien

Postkarte

Rückantwort nur auf
Postkarten in deutscher Sprache

Amsterdam - W.
Holland

Meine Lieben:

Hörte mit großer Freude von Lo
daß sie Bericht von Euch halte,
Wir sind gesund und habe manch
mal Bericht von ihr. Was macht
Flip? Herzl. Grüße und Küsse

Margot.

30. I. 44.

Dear Ones:

I hear with great joy from Lo that he had heard from you. We are healthy and get reports occasionally. How is Flip? Cordially and kisses, Margot.

(Charles Nolte to frere Dick, January 3, 1944)

Up betimes and to breakfast, and spying upon the table the most lovely
olive I did see in my life, and it all juicy and browned; and just before I made to leave the table, the waitress gave it me, and I did
deem it as nice and pleasant a thing as has ever made to happen; and
I taking it off and placing it in a drawer, and leaving it. And so to
the airport by omnibus, there to fly.

So to the flight office, and found nothing amusing there, it being the
Sabbath and no day to fly; but soon merrily learning there to be no
flying and as happy as can be; and so to the ready room for some fri-
volity. And many cadets danced and sang and made to play, and found
most of it amusing, but nothing so much as the news that we did not
fly, and thus whiled away the entire morning, and so by omnibus to
lunch.

Early up from lunch and to my room and drawer, there finding my olive,
and as nice a picture as I did ever see in my life, it being juicy and
brown. And not eating same, but, merrily enough to the airport, in
hopes not to fly, which thing was not to be, and me quite unhappy
when my instructor informed of my Stage 'A' check that day, and so
into parachute harness quite harassed, and not at all civil to flight
officer, either. Very betimes up into the air with check pilot, and
me quite worried, and the air unsteady, and not at all smooth. And
me flying in the air, thinking the while of my browned olive, and
quite forgetting my flying, and so doing much better at it, and check
pilot quite amazed, and me doing all low and high work with great
skill, and making out to be much a 'hot pilot' which thing I am not.
And so betimes below, still thinking of my browned olive, and thus
landed with all parts firm and no bumps the while, and not at all bad,
and thus taxiing to the strip, and there awaiting the verdict.

Up, and out of the plane, there still being no verdict, with check
pilot off and away without speaking, and me taking this an ill omen,
and so into office much worried, and not without fear; and there
finding all happy faces, and much talk, and so out of harness, and
to tables to sign papers, and me noting many two's among my grades,
which thing made me in a pleasant mind, and much happy, and finally
learning my check ride was '85', and so quite dazed, and up to seek
air outside.

And so to barracks, and still quite happy, and finding there my
olive and your letter, and cherished both, and did take them both
with me to the gentlemen's room, where I did eat former and read
latter, and quite happy and contented, and so to dinner, and Jack
Benny, which thing amazed me, as I had forgot the day to be the
Sabbath, and was quite amazed to find it so, and much pleased, too.

And so to bed, and much glad to get there, being weary and quite
tired, and very pleased over check ride, and olive, and letter.

                    Your devoted,

                    Samuel

This is a letter written by Charles Nolte to his brother Richard. Charles was at La
Mars, Iowa, in training to be a pilot in the Naval Air Corps. Apparently in a
whimsical mood, Charles chose to write this letter in the style of noted diarist
Samuel Pepys (1633–1703).

Somewhere In France.
November 2, 1944

Dear A.D.

Parlez vous francais!

I'm trying hard, anyway. We got a little French language guide and every chance I get I try to express myself in French. All the waitresses are French and speak no English so I practiced and asked the girl for a glass of water instead of gesticulating like the rest of the officers. She was so surprised!

Can't say just where I am or how long I'll be here — I have been in Paris, though — Saw the Eiffel Tower, Arch de Triumphe, etc. Yesterday was All Souls Day and the Unknown Soldier was honored beneath the Arc de Triumphe — Four of us got in the

The following two letters were written to William Schleppegrell's aunt Adolphine (A.D.)

live and paid our hommage by salutes.
Everything is la metro in Paris -
the subway - it's the only way to get
around - really isn't hard after
a few times.

Right now I am living in
a tent with 5 other fellows on the
front lawn of an old Chateau - we
have a stove now, but it sure
was cold before that came.

Well, guess that's all for now -
we flew over here from England.
Still no word from you at all -
Please write soon -

Love, Bill

January 24, 1945

Luftpost
Par Avion
Taxe perçue / PL

Kriegsgefangenenpost

-9.3.45.9-10 V

An Miss ADOLPHINE SCHLEPPEGRELL

819 SECOND STREET

123

Empfangsort: WOODLAND

Straße: CALIFORNIA

Kreis:

Land: U.S. OF AMERICA

Landesteil [Provinz usw.]

Gebührenfrei

Deutschland (Allemagne)

Lager-Bezeichnung: X. Stammlager Luft I · via X Stammlager · Pris...

Gefangenennummer:

9406

Vor- und Zuname: LT WILLIAM SCHLEPPEGRELL

Absender:

263

DEAR A.D. HOPE THIS HASN'T BEEN TO
GREAT A SHOCK FOR YOU - I WASN'T HURT
AT ALL IN MY JUMP, AND LOOK AND FEEL
THE SAME AS EVER. YOU MAY WRITE AS
MANY LETTERS AS YOU WISH BUT I CAN
WRITE A TOTAL OF 3 LETTERS AND 4 CARDS
A MONTH ONLY. WE HAVE ENOUGH FOOD THANKS
TO THE RED CROSS AND LOTS OF BOOKS TO
READ SO YOU SEE THINGS ARE PRETTY GOOD.
WISH YOU WOULD TELL MAJEL AND EXPLAIN
WHY I CANT WRITE BUT ASK HER TO DO SO.
LET'S HOPE THE WAR ENDS SOON. HOW IS
SCHOOL NOW? TAKE IT EASY AND BE VERY
CAREFUL. HOW I HATE TO PRINT! I PICKED
A GOOD DAY TO GO DOWN, DIDN'T I? WHAT
IS KNOWN AS A HAPPY NEW YEAR'S DAY.
THERE ARE 4 BOYS FROM MY SQUADRON
HERE WITH ME - A COUPLE WE THOUGHT
WERE DEAD, SO IT WAS A GOOD SURPRISE.

Not much I can say. I am reading "Mill on the Floss" - Just finished "Random Harvest". Write to the folks more now, will you, and assure them for me that I am ok. And will see you all looking same as ever All my love, Bill

Dear Miss Schleppegrell,

I've been waiting to hear from you; so that I could write you what I know. Bill had a good chance if he didn't fall into the hands of the front line troops. I was on the mission with him that day and felt terrible because I was powerless to help him. His plane was hit by anti-aircraft fire & his engine froze as he was trying to make it back to our lines. He had perfect

This is a letter to William Schleppegrell's mother in response to her previous letter regarding his welfare.

266

time he **bailed** out.

We sure miss Bill for we had a lot of fun together, playing bridge, etc. He had about 17 missions and was doing swell, too. His case was really tough luck. But then you may hear even before you get this letter that he is a PW. We all hope so fervently.

If there are any other questions I can answer for you I'd be happy to do my best.

Yours truly
Bob Guffud

Milaca Minn
March- 9- 1945.

Dear Lt. Scheffel:-
I am writing you at your home address in hopes of it being forwarded to you, as I do not know your other address. Our son, Lt. Wm Schleppegrell has been missing in action over Germany since Jan 1. On March 4th we received word from the War Dept that he was a P.O.W. in Germany — yesterday a telegram came from the Provost Marshal General that they had intercepted a message from Berlin sent by Bill

This is a letter written by William Schleppegrell's mother to one of his friends, inquiring about her son's whereabouts.

to us. We have since received over thirty cards and letters from all over from people who had picked up the message on their short wave sets. He told us not to worry that he was well and safe - he asked us to notify his commanding officer and he mentioned others. He wanted us to notify. and also "Wahl" now we don't know who he meant by that, and we feel thats an error and he meant Wall. I know he called you that, for he has talked about you a lot here at home. but I don't know whether you have been corresponding. or not. but just felt he said Wall and they got it as Wahl – he also mentioned a Warren if you have any idea who that could be please let me know – but we think they misunderstood that for Marilyn, his sister. We are at a loss to know how he got that message through to us from Berlin. He told us to write him often at Stalag Luft 1 – Germany – They are limited in their writing – so won't you please write him – I know how happy he will be to hear from you – We have been so terribly worried about him and was so happy to get the report that he was P.O.W. – for at least we knew he was alive – and now this message that he is well and safe, seems like a miracle. Our prayers have surely been answered and we are so grateful.

Sincerely

Mrs. V. L. Schleppegrell

Milaca Minn.

Print the complete address in plain letters in the panel below, and your return address in the space provided on the right. Use typewriter, dark ink, or dark pencil. Faint or small writing is not suitable for photographing.

To:
Miss A. Schleppegrell
819 2nd STREET
Woodland, Calif.

From:
Lt. Wm Schleppegrell
O-715009
Milaca, Minnesota
(Sender's complete address above)

[CENSOR'S STAMP]

Dear A.D.

Just a note to say that I'm still in France, still coming home, and very very disgusted with the way they are taking care of ex-POW's. Am feeling fine otherwise — hope you are also — No more "notes" 'till I hit the States — hope you understand —

Love, Bill

HAVE YOU FILLED IN COMPLETE ADDRESS AT TOP?

REPLY BY V---MAIL

HAVE YOU FILLED IN COMPLETE ADDRESS AT TOP?

22

16-28163-5 ☆ U. S. GOVERNMENT PRINTING OFFICE : 1943

William Schleppegrell wrote this letter to his aunt while he was awaiting his return home.

Robert Wick's letter to his parents in Iowa describing his trip to Pisa, Italy.

3 Dec '44
In Italy

Dear Folks:
This is note to let you
know that I am feeling fine
& getting along OK.
I visited Pisa & enclosed
you will find some cards that
may be of interest to you. I
spent about 3 hours around the
Leaning Tower, the Cathedral, & the
Baptistry. They are all together
as you can see on the card.
I climbed to the top of the Tower
& it was a magnificent view.
It was hard to realize that
here once stood Galileo &
here he worked out his
experiments on the laws of
gravitation. The tower leans
about 14 feet from the vertical.
Its about 181 feet high and

& the winding staircase has
293 steps.

It rained some today
& is rather chilly. The past 3
or 4 days have been rather
nice.

I just finished writing Alice
a letter & sent her some cards.
I can't help but wonder how she
is getting along. I'm afraid
it will be sometime before I
hear. None of us have received
any letter for a week. The Xmas
packages are interfering.

This will be all for now.
I hope to hear from you soon.

Love,
Robert

GENERAL HEADQUARTERS

ARMY FORCES IN THE PACIFIC

OFFICE OF THE COMMANDER IN CHIEF

A.P.O. 500,
April 30, 1946.

Mr. Joseph John Zylla,
731 Twelfth Avenue South,
St. Cloud, Minnesota.

Dear Mr. Zylla:

We have lost a gallant comrade in arms in the death of your son, First Lieutenant Frank L. Zylla, and I extend my sincere sympathy in your bereavement.

His service under my command in the Pacific was characterized by his complete loyalty to our country. In giving his life in this crusade for liberty, his name takes its place on the roll of our Nation's honored dead.

Very faithfully,

Douglas Mac Arthur

The official letter of condolence to Leonard Zylla's father upon the death of Leonard's brother Frank in the Pacific.

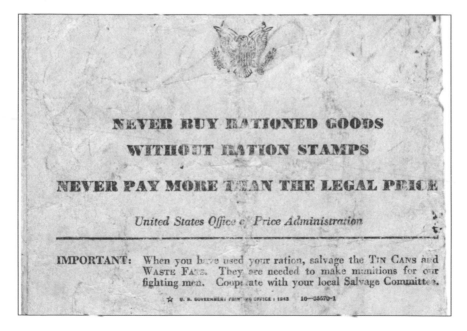

The U.S. government issued ration books which contained stamps for scarce items. Stamps were required in order to purchase those items. This was also done to prevent hoarding.

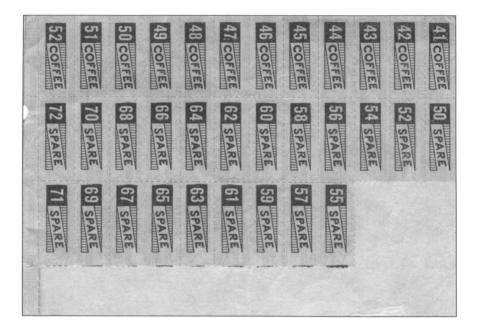

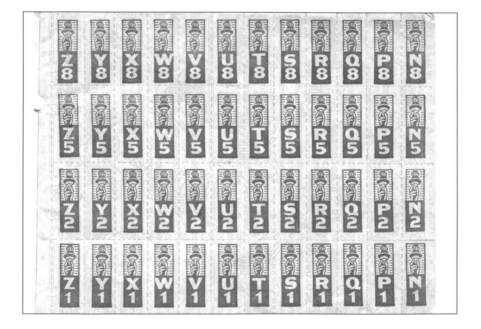

A photograph of the World War II Memorial in Washington, D.C. The memorial was officially dedicated on May 29, 2004. *Photograph courtesy of David Bilderback*.

PART IV

A Current Perspective

Andy and Adam Paulsen
(right to left)
2005

Born: 1982

Present home: Andy – St. Cloud, Minnesota
Adam – Moorhead, Minnesota

Military history: Enlisted; entered service 2001

Branch of service: U.S. Army Reserve

Length of service: To the present through 2009

Highest rank: Specialist (both)

Date/place of interview: July 9, 2005
Minneapolis, Minnesota

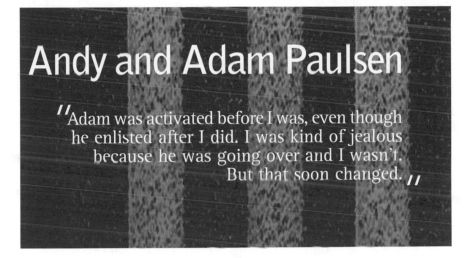

Andy and Adam Paulsen

"Adam was activated before I was, even though he enlisted after I did. I was kind of jealous because he was going over and I wasn't. But that soon changed."

RGP: First of all you are identical twins, right?

Andy and Adam: Yes.

RGP: What was it like growing up with a twin always there?

Andy: It was nice just because you always had someone to play with. If you looked for a neighborhood kid, he wasn't always necessarily there or able to come out and play. You always had a playmate.

Adam: It was nice to have someone who was there with you experiencing the same things.

Andy: The same likes and dislikes.

RGP: Did your folks dress you in sailor suits?

Adam: There is one picture where we are both wearing the same sailor-type of shirt that our grandma made for us.

Andy: Yes. Our mom dressed us the same when we were really young, but she could tell that that wasn't going to work because even our own mother couldn't tell the difference between us! *(Laughter)* So then she started dressing us differently.

Adam: Then it was one of those things where we were wearing the same types of clothes, just different colors.

Andy: One of us would have red shorts and one would have blue shorts with the same little stripes up the side.

RGP: You must have received some interesting reactions once you started school. Did your friends and teachers treat you differently?

Andy: We both had our own separate friends, but it was the same big group. We had our favorites from a bigger group. When we started school, we were living down in Nebraska. We grew up with the same group of people all the way through sixth grade. We really didn't get a lot of reactions like, "Wow, you guys are twins!" If the teacher said something, it was when we were younger, and we really don't remember it. We were always put into separate classes. Sometimes out on the playground or something, a friend would call to you and then he'd discover that you weren't who he thought you were. *(Laughter)*

Adam: For whatever reason, it was mom and dad's choice that we were to be in separate classes. Normally we had different teachers in different parts of the school.

Andy: I think that if I had twins, I would rather have them in separate classrooms so they would not be so dependent on each other and they could grow with other kids.

Adam: Maybe that is why we wound up going to different colleges?

Andy: Probably is.

Adam: At high school graduation, our relatives asked us where we were going to go to college, and one of us said St. Cloud State and the other said Moorhead. They were like, hey, you guys are separating?

RGP: As you reflect back on it, do you think going to different colleges was a wise decision?

Andy and Adam: Yes.

Andy: Different callings bring us different places.

RGP: Your major?

Andy: It was aviation, but I am switching over to mass communications because calculus and I go together like sunshine and chocolate chips. It is not a pretty sight. To get a degree in aviation, you need to have calculus. Besides, I would like to work more with people and do a job where I can be semi-creative.

RGP: Adam, what did you choose?

Adam: Recently I changed my major to film studies. I would like to produce or direct.

RGP: Now, let's talk about your involvement in the Army Reserve. Perhaps you could begin by explainng the difference between the Army Reserve and the National Guard.

Andy: The Army Reserve answers to the president, and the National Guard answers to the governor of the state. Both are funded with federal dollars.

RGP: I see. Regarding your service: Why did you join? Did you want to serve your country and go abroad and fight battles that weren't going on yet?

Andy: That is not necessarily what my intention was when I enlisted. I had seen movies and commercials about people who went through basic training. It looked like fun, and it looked challenging. Seeing those pictures of the obstacle courses is what really got to me. I think I enlisted for the adventure, and by going through the obstacle courses of basic training I could challenge myself. But it turned out at basic training that I didn't get to do as many strenuous exercises as I would have liked.

Adam: With me it was one of those things where I had always enjoyed WWII films, and I think essentially that is what put the military service in my mind. Of course, movies glorify war. But they "did the job" because they piqued my interest; and when my interest was piqued, I decided to sign on the dotted line. Afterwards, looking back, I really enjoyed it because it challenges you physically and mentally and it takes you to the peak and beyond. It is such a wonderful feeling to be standing there in formation at your graduation from basic training. It opens your eyes.

RGP: Were either of you motivated to join because it would help you pay for college?

Adam: Yes. Even Bosnia…it wasn't something that a lot of Reservists and Guard members had to do. The Gulf War was the last war when they called up Reservists and National Guard Units. 1991 was the last time when they started to pull people from the Reserve. The money for school was intriguing, of course. I won't say that it was the most important part of the reason why I enlisted, but it helped me decide to do it.

RGP: That financial package is a direct offshoot of the GI Bill.

Andy and Adam: Exactly.

RGP: Andy, how old were you when you enlisted?

Andy: I was 20. I think Adam was 20 at that time, too. *(Laughter)* I enlisted on August 29, 2001.

RGP: Did you say August of 2001? Good grief! You know what happened two weeks later?

Andy: I do.

RGP: How did that make you feel? That must have been a sobering situation for you because you thought it might affect you, right?

Andy: I don't really think it affected me. If I hadn't enlisted, I *would* have after September 11 just because I am intrigued by WWII aviation and just WWII in general. I think I would have wanted to experience—really experience—a historical moment. If we would have gone to war, I think I would have liked to have experienced it.

Adam: I didn't enlist until March 22, 2002. I wasn't even thinking about September 11 and the potential of going overseas. I just wasn't thinking about it. I felt the same thing that Andy did: The adventure was alluring. Also, when I get older and look back at my life, it is something I can say that I did and am glad that I did. That is really what drew me into service. Of course, when I was going through basic training and they were talking about Reservists going overseas, it was a little frightening just because of the fear of the unknown, but then you realize that it is not that bad. It is an adventure and something that everyone does not get to experience. It helps build your character and makes you stronger. I always liked that feeling when it came time for me to mobilize, but I was more excited than I was nervous. The fear was in my mind that anything could happen over there, but the idea that I was going to go out and travel and experience these new things was wonderful—I was very positive about the mobilization process.

Andy: It is really kind of funny: Adam was activated before I was, even though he enlisted *after* I did. After I heard he was activated, I was kind of jealous because he was going over and I wasn't, and I wanted my chance to experience it and see this different region of the world that was previously unknown to me. Yes, I was a little jealous. But that would soon change.

Adam: The funny thing was that it was the winter of 2003, and I got back from AIT (Advanced Individual Training) and was mobilized in…

Andy: Was it February of 2003?

Adam: Yup, in February. Then I went and sat at Fort McCoy for the first time until the very end of May, and then I was demobilized. Then in March, Andy—to relive a little bit of his jealousy—found out that he was mobilized. *He* got mobilized! About the time that I was demobilized to go home, he wound up going overseas. It was I who was a little jealous then because I had gone through the whole training and preparation process to go overseas only to find out that I wasn't going over after all.

Andy: You sat at Fort McCoy for a couple of months, and the government spent money on shots and all sorts of training only to find out that you were deactivated.

RGP: Now, Andy, you had joined before Adam, and yet he got called first, even though he didn't go overseas. And that didn't seem fair to you, right? Who made the decision about all of this? It reminds me of the film *The Fighting Sullivans*, where all five of the Sullivan brothers were killed on the same ship in the South Pacific in WWII. The "Sullivan Law" was put into effect shortly after that tragedy. It prohibited members of the same family from serving on the same ship or in the same area of battle. The film *Saving Private Ryan* is about this subject, too. Did that enter into this decision because you were twins?

Andy: I don't think being twins was an issue because we were with two completely different units. I was involuntarily transferred to the 244th out of Colorado, and Adam was activated with the Fargo unit.

Adam: Yes. I was activated with the Fargo unit, the 461st. That whole deal had crossed my mind a couple of different times while we were mobilized. What is interesting is when you look at it, when you look back at the whole last couple of years, I get mobilized and then demobilized, and Andy gets sent overseas. I was mobilized a second time. And then around the time that Andy came home—not even a month later—I went overseas. I guess that it was better for mom and dad that way. It is trauma enough to have one son overseas and constantly worrying about that one son; but then to have both sons overseas at the same time—well, it was nice that they always had at least one son home in the States.

RGP: Did someone plan the placement of you two in separate units? Is that how it worked?

Adam: Divine intervention? I don't know. That is just how it worked out.

RGP: Tell me about how long each of you were on active duty. How does all of that decision-making operate in the Army Reserves? Could they have extended your term?

Andy: Actually, from the time you get activated to the time you get deactivated, it is probably more like 15 or 16 months because you spend three months stateside getting ready with your unit. For me, that was the one that I was involuntarily transferred to. I spent four months at Fort Carson in Colorado Springs, and then we went overseas to Iraq. I was in Kuwait for a month, and then I was in Iraq for 11 months. When you come back, it takes about two weeks to out-process, and then you're released from active duty. My unit spent a year overseas. I could easily have been extended. About the time I was getting ready to come home from Iraq, there was a rumor which turned out to be true: If we would have stayed a couple days longer, we would have been extended for another month or two. There were people who were spending a deployment of 13, 14, even 15 months over in Iraq.

RGP: I heard it on the news, too. People were looking forward to going home and then they were extended.

Andy: Yes. Being told you have two more months—and then, during the course of those two months, what if something terrible happens and you don't make it back alive or are seriously wounded?

Adam: I spent three months at the immobilization station where you do all predeployment training. It is also where you go to get all sorts of equipment and gear that you need for the desert environments. That is where you spend your time stateside, depending on what unit you are with. After the stint at Fort McCoy in Wisconsin, we moved straight to Afghanistan. We spent our whole deployment in Afghanistan. Then a couple of weeks later, we were demobilized.

RGP: Can they ever take you back into active service once you are demobilized?

Adam: Yes.

RGP: I thought they could because otherwise they wouldn't have invested all of that time and money for training.

Adam: Right. They usually say that an individual can't be mobilized more than 24 months.

Andy: I think that is what it was.

Adam: After people get back home, they can get called back up. Ultimately it is up to our Commander in Chief, George W. Bush, to sign on the dotted line, and if he does, then we are off. Whatever we did before doesn't matter; it virtually disappears. We go out and do what we need to do again. They say one thing, but more or less it is really kind of a guideline to keep you at ease.

Andy: It really doesn't mean anything when they tell you that you can only be gone for two years and then you will be sent home. Kind of the opposite of the WWII veterans: When they started out, they stuck it out all the way to the end. In our situation, they told us that we could not be gone for more than two years, but it is up to the president. If he wants to sign on that line, then it wouldn't matter how long we stay over there.

RGP: How long after you are demobilized can they take you?

Andy: After you are demobilized, there is a safe zone where you have so many months where you cannot be touched, so to speak, or reactivated. After that deadline, then you can be activated again. I forget...is it 90 days?

Adam: It is 60 days; I thought it was 90, also. I found out it was 60 days. You are kind of in that "no zone" where you don't have to deal with the military.

Andy: "No touch" zone?

Adam: Yes. That's what it is called. After the 60 days, you have to go back, especially us Reservists. We have to move back into the Reservist mindset. Some people, while they were overseas, could volunteer to stay longer. Or as soon as they get back home, they can volunteer to go back over. You can go back after only three or four days of being back, if you want to.

Andy: But just because you volunteer after you get back, it doesn't mean you automatically go. You usually are put on a waiting list and taken to fill certain job positions that they need to fill.

RGP: Did you have a sense of patriotism before joining?

Andy: Not so much. We always had a flag hanging at our house, but there really wasn't a strong sense of patriotism. I suppose it's just like the 1940s before Pearl Harbor was bombed: There were families that loved their country, but it took a disaster like Pearl Harbor to really get people's inner patriotism to come out. When I enlisted, I was going to go through basic in January. I was going to do fall semester at St. Cloud State and then go to basic, but then I met a girl and decided to push the date back as late as I could. It was May of 2002 when I finally went to basic training. When I did wind up going to basic, I was kind of proud to put on the uniform. Before that, I really didn't have a strong sense of patriotism. Watching films and seeing what those WWII soldiers went through kind of makes you wish that you could have the same type of feeling: knowing that you are doing something for the betterment of mankind. It makes you feel good about yourself.

RGP: One major difference between WWII and what you both experienced is that we knew who the enemy was in WWII. That must have been difficult, Adam, when you think of Afghanistan and the Taliban. How do you know who the enemy is? And the same thing must have been true for you, Andy, in Iraq.

Andy: It is really tough in Iraq. I am not sure about Afghanistan; but in

Iraq, it is kind of like the Vietnam War, where you have people who are farmers during the day and at night they are trying to kill you by setting up IEDs (improvised explosive devices). As you would be convoying through different towns, you would look around and see these people. It is legal for them to carry weapons. However, we soldiers are not allowed to fire on them unless there is a hostile act or a hostile intent. Unless they are pointing a gun at you, you are not allowed to fire upon them. It was really crazy. While I was down in Kuwait for a month, the rules of engagement changed almost daily. When the U.S. first moved into Iraq in March of 2003, things were changing so much that they were constantly changing the rules. It was tough to distinguish between the old and the new rules. It was really confusing and frustrating because you really couldn't do anything. Part of you wanted to be alert and shoot someone with hostile intents, but another part of you thinks that if you do it, are you going to get in trouble?

Adam: Afghanistan was the same way. There would be farmers and peddlers in general during the day, but during the night, they were the ones who were setting up rockets and firing them into your compound. It was one of those things—unlike WWII, when the Germans attacked the Americans, and they stayed and fought. The Taliban use guerilla tactics. It is very effective and frustrating at the same time. Usually, when you get attacked, you want to take care of the problem and threat. But if they leave, then the threat is gone.

Andy: During WWII you had your uniforms, and the Japanese and the Germans had their uniforms as well. If you were sitting at some observation point, looking down a road to see if any enemy convoys were coming, you could see each country's symbol and unique uniform, and you could prepare yourself. You can see them coming and plan your attack. In Iraq and Afghanistan, you have these nationals, and you have no idea if they are enemies or not because there isn't a distinction in what they look like or what clothes they are wearing. It is really frustrating. I mean, insurgents don't wear uniforms!

RGP: Andy, as you know, there is a great sense of unrest in the U.S. in terms of our involvement in Iraq. The many thousands of casualties, both dead and wounded, have made an increasing number of Americans wonder if we should be in Iraq. While you were there, did you have any misgivings about taking orders, about being a part of this war?

Andy: Yes. When we were convoying into Iraq from Kuwait with our trailers, we were told to stop on the side of the road in the combat zone for 10 minutes, for whatever reason. If there were some Iraqi army personnel left or just anybody who hated Americans, it would have been easy for them to spot our convoy, and they could have shot a couple of mortars. By stopping, we had allowed ourselves to be set up for ambush too many times like that. There were several situations when we got up into Iraq at the main base we operated from, and we were required to have formations. We were never supposed to have formations in a combat zone because if there was an enemy sniper, it would be easy for the sniper to shoot whomever was in charge as well as any other soldiers. We would have formations in a combat zone! We would do physical training in the morning, sometimes in the combat zone! You are never supposed to do that.

It was really crazy. If you wanted to go out for a run, you could put your physical training uniform on—which consisted of a T-shirt, shorts, and running shoes, and go for a run. Nobody would know who you were. As soon as you were done running, however, you had to have your weapon and your helmet on. It seemed so odd that you could run around base if you wanted, but as soon as you did anything else, you had to have your helmet on and your weapon with you. It didn't make any sense. Also, the trucks we had weren't properly armed. We might have a 50-caliber machine gun but only a limited number of rounds of ammunition. We didn't get issued any grenades. The superior officers would do a complete inventory on ammunition, just at random. I don't know how, when you are sitting in a combat zone, you are supposed to inventory your ammunition. You should be given ammunition and as soon as it runs out, you should be constantly supplied with more just in case it would be needed. You would never know when you were going to need it or when the base was going to get attacked. There were several times when I wondered what we were doing and why we were doing it. We were in a combat zone. I didn't know what the reasoning was behind some of the rules we had to follow.

RGP: You couldn't talk to your superior officer?

Andy: That would only go so far. My platoon guide felt the same way about a lot of things, but it was beyond him to say or do anything. You've got your company commanders, and beyond that you have battalion commanders. You can only go so far with complaints, and then they get "lost" or get mixed in with everything else.

Adam: They try to explain to you that the complaints will go all the way up to where they are supposed to go, but somewhere along the chain of command, they just fizzle out. We had experienced the same things in Afghanistan when we were on convoys. We had limited ammunition. When we would stop, we would have to pull security around our vehicles, and we became vulnerable—plain and simple.

Andy: When we first went into Iraq, we had lightly armored Humvees, five-ton, and two-and-a-half ton trucks and flack jackets, some of which were from the Vietnam era. It was ill-advised that we would go into this combat zone with vehicles that weren't armored. We had these flack jackets that are like vests, but they would do nothing to stop the shrapnel. It was just extra weight. That is what it was. It was frustrating to be there without the armor on the vehicles. When we were in Kuwait, we had these five-ton dump trucks, and we did what we called "hardening." We bought lumber and fortified the backs of the vehicles with walls and sandbags. That is what we used when we got up into the country.

In Iraq we would have soldiers who would have their uniforms get destroyed from laying razor wire, which is like barbed wired, or they would just wear out. We couldn't get replacement uniforms. As soon as we got back down to Kuwait, we were able to trade in our worn-out uniforms for new ones. Before I came back, I had a pair of boots that was trashed, and I ended up getting brand-new boots right before I was ready to come home. It didn't make sense. It was not fun to have these uniforms that were just trashed or boots that had holes in them.

Adam: We had experienced the same thing in Afghanistan, where we had soldiers who had boots that were worn out but they couldn't get new ones. It was really unfortunate.

Andy: It was really tough for us in Iraq to get ammunition. If we needed to do some test firing or make sure that our weapons worked properly, we would make a bunch of fire pits where we would push dirt up into a pile and test fire our weapon. When we would test fire our weapons, it was tough for us to get replacement ammunition. A lot of times what happened is that we would build a picnic table or fix a shower for the active duty guys, and they would give us ammunition in return. The active duty guys had an unlimited supply of ammunition. For us, being that we were Reservists, I don't know if it was the battalion that wasn't issuing the ammunition or what, but they weren't giving us enough ammunition. It just didn't seem right not to have a constant supply of ammunition if we needed it. It was tough to get ammunition as a Reservist.

RGP: You know, this seems kind of odd to me as an outsider. You would think that with today's advanced technology and our planning, this would not be happening. Weren't there enough supplies produced by the Defense Department? Was it a supply problem? It must make you think that you weren't worth a damn.

Andy: That is really how it is. It was evident in Vietnam; it was evident in WWII, WWI—ever since wars have been waged. Foot soldiers and privates have always been expendable. If it takes 100 soldiers to clear one little town, as long as the town gets cleared and the mission is accomplished, it doesn't matter how many fatalities there are. You don't matter.

RGP: Isn't it more pronounced this time around because so many of you were just citizens who were called up? It is not like you had enlisted for a war that was already in progress. Also, you had not been drafted.

Adam: We are just pretty much Bush's "plastic army men" from his bucket called the military. He can pick us up—just like a little kid—and set us any place he wants. He can set up plastic tanks and drive them around. I hope he will never get to the point where he is bored with us. I mean, that is what kids do with their plastic soldiers: They lose them and destroy them. Hopefully, that won't happen with us.

RGP: Let's go to you, Adam. In Afghanistan, what kind of situations did you find yourself in where you were in mortal danger?

Adam: I was at Bagram Airfield, and that was the biggest military installation in Afghanistan. It was pretty secure, for the most part. We got rocketed once in a while. It would usually happen once a month, but then sometimes it didn't happen for three months. Right before we started to leave, it happened once a month again. When you are at Bagram, you are pretty safe. We had to walk around with our weapons; but when we would get out to these fire bases, we could leave our weapons behind and no one would say anything. I had never been in a real dangerous situation. We were in a combat zone, plain and simple. But everywhere in Afghanistan is a combat zone. I never really had to experience gunfighting or huge rocket attacks. It was better that I didn't because I went overseas to do some construction work, and that is what I did. I have heard about people who were at places where they got attacked a lot and had to pull security for extended periods of time. I never experienced anything like that overseas. It makes me kind of sad, in a way; but I am glad, too, because when rockets are flying and bullets are zipping by, you've got danger. I am glad I never had to experience that. The only time I fired my weapon overseas was when we were test firing before we left on a convoy. That is it. I am content with that. I have no problem with that.

RGP: Now, you were in the Army. Does the Navy still uses the word Seabees for people who do construction duties?

Adam: Yes, they do. I had worked with some people who were Seabees assigned to build some buildings. During breaks, we would chat with one another and discuss the differences between Army and Navy procedures. It was really fun. They do still call them Seabees.

RGP: I have learned something. I interviewed a guy who was a Seabee in WWII. I always thought that it was "Seabee," and it is—but it stands for CB: Construction Battalion.

Andy: That is kind of funny because for my advanced training, I went down to Gulfport, Mississippi, which is a Navy Scabee base. They were training Army, Navy, and Air Force personnel at that place, but it was a Seabee base. When I was down in Gulfport, it was spelled out like you had mentioned before— "Seabee"—and it really wasn't CB. That is funny that you said that because it was the first time I had heard that connection.

RGP: How near were you to some serious danger?

Andy: I was on a convoy out in the middle of nowhere. We were working on a job, fixing up a bridge. There were a couple of pop shots fired at our convoy. It was kind of off in the distance, so we didn't know where it came from nor how far away it was. That was the only time I was on a convoy when shots were fired. I was on a convoy another time when we were going out to a job site, but for whatever reason, our convoy didn't leave when it was supposed to. We were delayed by five minutes. On the way to the job site, the convoy was stopped because traffic had stopped. On the bridge that we crossed, there was an IED that blew up, and a different military convoy had casualties. If I remember right, there were two casualties and one seriously injured. It makes you really think about things, knowing that our convoy was delayed for five minutes and that on the way over the bridge there was an IED that went off right before we got there. It really makes you wonder and think about how quickly something can happen. Another time I was at a different base that was mortared about two or three different times. It was at night. First we heard the noise of the mortars being launched from their tubes, and then we heard some explosions. That was really kind of nerve wracking. We threw our body armor on and grabbed our weapons and headed to the bunkers. Those were the only two times I was really, really close to a combat situation, if you want to call it that.

RGP: Did you ever see someone killed right next to you?

Andy: No, I did not.

Adam: Thankfully, neither did I. I don't think I know how I'd take that. People can say that they'd do one thing in a situation, but when you are in the situation…

Andy: It is completely different.

Adam: Exactly.

Andy: At one of the different forward operating bases, there was some sergeant who was using a skill saw. He didn't hear this mortar launch, and he wound up getting a sliver of shrapnel in his butt. It was a small sliver that didn't wound him at all, but it was kind of comical at the same time. They wound up pulling it out with a tweezers. It was kind of funny because in the film *Forrest Gump*, he was shot in the butt. It is just kind of funny when someone gets shot in the butt—especially when there's no serious injury as a result.

RGP: I have heard again and again in these interviews with WWII vets their sad stories of great delay in getting news from home. For example, their wives having a baby back in the States, and they would not hear about it until three months later, when the Red Cross got the communication to them. Soldiers would write letters home which, of course, were censored by the military, and it might take weeks for the letters to get home. You were in a different situation, weren't you?

Andy and Adam: Yes.

Adam: As far as technology goes? Yes, we were fortunate.

Andy: Down in Kuwait, there was an Internet setup. After a while, after being in Iraq for a couple of months, every once in a while you would see a little Internet café pop up at one of the bases. My unit had a satellite phone, and it would travel to the different companies during the month We were given one 10-minute phone call a week when we had the phone. It was really nice that we had the satellite phone for most of our deployment. By the time I left, there were several cafés set up and an AT&T phone bank setup where you could just use a calling card. It was nice to be able to call home and hear familiar voices. There were several people who had bought cell phones down in Kuwait with prepaid minutes, and they were talking to their loved ones. We were very fortunate.

RGP: Even e-mail. I know it is just written words—but the thought that it is instantaneous communication compared to the 1940s, when people were waiting months and months.

Andy: It can really help the morale of the troops when you can pick up a phone and call home or just type out an e-mail. You can hear good news right away—but you can also hear bad news as well. There were some guys who had experienced some bad times. They had been dating these women before going overseas, and then their lady friends decided to break up with the— and told them that by e-mail. There were a lot of messages coming through like that. We had one guy who had a joint banking account with his girlfriend, and that was not good. She pretty much wiped him out.

RGP: You know, that reminds me of someone in prison. They are helpless when they hear that kind of news.

Adam: That is how we are overseas: helpless. There were several incidents involving married guys whose wives took all their money and then wanted a divorce. There were too many situations like that.

RGP: You had a lot of women in the service with you in this war. That was not the case so much in WWII. What was that like?

Adam: I was part of a Headquarters Company. All of the females were sent to the Headquarters Company. These women can be part of the line companies for drill weekends; but once you moved to a combat zone, they weren't allowed to be involved much. It was interesting and nice to have females around. When I went to basic training, I went with all males. I liked it, but it is nice to have females in the company, too. For the most part they worked just as hard as the guys, but there were a few who shouldn't have been there at all.

Andy: There are always exceptions.

Adam: In the National Guard and Reserves, a lot of females had used the military to pay for their schooling. A lot of the females you see in the military are there because they couldn't get into college or they couldn't even get into community college. They didn't have any other place to go, and their road was coming to an end. As far as active duty goes, you get that a lot more.

Andy: When I was in Iraq, I had the motivation to stay in school. I talked to some of those people about their life experiences. It just…it makes you push yourself a little more. I didn't want to end up like that.

Adam: That is another reason why I am excited to go back to school to further my education.

RGP: In a way, you both have been addressing this all through your interview—but one of the reasons I asked you to talk with me about your experiences was to give a perspective on what military life was for you compared with what you've read about WWII veterans' experiences. That is, you young ones in the current situation compared to those who lived through WWII.

Andy: I think it is mainly the degree of tolerance in a situation. As a society today, we like things to happen quickly. We don't like to wait; and when we have to wait, we have no patience. There were a lot of people who didn't like to have to wait for the phone to talk to their girlfriends and family members. This is unlike WWII, where they had to wait months and months. In my experience, our soldiers only had to wait a week, at the most. We expect so much more immediate gratification today. We expect to have the communication right now—when we want it. We have this expectation that everything will happen right away.

Adam: In many ways, the guys who went overseas in WWII had the same experience as we did. They were far away from home. But our stay overseas was a lot shorter than theirs. People now think that being overseas for a year is a long time but it really isn't, compared to the amount of time people were separated from their families in WWII. I know that our living accommodations are also a lot better now. We were provided with air conditioning in the desert and stuff like that, so it is more comfortable. People complain about the heat—but back in WWII, they didn't have those types of comforts.

Ronald G. Perrier was almost two years old when Pearl Harbor was attacked. Since early childhood, he wanted to be a teacher, and he has taught at the secondary and college/university levels for 40 years. He holds the B.S. degree from the University of Wisconsin–River Falls and the M.A. and Ph.D. degrees from the University of Minnesota in Minneapolis. He is Professor Emeritus of Film Studies at St. Cloud State University in St. Cloud, Minnesota, where he taught for 27 years prior to his retirement in 2002. In his teaching career, Dr. Perrier has had nearly 50,000 students in his classes.

Other Books by the Author

– Text/Workbooks –

Introduction to Theatre and Film (1977; sixth revision 1998)

The Great Escape: Film and the 1930s (1995)

Films of the 1940s (1997)

– Drama Anthologies –

Plays for Stage and Screen, Volume I (1989)

Plays for Stage and Screen, Volume II (1990)

Plays for Stage and Screen, Volume III (1998)

– Anthology of Fiction Sources for Films –

From Fiction to Film (1992)

– Nonfiction –

Growing Up Male in America (2002)
Interviews with young men in their 20s

A Sense of Honor: Remembrances of WWII Veterans (2004)
A series of interviews